Book Talk and Beyond

Children and Teachers Respond to Literature

Nancy L. Roser
University of Texas at Austin

Miriam G. Martinez
University of Texas at San Antonio

Editors

International Reading Association
Newark, Delaware 19714, USA

Director of Publications   Joan M. Irwin
Managing Editor   Anne Fullerton
Associate Editor   Christian A. Kempers
Assistant Editor   Amy L. Trefsger Miles
Editorial Assistant   Janet Parrack
Production Department Manager   Iona Sauscermen
Graphic Design Coordinator   Boni Nash
Design Consultant   Larry Husfelt
Desktop Publishing Supervisor   Wendy Mazur
Desktop Publishing   Anette Schütz-Ruff
                         Cheryl Strum
Proofing   David Roberts

Cover and section introduction illustrations by Barbara Tidman

Every effort has been made to trace and acknowledge copyright holders of material from other sources included in this work. The publisher welcomes any information that will lead to correction or clarification of such acknowledgments in future printings.

Copyright 1995 by the International Reading Association, Inc.
All rights reserved.

Library of Congress Cataloging in Publication Data
    Book talk and beyond: Children and teachers respond to literature/Nancy L. Roser, Miriam G. Martinez, editors.
        p.   cm.
    Includes bibliographical references and indexes.
    1. Literature—Study and teaching (Elementary).   2. Children—Books and reading.   3. Reader-response criticism.   I. Roser, Nancy.   II. Martinez, Miriam G.   III. International Reading Association.
LB1575.B58   1995   94-42224
372.6044—dc20   CIP
ISBN 0-87207-129-4

Contents

Guiding Book Talk

Contributors

Kathryn H. Au
  Pacific Literacy Center
  Honolulu, Hawaii

Jennifer Battle
  Southwest Texas State University
  San Marcos, Texas

Karen Bromley
  Binghamton University, SUNY
  Binghamton, New York

Bernice E. Cullinan
  New York University
  New York, New York

Maryann Eeds
  Arizona State University
  Tempe, Arizona

Cindy Farest
  Texas Tech University
  Lubbock, Texas

James Flood
  San Diego State University
  San Diego, California

Linda D. Fry
  Braun Station Elementary
  San Antonio, Texas

Lee Galda
  University of Georgia
  Athens, Georgia

Virginia J. Goatley
  Michigan State University
  East Lansing, Michigan

Joanne M. Golden
  University of Delaware
  Newark, Delaware

Veronica González
  Braun Station Elementary
  San Antonio, Texas

Elaine Handloff
  The Independence School
  Newark, Delaware

Janet Hickman
  Ohio State University
  Columbus, Ohio

James V. Hoffman
  University of Texas at Austin
  Austin, Texas

Mary Ann Jones
  San Diego Unified School District
  San Diego, California

Julie V. Jordan
  Braun Station Elementary
  San Antonio, Texas

Gloria Kauffman
  Maldonado Elementary School
  Tucson, Arizona

Carol Kibildis
  Granger Junior High School
  Chula Vista, California

Barbara Z. Kiefer
  Teachers College, Columbia University
  New York, New York

Linda D. Labbo
  Region XX Service Center
  San Antonio, Texas

Diane Lapp
  San Diego State University
  San Diego, California

Judith Wells Lindfors
  University of Texas at Austin
  Austin, Texas

Sylvia Lopez
  Braun Station Elementary
  San Antonio, Texas

Miriam G. Martinez
  University of Texas at San Antonio
  San Antonio, Texas

Diane McAdams
  Murray Boone Elementary School
  San Antonio, Texas

Amy A. McClure
  Ohio Wesleyan University
  Delaware, Ohio

Lea M. McGee
  Boston College
  Chestnut Hill, Massachusetts

Susan I. McMahon
  University of Wisconsin
  Madison, Wisconsin

Juel Moore
  San Diego Unified School District
  San Diego, California

Joy F. Moss
  University of Rochester and The Harley
    School
  Rochester, New York

Marcia F. Nash
  University of Maine at Farmington
  Farmington, Maine

Ralph L. Peterson
  Arizona State University
  Tempe, Arizona

Taffy E. Raphael
  Michigan State University
  East Lansing, Michigan

Nancy L. Roser
  University of Texas at Austin
  Austin, Texas

E. Wendy Saul
  University of Maryland–Baltimore County
  Catonsville, Maryland

Kathy G. Short
  University of Arizona
  Tucson, Arizona

Cynthia L. Sloan
  Braun Station Elementary
  San Antonio, Texas

Deborah Wells
  Slippery Rock University
  Slippery Rock, Pennsylvania

Jane West
  Agnes Scott College
  Decatur, Georgia

Deborah A. Woodman
  Lansing School District
  Lansing, Michigan

Foreword

PEOPLE LIKE TO talk, and they like to listen to other people talk. Some say talk is cheap, but it is also a basic way to learn literacy. Noted British linguist and educator Jimmy Britton (1983) says that "reading and writing float on a sea of talk."

We walk past a group of people, hear them talking, and join in the conversation. We see a neighbor or colleague and stop to chat or gossip about the latest news. When we turn on a radio, most likely we tune into a talk show. When we turn on the TV, we may watch Oprah Winfrey, Phil Donahue, or David Letterman. New programs, called "TV Live," are cropping up, featuring ordinary people talking spontaneously about anything and everything. Hundreds of people volunteer for MTV spots just so they can talk, be themselves, and be on TV.

Much of our thinking seems to take the form of inner conversation or debate. Speech for oneself can be internalized as inner speech, or thinking, or it can be verbal thinking, or outward speech. We clarify our thoughts when we talk about them with another person. And when we read Shakespeare or Mark Twain, we carry on a dialogue (either inwardly or outwardly) with the writer. Children, most of whom are prolific talkers from about the time they are two years old, also use talk to clarify their thinking and to deepen their learning.

Nancy Roser and Miriam Martinez capitalize on our tendency to talk and show us how to turn talk into valuable classroom currency. We discovered long ago that silent classrooms are not the best kind for learning: children talk to learn, teachers talk to teach. The wealth of resources Nancy and Miriam provide focuses on classroom talk about book-related topics. They encourage "book talk"; the "beyond" is what happens when rich, fulfilling literature surges into the classroom.

The teachers represented here not only make literature in classrooms available, they make it unavoidable. These teachers initiate literature discussion groups, book clubs, and literature circles—small groups of students who read a common text and come together to talk about it. Students share the thoughts and feelings that reading a book stimulates. By experiencing a story, students discover literature's potential to illuminate life. They are young travelers on life's road: they learn from mentors and classmates who lead the way or walk beside them through literature.

Book Talk and Beyond is divided into four sections. "Getting Ready for Story Talk" focuses on the preparatory steps that are necessary for ensuring aesthetic, defensible responses in the elementary classroom. Janet Hickman describes the social and physical contexts that foster responses to literature—the spaces, places, times, opportunities, and invitations that result in literary communities. Maryann Eeds and Ralph Peterson deal with the information about literary elements, techniques, and styles that teachers may rely on to nurture children's insights into literature. Wendy Saul addresses a preparatory process that enables teachers to guide conversations about books and stories more effectively. Miriam Martinez and Nancy Roser address the effects of book choice on the types of responses children make to literature, and they propose guidelines that lead to selecting books that promote varying kinds of talk. Diane Lapp, James Flood, Carol Kibildis, Mary Ann Jones, and Juel Moore round out this section by focusing on teachers' developing awareness of the potential of book talk—as well as how that awareness transfers to the classroom—through participation with peers in literary discussion groups.

The second section highlights the tools of story talk. Joy Moss describes the procedures for promoting children's awareness of the connecting threads that join stories—their themes and forms. Taffy Raphael, Virginia Goatley, Susan McMahon, and Deborah Woodman describe book clubs as opportunities to help students learn what to share about the literature they read and how to share it. Nancy Roser and James Hoffman with Linda Labbo and Cindy Farest discuss how to record story talk and offer specific procedures for recording children's language of response. Webbing is the focus of Karen Bromley's chapter as she describes the varying uses of semantic webs as tools for promoting thinking and talking about books.

The authors who write the third section "Guiding Book Talk" turn their attention directly to book talk. Lea McGee discusses broadly what teachers should do before and during literature conversations—including how to select quality literature—to promote children's discoveries about texts. Amy McClure offers help for the often neglected, feared, and abused discussion of poetry across all grades. The focus of Deborah Wells's chapter is on teacher's decisions and procedures that successfully foster in-depth and insightful discussions of novels and avoid question and answer exchanges in book talk. Kathy Short and Gloria Kauffman demonstrate the power of children's conversations when a teacher moves to the periphery of classroom discussions. Kathryn Au suggests ways to build on children's experiences and culture as the basis for talking about literature. Next, Jennifer Battle discusses story talk in a bilingual kindergarten. In the final chapter in this section, classroom teachers. Veronica González, Linda Fry, Sylvia Lopez, Julie Jordan, Cynthia Sloan and Diane McAdams relate the evolution of story time talk in their own classrooms from kindergarten through grade four.

Children often express their responses in ways other than through talk, and the final section of the book discusses ways in which teachers can most profitably foster those divergent forms of response. Lee Galda and Jane West suggest ways to encourage responsive classroom drama in all its forms. Barbara Kiefer helps teachers understand and appreciate art forms in picture books as a way of encouraging artistic responses to those books. Elaine Handloff and Joanne Golden discuss the craft of writing and its ability to help children express their thoughts about books. Finally, Judith Lindfors and Marcia Nash, in separate chapters, describe how teachers can use response journals to promote and support students' discoveries about themselves as readers and writers as well as encourage exchange about good books.

Writers in this volume emphasize the importance of children observing the way adults think and learn. Children learn from seeing demonstrations of higher level thinking and observing informed responses to literature. Teachers need to be a part of literature discussion groups so they can "shoot literary arrows" guiding students toward intertextual links and more literary ways of responding to books.

Read and enjoy the conversations in this book. Talk with your colleagues about the ideas presented here. Invite your students into conversations about books and what they mean—the same way these writers have done with us.

Bernice E. Cullinan
New York University

Reference

Britton, J. (1983). Writing and the story world. In B. Kroll & G. Wells (Eds.), *Explorations in the development of writing*. New York: Wiley.

Getting Ready for Story Talk

CHAPTER 1

Not by Chance: Creating Classrooms that Invite Responses to Literature

Janet Hickman

IN MANY EXEMPLARY, literature-rich class-rooms, a visitor's first impression is that good things just *happen*: children read and listen eagerly to stories; they engage in real conversations about books with their teacher and one another; they share their ideas in writing, art, drama, or other interpretive activities. Students seem enthusiastic about their work, enjoying themselves and learning at the same time. It all seems so natural and effortless that even at second glance, some observers conclude that only privileged super-kids could be this responsive. Yet my own contacts with schools (Hickman, 1983; 1992) and many published descriptions of children at work with literature (for example, Holland, Hungerford, & Ernst, 1993; Mills & Clyde, 1990) show that lively, book-loving classrooms of children can be found almost anywhere.

These classrooms cannot be accounted for in terms of special student abilities nor are they matters of happy accident. They exist because teachers planned them. They are care-fully structured creations in which children respond because the classroom invites response, because the books and materials to work with are there, because appropriate times and spaces are provided, and because the activities associated with being a reader are modeled, supported, and encouraged.

What are these successful literature classrooms really like? How do teachers construct them? I have spent countless hours observing and talking with many effective teachers in order to suggest answers to these questions. In every case, the teachers have worked very deliberately to create physical and social contexts that enabled more children to make more connections with more books. Much of that work goes on behind the scenes in careful planning for space, time, materials, and activities. Of equal importance are day-to-day interactions as teachers encourage children to read and to both develop and express their responses. Those who successfully engage children with literature have not all worked in just the same ways, of course, but what they do and the contexts they create have many common features.

Planning Behind the Scenes

Planning, arranging, and thinking ahead are a basic part of what all teachers do. Here I want to focus on planning, not as a day-to-day activity, but in terms of the larger frameworks that some teachers establish to guarantee their students certain kinds of reading and responding experiences.

Books and Materials

First and foremost, teachers who want their students to be responsive readers provide access to books. They take full advantage of school libraries and promote the use of public libraries, but they know there is no substitute for books in the classroom, books immediately at hand. Some of these are borrowed, some may "belong" to the classroom, others are from the teacher's private collection. Some are paid for with book-club bonus points or gift allowances from parent organizations; some may be purchased with a teacher's own funds. However the books are provided, they are there.

There seems to be no magic number of books for classroom libraries, but they do need to contain enough titles to give every child an opportunity to make choices. Most classrooms have a core collection of established favorites that are always available. Other titles come and go, so that there is always something new to draw prospective readers to browse and choose. Both kinds of offerings are important.

Book collections in the successful classrooms I have visited are not assembled at random. They are chosen with care and for a variety of reasons. An all-day, urban kindergarten

has an ample supply of simple nursery tales highlighting patterns of three, including Jan Brett's version of *Goldilocks and the Three Bears* and Marcia Brown's *The Three Billy Goats Gruff*, plus many other picture books chosen to appeal to children who are building their familiarity with stories in print. An intermediate classroom engaged in a unit study of state history is temporarily well stocked with historical fiction and relevant informational books, paperback novels for both able and struggling readers, and many titles designed to feed interests developed in previous thematic studies.

Just as there is no magic number of books that guarantees children will read and respond, there are probably no magic titles either. Of the thousands of commendable children's books in print, some obviously serve particular purposes or audiences better than others. It is not the provision of specific, absolutely-can't-miss titles that seems to be important; rather, it is the fact that the selected books have been deliberately collected by someone who knows and cares about a certain classroom full of children and their reading.

Planning ahead for a range of responses to reading usually means providing other materials in addition to books. One second grade teacher urged parents to contribute to her growing collection of interesting papers, booklets, envelopes, and writing instruments. This spurred increased attention to writing in general and made it possible for children to offer creative responses to *The Jolly Postman* by Janet and Allan Ahlberg. Props and dress-up clothes increase the acting out of stories in primary classrooms, although children encouraged in drama seem to make do with a minimum of "stuff." Art materials are absolutely necessary to some forms of interpretation, but they may be hard to obtain on limited budgets. Teachers in underfunded classrooms often assemble collections of scrap paper, fabric, and wallpaper samples for collages, or household discards (egg cartons, plastic bottle tops, ribbon spools) for construction and sculpture. Tape recorders and blank tapes allow for storytelling responses or for recording background music to fit poems and stories. Any of these materials can be brought into the classroom to support responses to particular books. However, in some schools I have visited, materials like these are considered regular classroom tools, and they are almost always available to children as they stretch their thinking about what they have read. Certainly the books and materials to which students have access help to shape the kind of readers they become.

Spaces and Places

It takes both ingenuity and strong arms to keep a classroom well supplied with books, and those qualities are equally useful in arranging a room's actual physical environment. Every literature-friendly classroom I have visited has some fixed space for books, such as a library corner or special shelving. Frequently, however, the books that are most current to the work of that class are displayed somewhere else. Although shelves make efficient storage, they hide the enticing covers that attract students. Consequently, the books that teachers want children to notice appear cover forward on chalk troughs, windowsills, cabinet tops, and tables. The spaces they occupy may be related to their content or to their purpose within the classroom. Bruce McMillan's *Mouse Views* lies open in one first grade classroom beside the gerbil cage; in another it stands with Gail Hartman's *As the Crow Flies: A First Book of Maps* alongside a half-finished map of the school.

Making space for interacting with books is as important as finding places for the books themselves. Most of the teachers I know, taking a cue from the habits of readers in non-

school settings, make an effort to provide comfortable and inviting places where children can browse, read, or gather to hear read-alouds. Bright rugs, soft pillows, rocking chairs, carpeted platforms, and sturdy lofts with wooden ladders—the form of these enticements depends on resources and inventiveness (and sometimes local fire codes), but the simplest may be as effective as the most elaborate in making the point that reading is a pleasurable, natural activity.

Teachers also recognize the collaborative nature of responding by finding space for children to read, talk, and work together. In older buildings, space has been commandeered from coat rooms, alcoves, and wide hallways for small group discussions, practicing Readers Theatre, mural making, and many other activities. Most teachers, however, make spaces by arranging—and frequently rearranging—desks, tables, and bookcases or cabinets, which gives children room to work in pairs or small groups of various sizes.

Space for displaying children's work is another constant in classrooms that successfully invite children's responses to literature. One primary group that was preparing for a visit from author-illustrator Tomie dePaola imagined what he would look like and painted large pictures of their speculations. Their teacher fastened these and other pictures and stories they had made as responses to dePaola's books along the walls at the entrance of the classroom to greet their guest. Encouraged by their teacher to share their thoughts about *Shiloh* with author Phyllis Reynolds Naylor, a group of fifth graders drafted and posted on their bulletin board several versions of a letter to her before deciding which to send and how it should be revised.

Displaying children's work allows them to collect and share needed information. It also serves as testimony to a responsive climate

As the Crow Flies
A FIRST BOOK OF MAPS

by Gail Hartman • illustrated by Harvey Stevenson

Cover illustration from Gail Hartman's As the Crow Flies: A First Book of Maps. Illustration ©1991 by Harvey Stevenson. Reprinted by permission of Macmillan Books for Young Readers, an imprint of Simon & Schuster Children's Publishing Division.

and can make a classroom more attractive if products are given colorful backgrounds and careful arrangement. Most important, displaying children's interpretive and creative work affirms its value and provides a reason for them to revise and attend to quality in their work. Conventional display space comes at a premium in most active classrooms, forcing innovations such as strings hung from the ceiling with plastic clips attached or a tabletop triptych of sturdy cardboard. Children's pleasure in seeing others notice their work makes the effort it takes to create display spaces worthwhile.

Finding Time

Plentiful space and books by the hundreds are virtually worthless unless there is time to make use of them. In the classrooms most familiar to me, teachers plan time daily, or almost daily, for the following experiences:

- listening to read-alouds;
- reading alone or with a friend from self-selected material;
- talking about books—providing opportunities for spontaneous comments and substantive guided discussions;

6

- responding to books in writing or through other interpretive activities that extend children's thinking; and

- sharing finished products, which often leads back to talking about books.

These experiences serve as a framework across grade levels, although there are variations in emphasis and interpretation. For example, there are usually more opportunities for reading aloud in early primary grades, where children may hear stories three or more times per day. At this level the talk and writing about books may be more closely interwoven with discussion about the characteristics of print and the conventions of reading and writing than with older students. A teacher's planning in terms of these broadly defined experiences has the advantage of specifying children's activities in fairly concrete terms while leaving plenty of room for incorporating particular intents and objectives.

Still, the most common complaint in literature-rich classrooms, as in most classrooms, is, "There's never enough time." Schedules crowded with "specials" and mandates that prescribe schedules make it especially challenging for some teachers to plan for the work with literature that they think is really important. In some schools this problem is addressed through the use of literature across the curriculum. Third graders engrossed in Seymour Simon's *Our Solar System* make their time count for both reading and science, just as middle schoolers do for reading and history by discussing their responses to the working conditions of the 19th century mill described in Katherine Paterson's *Lyddie*. This sort of integrated learning has benefits that go far beyond the reading program, but it requires careful planning and consistent monitoring.

The Teacher in Action

Unlike the hard work teachers do behind the scenes to make children's ready engagement with literature seem easy, their classroom interactions are immediately visible. The teacher's demeanor and ways of working with students set the tone of the classroom and contribute significantly to the social context within which children learn (see also the section on "Guiding Book Talk" in this volume).

A Reader Among Readers

The teachers whose work I have been describing are very different in personality, but they have at least one trait in common—knowledge about and enthusiasm for books and reading. Each one recognizes and accepts the role of chief reader, that is, the most experienced reader and responder among fellow readers who are younger and less experienced. Teachers in classrooms that nurture children's responses model how readers act, not in a staged or exaggerated way but through their own genuine interest in and observations about books. "I love the way this sounds. Listen to it again," one teacher says about a lyrical passage in *Missing May* by Cynthia Rylant. Another proudly displays a collection of picture books autographed by their illustrators at meetings and conferences; he can describe how the artwork was done for each one. Still another tells her students how she haunts the public library looking for new titles by her favorite author; she well understands how much they would like Beverly Cleary to write just one more book about Ramona.

Knowledgeable readers notice the craft of books—connections to other stories, stylistic patterns of one author, story structure, nuances of character, and the components of finely wrought illustrations. Readers who entertain such ideas are eager to share them. By talking with students about such perceptions in the way one reader talks to another, teachers introduce children to broad perspectives on literature that may go well beyond the expectations of the formal curriculum.

In a classroom community of responsive readers, of course, the child's perspective also has high value. Teachers who are fellow readers with their students listen with care as children talk about books. They listen to children's ideas with the same kind of attention they expect for their own, modeling a standard for classroom conversation and getting important information about children's thinking in the process.

Invitations and Opportunities

Personal invitations to read and respond are common in classrooms where literature is valued. Some of the best teachers I know seem to be playing host at a party as they introduce books to their prospective readers. "I thought of you right away when I saw this book," they say, or "The main character reminds me so much of you." These are invitations hard to resist because there is nothing generic or impersonal about them. Occasionally the key will be a comment about the content of a book or the casual mention of a character's name to save the reader from struggling with an unfamiliar pronunciation. (As a child I would never have read Rachel Field's *Hitty, Her First Hundred Years* if a kind adult had not given voice to the name Phoebe when she handed the book to me.) And, of course, the surest invitation into a book is to read it, or a portion of it, aloud—a daily practice among these teachers from kindergarten to middle school classrooms.

> *"Personal invitations to read and respond are common in classrooms where literature is valued."*

Teachers have many ways of creating opportunities for children to respond. They allow time to think; they offer choices of response modes and materials; they recognize the beginnings of good ideas and encourage them; and they offer support for further response.

Arranging for children to talk and work together seems to be an important contribution that many teachers make. Most children have a natural inclination for fellowship; they need to test their ideas about stories and the world in the company of others. Not surprisingly, classrooms where such collaborative work is the norm are not always the quietest or tidiest places in the school. Valuing social interaction usually means adjusting rules accordingly. For instance, where children are to read together or share spontaneous comments, strict silence should not be required.

Making It Happen

Looking at all the components of classrooms that invite children to literature can be daunting, especially for those new to teaching or those whose classrooms are organized differently. It is important to remember, then, that no two classrooms, even exemplary ones, are just alike. Although the descriptions I have given here are composites based on common features, I have not described the work of any individual teacher. Many classrooms that effectively bring children and books together may not show all these characteristics. However, there does seem to be some sort of critical mass of attention to stories and responses that produces the effect we are after. Just reading aloud will not do it. Occasional opportunities to discuss a book in a small group will not do it. Story-inspired artwork hung for open house will not do it. All these could be beginnings, but more is needed. To create classrooms that nurture children's responses to literature, successful teachers provide multiple avenues to reading and responding, and they do so consistently. And we can be sure it does not happen by chance.

References

Hickman, J. (1983). Everything considered: Response to literature in an elementary school setting. *Journal of Research and Development in Education*, 16, 8–13.

Hickman, J. (1992). What comes naturally: Growth and change in children's free response to literature. In C. Temple & P. Collins (Eds.), *Stories and readers: New perspectives on literature in the elementary classroom* (pp. 185–193). Norwood, MA: Christopher-Gordon.

Holland, K., Hungerford, R., & Ernst, S. (Eds.). (1993). *Journeying: Children responding to literature*. Portsmouth, NH: Heinemann.

Mills, H., & Clyde, J. (1990). *Portraits of whole language classrooms: Learning for all ages*. Portsmouth, NH: Heinemann.

Children's Literature

Ahlberg, J., & Ahlberg, A. (1986). *The jolly postman*. New York: Little, Brown.

Brett, J. (1987). *Goldilocks and the three bears*. New York: Putnam.

Brown, M. (1957). *The three billy goats Gruff*. San Diego, CA: Harcourt Brace.

Field, R. (1929). *Hitty, her first hundred years*. New York: Macmillan.

Hartman, G. (1991). *As the crow flies: A first book of maps*. Ill. by H. Stevenson. New York: Bradbury.

McMillan, B. (1993). *Mouse views*. New York: Holiday House.

Naylor, P.R. (1992). *Shiloh*. New York: Atheneum.

Paterson, K. (1991). *Lyddie*. New York: Dutton.

Rylant, C. (1992). *Missing May*. New York: Orchard.

Simon, S. (1992). *Our solar system*. New York: Morrow.

CHAPTER 2

What Teachers Need to Know About the Literary Craft

Maryann Eeds and Ralph L. Peterson

WHEN PEOPLE WHO have read the same good book talk about it with others, whether they are children or adults, certain kinds of talk can be expected to occur. Sometimes confusing parts need to be clarified, and the group figures them out together. Sometimes connections are made with readers' personal experiences or with other books they have read. And because it is almost impossible to talk about a book without doing so, readers often discuss literary elements. They may not realize they are doing this, and they may not use particular literary terms, but they do discuss, for example, memorable characters and characters coping with the events of the story. They discuss place and time. They talk about tension and what they thought the story was really about. They reveal what made them laugh ("I liked the part where...") or cry or shiver. They often notice language and the voice of a narrator.

Drawing from years of observations of literature studies and participation in book talk,

we have come to the conclusion that you can trust that when something is important in a story, it will get talked about. It does not appear to be necessary for a leader to be present to have such talk occur, but we have also found that less experienced readers, even when discussing literary elements, are often unaware of the good work they are doing. They may not notice, for instance, how an author has worked to create multiple layers of story meaning and how this contributes to the overall unity of a work. It is our belief that we as teachers, through our own growing awareness of literary elements and of the kinds of talk that may be expected to occur in literature study groups, will often have opportunities to move talk beyond mere sharing of impressions and reactions toward that deeper level of noticing and insight that we call *dialogue*. It is in these moments of dialogue with others that our understanding and appreciation of literature are deepened. We have learned that a gradual increase in awareness of how various authors use literary elements within particular stories enables readers to enter even further into a story world and greatly enrich their reading experiences. And we believe that awareness of literary elements and of their function in a story nurtures the development of children's ability (and our own) to respond imaginatively to a text, opening the way to dialogue and providing insight into layers of story meaning that may otherwise go unremarked.

Consider the layers of meaning in Mildred Taylor's *Roll of Thunder, Hear My Cry*, for example. We can read this book at an action level and suffer with the characters as they avoid the yellow school bus and finally bring its driver and passengers to their knees. We can empathize with Cassie as she experiences the injustices of living in a world where arbitrary acts exist and the causes for them are nothing more than the fact that one race feels itself superior to another. But we are going to be doing shallow reading unless we attend to the place where the action occurs and take great pleasure in the land and in the loving relationships that hold Cassie's family together. Being aware of multiple levels means we are aware of symbols such as Uncle Hammer's car—how it encapsulates the Logans in elegance and moves them through the countryside, making them equal to all. We miss the essence of the story if we do not see the conflict parents face as they rear their children in the home with expectations both of their being just and being treated justly, only to take them into a community where the color of skin defines who and what is of value. Insight is gained, too, by appreciating how Uncle Hammer stands up for himself, succeeds, and is proud, but at the same time puts the Logans in jeopardy by possibly releasing an existing anger and bigotry that may destroy the family through hanging or burning—all that the Ku Klux Klan represents. It is also in seeing the story as a metaphor for

growing up, Cassie's growing into womanhood, that the story becomes more than entertainment and illuminates real life. In the beginning Cassie is self-centered, wanting her pa, her mother, and Big Ma to support her rights and ensure her place in a racist world. At the story's end, she is concerned about the land payment, as she has grown to understand the world from a perspective that is not "me and myself" but "we." Now the question is: "How are *we* going to make that payment?" How will the family hold together, hold on to one another, keep the land, and save the spirit?

When readers are able to raise the lived-through experience of reading a book to a conscious level and reflect deeply to create a unity from the events, symbols, mood, place, and character, it is also possible that perspectives may be changed. For example, we can see *Roll of Thunder, Hear My Cry* as a metaphor for growing up or for family—what it means to belong and to be a part of a group that cares for and loves one another. But we can also see it as a message about what happens in life when people are not treated justly—when the law is the province of one group and used like a whip against others. Awareness of multiple levels of story meaning can cause us, as readers, to question ideas that are taken for granted or critique prevailing social practices. In reading Taylor's book, many see for the first time the pain caused by racial epithets or the power of institutions, such as a bank or welfare office, to perpetuate injustice. What happens to Cassie's family is representative of what can happen to other families.

We believe that the ability to engage in deeper levels of interpretation and critique develops gradually through dialogue with other readers and with teachers who are increasingly aware of the layers of story meaning and how the elements of literature work to create them. We favor allowing awareness to grow by only naming literary elements within the context of sharing the story. We believe we should use the language of literature naturally by listening carefully to what students talk about—constantly looking for opportunities (which we can expect to arise in any discussion) to "shoot literary arrows" (Peterson & Eeds, 1990).

To become more sensitized to the possibilities for dialogue that good stories offer, we have found it helpful to read any book chosen for literature study at least two times to ourselves—once so we can "lose ourselves" in the story and the second time to pay attention to literary elements and multiple layers of story meaning. We use William Steig's (1972/1984) wonderful book *Dominic* as an example for talking about both the literary elements and about how we go about preparing for a literature study.

Preparing for Literature Study: Considering the Elements

Structure

Structure gives unity and coherence to all the elements of story. It encompasses story incidents that cause action at various levels and resolve dramatic tensions. In thinking about structure, it is helpful to be aware of *plot* and *tension*. Plot may be focused on too much in traditional classrooms where literature is dealt with at a basic level, as students are required to list story events in a book report, for example. But the meanings we make in reading are dependent (at the very least) on responding to the plot—the narrative sequence—by interpreting how incidents are related and how one event adds to another. It is through the ordering of incidents that the author evokes the feelings readers experience. At a plot level,

Dominic is about the picaresque adventures of an admirable dog who sets out to seek his fortune. He runs into a "witch-alligator" who offers to tell his future, but he refuses in favor of savoring each moment as it comes. He has recurring encounters with the evil Doomsday Gang and always emerges triumphant. He befriends a dying pig who makes Dominic his heir, and through this fortune, Dominic is able to help many of those who have been victimized by the Doomsday Gang. In the final episode, he encounters a sleeping beauty of a female dog, awakens her with a touch, and eventually travels with her on a new adventure.

Even more important than plot in story structure is *tension*. We only know the plot of a story after it happens, but the notion of tension is always present in our reading, pulling us along and challenging us to stretch our imaginations. Tension might be referred to as

Illustration from William Steig's Dominic. ©1972 *by William Steig. Reprinted by permission of Farrar, Straus & Giroux, Inc.*

the suspense, anxiety, nervousness, strain, urgency, excitement, or fear that grips us as we read. In most books, there are many story events that are full of tension and keep us turning pages. But there is generally a central tension—one that can often be identified by asking ourselves what the story is *really* about. Plot will give us a surface answer; the central tension will be the underlying one. As we read, we can be expected to make adjustments in what we think the story is about. If the meaning we are constructing ceases to make sense, we have to back up, change our perspective, and start again. This is where talk makes all the difference. Dialogue can help put events and relationships into a new light, and the interpretations of others can change our own ideas of what we think a story is really about. In working together to disclose a deeper level of meaning, all our imaginations are enriched. This is why many of us enjoy reading the interpretations of professional critics—because they may have original interpretations that have not occurred to us.

In *Dominic* there is one incident after another in which tension is evident—incidents that make us feel anxious and hold us in suspense. We are first concerned with Dominic's reaction to the witch-alligator: "Though all smells engaged his interest, he wasn't sure he liked her particular one, and it seemed to him that she had many more teeth than were necessary for any ordinary dental purpose" (p. 5). But when he not only survives his encounter with her but learns which road he should take for adventure, our anxiety is relieved and we go on to the next episode—one in which Dominic is almost immediately trapped by the Doomsday Gang. The tension then is whether he will be able to escape from the dark hole dug by the gang who "robbed, ravaged, cheated, attacked innocent creatures at large and travelers especially, and did all sorts of dam-

aging mischief" (p. 12). This continues throughout the many adventures in the book, each one building to greater tension until the exhausted Dominic is finally truly in danger of death at the hands of the evil gang—"Now they intended," writes Steig, "to subtract him from the sum of existing things" (p. 135). But this final close call is thwarted by the interference of the trees, that, realizing Dominic is about to be killed "in their midst, in the very heart of the woods" (p. 136), spoke out and woke him. The "terror of this experience, the condemnation from the lords of the hitherto silent vegetable kingdom" (p. 136), at last stops the Doomsday Gang.

All the individual events and incidents that make up the book reveal the nobility of Dominic, who is able to surmount each challenge with vigor and honor. But the central tension of the book comes from another plot that Steig has created. Dominic is suffering from a kind of unknown longing, which has, in fact, caused him to leave home in the first place. It has caused him to howl to the moon his "burden of love and longing in sounds more meaningful than words" (p. 92). And when he finds a worn-out, little, stuffed doll puppy, he is overwhelmed with feeling and declares to the heavens: "Oh, Life, I am yours. Whatever it is you want of me, I am ready to give" (p. 92).

So the central tension we feel through the book is wondering whether Dominic will discover what he is searching for—the secret of life, the reason for his long, adventurous journey. At the end of the book when he finds the beautiful sleeping dog in the garden and wakes her with a touch, she asks, "Are you the one?" and he answers, "I think I am" (pp. 143–144). As they go off together to start a new life adventure, we feel that Dominic has indeed found his answer.

Character

Characters are all-important to story. When characters cope with problems and circumstances that seem universal, they teach us to see the rich potential for goodness, love, faith, hope, and honor (as well as fear and evil) that is in all of us. Were it not for the artfulness of Steig's constant references to dog-like behavior, it would be easy to forget that Dominic is a dog. His delight in living every moment with zest, his kindness, his wonder at the marvelous cycle of life as he mourns for the old pig, and even his overconfidence make him a memorable character. We know Dominic by what he believes and values:

> Life wasn't dull along this road. Fighting the bad ones in the world was a necessary and gratifying experience. Being happy among the good ones was, of course, even more gratifying. But one could not be happy among the good ones unless one fought the bad ones. He felt he was serving some important and useful purpose (p. 132).

We know him by how he behaves in action that is significant to the story. Dominic never backs off from encounters with evil; he is unfailingly kind to the weak and unfortunate—especially to children. In one incident he even frees a wasp that has been trapped in a spider web just because of his undying love of liberty. We know Dominic by what he says ("Wow, wow, wow, wow." "Here's to unending love!" "Happy Day to us all!"), by what he thinks, and by what Steig says about him: "Dominic couldn't abide being in the doldrums for long. The doldrums were dreary, and Dominic's spirit was sprightly, it liked to rollick" (p. 36). Dominic is believable because his behavior is always true to his character—a larger-than-life hero. It is always dog-like as well: in his farewell note to his friends he writes, "I embrace you all and sniff you with love" (p. 4). He loves bones—especially those to which age "added a rich musty tang which only a connoisseur of bones could properly appreciate" (p. 68). He is also always a noble, honest, stout-hearted, generous dog.

Authors bring characters to life in many ways: through metaphor, simile, and naming; through the actions they take and the thoughts they have; through what they say and what others say to and about them; through the reactions others have to them and those they have to others; and through narration. We identify with the protagonists and feel negative toward the antagonists—the characters (or things) that keep the main characters from achieving their goals. Both these types of characters are generally fully developed and often change over the course of the book. Most books also contain one or more pasteboard characters who are not fully developed but without whom the story could not be told. These are often stereotypes—such as evil stepmothers and crotchety neighbors. In *Dominic*, the main character is certainly well developed, and Steig has a way of making even minor characters memorable. The evil Doomsday Gang is a kind of group antagonist comprising weasels, stoats, foxes, ferrets, and other stereotypically repulsive creatures. It is helpful to think about how all these characters come to life when preparing for a literature study.

Place

Imaginary places created by authors are some of the best-known places in the world. Place—an intricate part of a story's whole—contributes to story illusion. Understanding place helps readers bring story to life in their imaginations and adds to meaning construction. Place may contribute to the mood or feeling of a book, influence character and action,

Illustration from William Steig's Dominic. ©1972 by William Steig. Reprinted by permission of Farrar, Straus & Giroux, Inc.

be used to inform the reader about the period in which the story occurs, or to show the passing of time. Place may contribute to believability in other ways as well, perhaps by giving insight into the interests, values, or commitments of the characters. The importance of place varies with each story. In *Dominic*, place is unnamed but is clearly one where courageous dog heroes battle foul villains, where magical things happen as a matter of course, and one that inspires Dominic and many of the other inhabitants with its great natural beauty. As Dominic starts on his adventures, he travels through a shady wood "smelling all the wonderful forest odors, alert to every new one, his nostrils quivering with delight. He smelled damp earth, mushrooms, dried leaves, violets, mint, spruce, rotting wood, animal droppings, forget-me-nots, and mold, and he savored all of it" (p. 9).

After escaping from the Doomsday Gang the first time and freeing the trapped wasp, Dominic sets off feeling on top of the world.

Steig's descriptions of place at this time match such a joyous mood:

> "What a wonderful world!" thought Dominic. "How perfect!" Had it been up to him when things were first made, he wouldn't have made them a whit different. Every leaf was in its proper place. Pebbles, stones, flowers, all were just as they ought to be. Water ran where water should run. The sky was properly blue. All sounds were in tune. Everything had its appropriate smell. Dominic was master of himself and in accord with the world. He was perfectly happy (p. 22).

When he asks Mrs. Fox, who is a goose, what she likes to do best—walk, swim, or fly— her answers, especially about swimming, again evoke a mood inspired by place:

> "Swimming is not as good for thinking as walking is, but swimming is wonderful for woolgathering. I love to float with the current of the stream, listen to the gentle lapping by the shore line, and dream whatever daydreams want to be dreamed. It's so peaceful" (p. 77).

Dominic refers to Mrs. Fox's little house as her Garden of Eden. At the end of the book, when Dominic finds his sleeping Eve(lyn) in another fabulous garden, we realize that he, too, has found his own place in life—his own Eden.

Time

The art of storytelling is in part dependent on how the teller controls the passing of time. There is no story, of course, if time does not pass. Time may be chronological, signaled by the orderly passing of hours, days, weeks, seasons, and centuries. Stories may also start at midpoint in the life of a character, with flashbacks to earlier times or jumps ahead to the future. The ordering of time can create suspense and move a character along psychologically. Pace can slow to a near standstill or advance to match a charged central tension. Awareness of how time is structured in a story can contribute to our interpretations and our appreciation of the writer's craft. In *Dominic*, time passes straightforwardly, beginning with Dominic's leaving home to go where his fortune tells him to go. He immediately encounters the witch-alligator, who "can see the future just as clearly as [she] can see the present and more clearly than [she] can recall the past" (p. 6). When Dominic tells her he prefers not to know the future, she commends him for being so wise and tells him about the fork in the road—with one road leading nowhere and the other to where "things will happen that you never could have guessed at—marvelous, unbelievable things" (p. 8).

Dominic almost always moves at a feverish pace throughout his adventures. His restlessness is only abated when he unwraps the little doll puppy and examines it. He asks himself why it holds such magic for him, and as he dreams of things to come, he is unaware of the passing of time. We find out at the book's end that the doll was something lost by his sleeping love and is the key to their finding each other. She, of course, has been sleeping for years, just waiting for her Dominic prince to find the doll. There is a time mystery here, too, involving the witch-alligator, who put Dominic's love under the sleeping spell.

Point of View

Authors take a position within the imaginary worlds they create. This point of view sets the rules for how much the narrator can be expected to know about the story characters and events. Determining if the story is narrated in the first or third person helps readers identify point of view. A first-person point of view is familiar to anyone who has ever told a personal narrative but can be limiting when telling a story. First-person narrators have no certain way of knowing other characters' feelings and thoughts, so readers only know what the narrator thinks and feels and how he or she reacts to others.

When telling a story from a third-person point of view, however, the narrator can be all-knowing, all-seeing, all-wise, and unlimited by time and distance—empowered to know the innermost thoughts and motivations of all the characters. Or, the author may choose to concentrate on just one or two of the characters, letting us know everything that happens from their particular perceptions. Sometimes authors elect to reveal little about characters' thoughts and feelings and tell the whole story in an objective or dramatic point of view—through dialogue and action only—letting us make our own interpretations about characters' motivation.

In *Dominic*, Steig acts as all-knowing narrator, but the point of view is almost always Dominic's. The author most often informs us of what Dominic is thinking and feeling, but there are times when he departs from this limited stance and even lets us know what the trees are thinking.

Mood

The story element of mood stimulates our imagination and calls on us to make personal connections. Our own daily life and our literary life are put in touch with each other through mood. As created through words, rhythms, sounds, and images, mood intensifies our perceptions and aligns our hearts and minds with what is happening in the story world. The function of mood is to have readers go beyond what is actually said in the text. For example, tension may be relieved by laughter and light-heartedness. There are times when we might react with fear or horror or cry in response to a created mood. Mood concerns the author's feelings as well as our own. We may be excited or terrified or puzzled at a particular moment in the book, but the author's mood—the attitude he or she had while writing—is often what triggers our response.

In *Dominic*, the prevailing mood is light-hearted delight—in Dominic's adventures, in his total plunge into life and all that it brings, and in the words Steig uses to bring all this to us. We are also deeply touched by universal themes. For instance, when Steig writes about Dominic's reverie on the death of the old pig, we feel beauty, mystery, and sadness:

> Dominic went out for a long walk and did a lot of thinking. He was still walking when the stars came out. Mournful, he lay down on the ground and looked at the stars. Life was mysterious. Bartholomew Badger [the old pig] had been alive long before there was a Dominic—long before anybody had even thought there would ever be such a dog (p. 34).

And later:

> Somehow this kind of thinking made Dominic feel more religious than usual. He fell asleep under the vast dome of quivering stars, and just as he was falling asleep, passing over into the phase of dreams, he felt he understood the secret of life. But in the light of morning, when he woke up, his understanding of the secret had disappeared with the stars. The mystery was still there, inspiring his wonder (p. 35).

As readers remember that feeling of mystery and wonder they may have had from incidents in their own lives that have led them to an acceptance of what life has brought so far and inevitably will bring, they can empathize with Dominic.

To highlight how mood works in story, it may be helpful to first identify what we read that made us feel a certain way, and then look at how the author did this. What did the author do to grip us or put tears in our eyes?

When children share the parts of a story they found funny, sad, or uncomfortable, it is likely they are talking about mood.

Symbol and Extended Metaphor

In story, symbols act to put us in touch with abstract meaning or meaning that cannot be stated directly—the extended metaphor of the work. Symbols influence our interpretations often without our realizing it. It is often through talking with others about a work that we consciously interpret a symbol's significance. Readers of Steig's other works may notice he often describes a dome of quivering stars, as the one mentioned in the *Dominic* text earlier, in which characters have questions of deep wonder and mystery.

In representing a feeling, force, or concept in a story, symbols contribute to developing story tension and resolution. Symbols can also influence story characters and actions as well as intensify mood. In *Dominic*, the little toy puppy symbolizes the thing that Dominic is missing: his love, his mate, and a mother for his children. It leads us to a possible extended metaphor for the book—one of finding a true mate (and achieving a kind of immortality through having children) as life's quest. On his adventures Dominic has many encounters that indicate this metaphor. For example, the dying old pig's wish for Dominic is that he have many heirs. Readers see the delight that Dominic takes in the young of all species, which foreshadows what kind of father he will be. He is overcome with pent-up feelings when he finds the little doll, which inspires that unidentified longing in him. He sniffs the little dog doll, and his heart is "pierced with yearning he didn't understand" (p. 107).

Later, as he awaits the wedding he is attending, he takes out the little doll again. It makes him dream of things to come, and suddenly he knows he is going to be pleased with his future. He dreams of springtime, flowers, pools, and forests—a time of peacefulness and new beginnings.

Finally, Dominic finds the garden where his beautiful mate is sleeping. He awakens her and is told that because he has the doll, he is "the one." All his longings are resolved as he gives her the doll, and she hugs it "like a long-lost child" (p.146). They leave together, and Dominic realizes that he is at the beginning of a great new adventure. All this can be read as an extended metaphor of the meaning of life's journey—the joy of the adventure, the search for the perfect mate, and the possibility of eternal life through one's children.

On the other hand, readers may see the book as a blueprint for functioning in the world—a kind of guidebook for living. Dominic, of course, is a model for facing evil head on. The other characters might also suggest different ways to approach living in the world. Barney Swain (a boar) is a bit of a bore and tends to sit down and wail if things do not go right. Lemuel Wallaby (a turtle) just plods along, happily taking in the world at a very slow pace. Bartholomew Badger accepts that he is at the end of his life—a long and happy one, marred only by the regret he feels over never having had piglets. Elijah Hogg (a donkey) decides that he needs no wealth to be happy; he would rather spend his days browsing in alfalfa. Matilda Fox is the intrepid single mother of five goslings, making the best possible home for them that she can and welcoming all her responsibilities.

But Dominic is the most admirable character of all. He loves the world passionately. He loves his fellow animals and expects that there is good (or was at one time) in everyone. He cares for the old pig out of the goodness of his heart, and although rewarded with material goods, he finds them a great burden and

gives them away. Some have suggested that perhaps the religious order of Preachers or the Dominicans, who were said to be poor and travel on foot, were an inspiration for his character. In this way, for some, *Dominic* can be read as a model of different ways of looking at the world and living one's life.

As readers, we are at our best when we are up to the challenges a good story poses and we are able to successfully bring a unity to the literary experience. When this happens, the story becomes an extended metaphor. The author's aesthetic weaving of story events, images, words, and symbols illuminates the stuff life is made of, helping us contemplate our own experiences, concerns, and commitments. In our reading we seek out encounters with literature that call on us to construct metaphors that open us to the world, jar us into living more consciously, and help us appreciate the human experience.

Teachers and Students at Work

Sometimes it is helpful to look at transcripts of literature studies to see where opportunities to shoot literary arrows have occurred and been taken. The following excerpts are from such conversations in three classrooms. Here, Barbara Hancock's first graders talk about *Sylvester and the Magic Pebble*, another work by Steig:

Joey:	It was neat when the lion was looking at him.
Teacher:	Why did you mark that part?
Joey:	Because the lion is looking at him.
Teacher:	Because it's beginning to get exciting when the lion comes into the picture?
Joey:	Uh-huh.

Teacher:	How do you suppose Sylvester is feeling there?
Joey:	Scared!
Teacher:	Yes. Do you feel the tension building in the story? All of a sudden Sylvester, who is out in the sunshine having a good time playing, finds this little pebble. And bingo! A lion comes upon the scene, and we start to feel the tension building up.
Michelle:	I think it's happy. Because he found a magic pebble, so he might be happy. So I think he is happy.
Alex:	Can I tell you the part I liked because I have the real book at home? I like it when he got home to his parents.
Teacher:	That was the best part of the whole story, wasn't it?
Dominique:	I like the part where the father put the magic pebble on the rock so he could turn into Sylvester again.
Joey:	I know what part. I liked this part where they were sad, and the part where he became the donkey. [He reads the part that says,] "I wish I were myself again. I wish I were my real self again."
Teacher:	That was the part of the story that was filled with pain and tension, wasn't it?

Each teacher will find her or his way of working, but in this excerpt, Barbara picks up on Joey's mention of the lion early on and uses it to talk naturally about the idea of tension and how it builds when there is an incident that makes a reader or a character feel scared. Michelle talks about mood, and Alex skips to the resolution at the end. Joey brings the discussion back to the suspenseful part just before the character is turned into himself again.

Barbara again confirms that feeling of suspense and uses the word tension to label it. Her use of the term is a natural part of the conversation, but she most likely would not have used these "arrows" if she had not been listening to what the children were saying while she was in the midst of the conversation. She chose to focus on suspense and conflict as ways the author pulls us along, but she could have shot arrows about mood (Michelle's happy feelings) or continued to talk about the central tension—what the book is really about—when Alex spoke of the family being reunited.

In this transcript, Josephine Roberts's third graders talk about Patricia MacLachlan's *Sarah, Plain and Tall*:

Kara:	I thought it was a very good story because there is this one part in the story I really connected to. When the storm was coming, Jacob called it a *squall*. I looked it up. And it's only like a vicious storm with wind and thunder. It's like emotions with the characters. They didn't know if the roof would hold up. I could really feel the emotions.
Teacher:	How were some of the characters reacting? You called it a squall?
Kara:	The character, the father, said or called it a squall. I didn't know what that means, so I looked it up.
Teacher:	Is that when lightning is hitting really hard but there is no rain? What were you identifying with with the characters? Let's see if any of the rest of you thought of this. Do you remember what any of the characters were going through?
Kara:	Jacob was really worried that the roof wouldn't hold up, because just before the storm they were about to fix the roof.

Teacher: His concern—wondering if it was going to hold up. How about any of the other characters?

Kara: Sarah is very frightened and Caleb was. It was kind of a scary moment.

Teacher: Why do you think Sarah might be even more upset than Jacob during the storm? Think about what we know about the characters.

Chris: Because she is a girl and she might get more scared.

Teacher: So you think a girl could get more scared? That's one idea.

Michelle: Maybe she wasn't used to that kind of storm.

Teacher: Did she ever mention that kind of storm where she's from? So that's another idea.

Talia: Well, Sarah was very brave when she ran out into the storm.

Chris: She was real brave in the part when the buzzards are around the lamb that was dead. She tried to go in and scare them all off. If they get really mad, they could tear you all up.

Michelle: When Jacob said, "I've got to fix the roof," Sarah said, "No, *we've* got to" because she didn't want to feel left out and think that she was just too girlish to just stay inside and take care of the kids and stuff. She wanted to try and get some action and do other things sort of dangerous. She could have fallen from the roof.

When this transcript was made, Josie and her class were just beginning literature studies. Some of her responses illustrate how difficult it is sometimes to hear and respond to the connections and comments that children make—especially when a teacher tries it for the first time. On the other hand, we can see that she genuinely takes part as a group member, constructing meaning (about squalls) with the others. And although she does not label it with a "symbol" arrow, she builds on Kara's insightful equating of the characters' emotions with the storm. The children take the lead in several spots: Kara says, "It was a scary moment"—a terrific opportunity for talking about tension created through character interaction with event. The group also attempts to refute Chris's first assertion that Sarah may have been afraid just because she was a girl. Their comments illustrate how much the children knew about Sarah's character and how they knew it, and they give opportunity for talking about how an author works to create character.

There will always be missed opportunities to shoot arrows because children's talk is so rich we cannot possibly respond to it all. But the comforting thing about working this way is that there is always another chance tomorrow. In listening to transcripts of our own talk with students, we are constantly as humbled by missed opportunities as we are thrilled by our students' insights.

Here, in another excerpt, Grainne Gardiner-Gay's sixth graders talk about A Day No Pigs Would Die by Robert Newton Peck:

Priscilla: There was a cow in the beginning who was having a calf and it was bleeding all over and it had a hard ball stuck in her windpipe and...

Heather: What was that thing? It said it was called a something...

Priscilla: It was a hard ball. And he had to just, like, get it out and when he got it out, she started running and his arm got stuck in the cow's mouth.

Lauren: He had to use his pants to pull out the calves.

Theresa: I thought it made it more interesting how they made it in details.

Heather: Yeah, he was so detailed about it and how he said he got his hand out of the mouth. He got this big gouge out of it.

Theresa: I thought there were two things. One where, like, everybody dies and you have to live with it. Another is becoming a man is, like, when you do something that you don't really want to, but you have to.

Heather: Yeah, you have to just live with it.

Teacher: So you think that would be the theme of the book, Theresa?

Theresa: Yes, because they mention that more than once—about being a man.

Lauren: It was also funny when he went to the fair with Pinky and he threw up before all...

Heather: Like when he was out there in front of all...

Lauren: Yeah, and it was right on the judge's shoe. And then when Rob's aunt was trying to tutor him because he got a D and he didn't understand what a "tooter" was.

Heather: He thought it was like a clarinet or another instrument.

Theresa: She said, next time I'll teach the pig or something.

In this beginning session, the students are sharing thoughts and impressions and seem truly immersed in recalling the joys and sorrows they experienced in reading the book. Grainne does shoot an arrow to confirm the central tension or theme: becoming a man is doing what has got to be done. And the students roar on, talking about the funny parts—the mood created by all the incidents that made them laugh.

In a later session, the class discusses the extended metaphor in the book of the cycle of life and death and the symbols and foreshadowing of the father's death in more detail:

Lauren: Before, it's like a little bit before they talked about how his Dad was going to die, it talked about how the apple crop was bad. They couldn't have the apples to make pies and stuff. They were having trouble getting their food because the Dad couldn't shoot anything because he didn't have the right kind of gun and stuff.

Theresa: And being poor on the farm made them accept the deaths. It was either the animal dying or they would die.

Teacher: Lauren, when you were talking about the apple crop, maybe that symbolized what was to come that winter. The apple crop wasn't really prosperous, so maybe it was showing what was going to come that winter for the father.

Heather: You could tell that Robert wanted to be closer to his Dad, too. He would be thinking in his head how he would want his Dad just to put out his arms and hug him and say, "I love you." He really didn't get a chance to do that.

Lauren: It seemed like his Dad, his way of loving Rob was sending him to school so he could have a better life than he did.

Teacher: It seemed there were many deaths in the story that foreshadowed the father's. There was a hawk...

Theresa: The rabbit...

Heather: A squirrel.

What Teachers Need to Know   21

Lauren: There was the rabbit because they were out in the field and Rob was sitting with Pinky and this hawk came and pounced on the rabbit. It tells about how he heard the death cry of the rabbit and it was the only time rabbits ever made a noise, when they were dying. It talked about how sad it was.

Teacher: Yes, and the smell of the butchered pigs was like the smell of death.

Heather: When his Dad came home, he could smell it on his fingers and smell it on his clothes, and it never went off his Dad. When they were walking around and stuff, he said there was, like, a stench that would follow him.

Lauren: And that one man who went to dig up the little girl. She was his daughter. She was buried in the wrong place.

Theresa: Well, the deaths in A Day No Pigs Would Die, they were, like, you could tell that they were meant to be because it brought more peace I guess. But in Good Night, Mr. Tom it was sadder because the deaths were more tragic. I guess the baby dying and Zack—that was real sad and the deaths in A Day No Pigs Would Die—they were leading up to the deaths, and in Good Night, Mr. Tom, they were, like, all of a sudden they happened.

Michael: After his Dad died, it seemed like he was more grown up when he got all the people and set up the funeral. He let his mom and aunt go upstairs and he finished the work downstairs.

This discussion is rich. Grainne points out how Lauren's noticing the bad apple crop may have foreshadowed the death coming that winter. She uses the term *symbolic* in a very natural way, building on what the students have noticed. She is listening carefully and shooting literary arrows when appropriate. The group understands the death images and the time concept of foreshadowing as they remember all the incidents dealing with death in the book. They indicate in their remarks how deeply they understand and know the characters of Rob and his father. Theresa compares the story with another they have read, where deaths were shocking—not foreshadowed and not peaceful. And Michael brings the group around again to what perhaps spoke most to him—a young man's painful coming of age.

Final Words

An awareness of an author's literary craft should fill us and our students with delight. Some have worried that a teacher's presence in a group will intimidate and silence students. We have not found this to be the case. In fact, we believe the teacher's presence dignifies and honors the group and the students' individual contributions. If we work from a point of view of sharing our insights and interpretations with other readers of any age, no one should feel that one interpretation or insight is better than another. As alert readers, we share our interpretations with our students, and they share theirs with us. Sometimes there are small epiphanies that make us rejoice in a fellow reader's insights; always there are opportunities for dialogue. Our advice is to plunge in, make it up, and teach like Dominic lived: "Dominic wasn't a bit worried. Challenges were his delight. Whatever life offered was, this way or that, a test of one's skills, one's faculties; and he enjoyed proving equal to these tests" (p. 15).

Reference

Peterson, R., & Eeds, M. (1990). *Grand conversations: Literature groups in action.* New York: Scholastic-TAB.

Children's Literature

MacLachlan, P. (1985). *Sarah, plain and tall.* New York: HarperCollins.

Magorian, M. (1981). *Good night, Mr. Tom.* New York: HarperCollins.

Peck, R.N. (1972). *A day no pigs would die.* New York: Knopf.

Steig, W. (1967). *Sylvester and the magic pebble.* New York: Windmill.

Steig, W. (1984). *Dominic.* New York: Farrar, Straus & Giroux. (Original work published 1972)

Taylor, M.E. (1976). *Roll of thunder, hear my cry.* New York: Dial.

CHAPTER 3

"What Did Leo Feed the Turtle?" and Other Nonliterary Questions

E. Wendy Saul

I hate it when teachers ask skills questions. You want to do well, so you redirect your reading to focus on those kinds of things. It's so insulting, and what's more, it spoils books.

—Mary Posek, English major, recalling her precollege reading experiences

THROUGH UNIVERSITY COURSES in children's literature, reading, and language arts, I teach that young people are best served by real books, conceived and written by authors who care about ideas and language. But privately I worry.... If teachers do not know what to do with a book (and feel that they must do something), will they turn to the skills lists for questions and activities? In short, why is it that the questions my students plan to ask children following the reading of a story, poem, or novel sound like they were manufactured in basal land?

This chapter is premised on two assumptions: first, that interpretation is key to literary comprehension, conversation, and enjoyment, even in the primary grades, and second,

that skills instruction often takes away from literary discourse. At present there is considerable support in the schools for the marriage of literature and skills. This approach makes about as much sense as teaching painting by directing children to hold sticks and wave their hands up and down. Through my own classes I sought to examine how prospective teachers might better understand the importance of interpretive moves and become more adept at asking literary questions.

The work that I report here took place over four semesters. About two years ago I identified what seemed to be the problem: if students were unfamiliar with the pleasures of and meanings evoked through literary conversation, how could I expect them to appreciate the importance of making such talk part of classroom life? I, like most of my colleagues, saw the problem as conceptual. Students had too little experience reading and discussing books. Until they could distinguish between a literary discussion and a teacher-directed reading activity, I could not expect them to ask literary questions.

Teacher-directed reading questions were relatively easy to define. The categories are seemingly neat—main idea, detail, inference, sequencing, vocabulary, opinion—and apparently familiar to students who hadn't yet had a reading methods course. I assumed that these prospective teachers were attracted to reading skills questions, at least in part, because they knew what a reading skills question looked like. But literary conversation is more illusive. They needed examples. They needed models. They needed to experience the satisfaction of feeling how a work, through oral or written communication, becomes one's own.

My students are required to read widely in children's literature, but generally I lead class discussions. To help them better understand interpretation I sought a method that might make them more self-consciously literary in their thinking. I began by reading aloud Cynthia Rylant's (1985) well-crafted and moving story "Slower Than the Rest," which follows Leo, a 10-year-old boy who's been assigned to a class for "slow" children, as he finds and befriends a turtle he names Charlie. During "Fire Prevention Week" Leo brings Charlie, a congenial turtle, to class as part of his presentation.

> "When somebody throws a match into a forest," Leo began, "he is a murderer. He kills trees and birds and animals. Some animals, like deer, are

> fast runners and they might escape. But other animals"—he lifted the cover off the box—"have no hope. They are too slow. They will die." He lifted Charlie out of the box. "It isn't fair," he said, as the class gasped and giggled at what they saw. "It isn't fair for the slow ones."

Leo said much more. Mostly he talked about Charlie, explained what turtles are like, the things they enjoyed, what talents they possessed. He talked about Charlie the turtle and Charlie the friend, and what he said and how he said it made everyone in the class love turtles and hate forest fires. Leo's teacher had tears in her eyes.

Leo follows his class to the "Prevention Week" assembly and mentally drifts off. He is brought back suddenly by a classmate, "Leo it's you...you won!" He had received a plaque for the best presentation in the school. As he shook the principal's hand, "he thought his heart would explode with happiness." The story concludes:

> That night, alone in his room, holding Charlie on his shoulder, Leo felt proud. And for the first time in a long time, Leo felt *fast*.

To see if I was correct in my assumptions about the students' literary orientation (or lack thereof), I asked them to list some questions they would ask children about this story. The majority of questions called upon students to rehearse the text and could be answered with one or two words (although my guess is that children would be asked to write out answers in complete sentences):

- What type of animal was Charlie?
- Why was Charlie special to Leo?

> **"If teachers do not know what to do with a book, will they turn to the skills lists for questions and activities?"**

- What happened to Leo that made him feel fast?

- What did Leo feed the turtle?

- How did Leo feel about himself before the award?

- How did Leo feel about himself after the award?

- How did Leo meet Charlie?

- What does "congenial" mean?

- What made Leo feel unhappy in school?

Another group of questions seemed almost independent of the text:

- Do you think that it is fair to label people?

- Have you ever had a pet?

- How would you feel if you had to be put in a special class for slow learners?

- Would you like to have a pet turtle? Why?

All the queries in group A could easily be marked right or wrong—these are what my students refer to as "fact" questions. The questions in group B are what students call "opinion questions"; here, any answer is welcome.

Finally, there were two questions that might lead children into the story and help them consider the work as a human construction in which craft and effect are taken seriously:

- Were Charlie and Leo alike in any way? How?

- What else could Leo have meant when he said "It isn't fair to the slow ones" during his presentation?

These questions seemed better—they were at once story-oriented and appropriately complex.

My next goal was to find a way to engage these preservice teachers in a literary discussion so that they could better appreciate its value. I wanted to model a teacher style that is at once active, accepting, and critical. I sought an approach that might invite even young children to see that literature can be discussed holistically. I looked for a situation in which there were no right and wrong answers but where textual support for an interpretation would clearly be valued. Here it was: an idea I call "diagramming stories."

The purpose of this exercise is to find a shorthand way to focus on the structural peculiarities of a text, to comment on what in the book or story looms largest to the reader, and to describe, in something close to metaphorical terms, the essence of the book. Moreover, the diagram is seen only as the starting point of a conversation. It is important that we work on a blackboard with chalk. The diagram in this way becomes the visual analog of a conversation—transient but useful in, for instance, writing a paper or centering on a given text.

And my diagrams answer yet another problem—the dilemma of what to do with students who come to class believing that the task of people in literature is to unearth the bizarre in a text, to go where no reader has gone before. Mechanically they set about their business, seemingly untouched by the book and ready to pounce on unsuspecting pupils with queries regarding hidden meaning. The beauty of the diagramming approach recommended here is that it is based largely on a naive reading of the work—it invites students to think about how a given tale is shaped and how it moved the reader. In short, there is no hiding behind literary devices.

Figure 1

I talked with students about interpretation and had the framers of the questions cited earlier work together on a diagram on the blackboard. The original blackboard diagram began like most first attempts—a linear, chronological accounting of the tale. In this instance my student "K." had Leo pictured in a class with several other children. His mouth was down-turned. Another student suggested to K. that she make Leo's head appear square because everyone else in the diagram had round heads. K. thought that was a good idea. Then someone else suggested the possibility of steps to signify important changes in the rhythm of the story. Again there was erasing and discussion. It was at this point—when the discussion grew animated—that I asked students to begin work on their own interpretive drawings. I present three here, accompanied by the students' own (transcribed) comments as they introduced their representations to the class.

I start out with Charlie with a stack of books and him being a little bit bewildered [see Figure 1].

And then he goes and takes a step down when he's put in special ed. He's in there with all the other children, he's the last one with a sad face. I don't know. He feels kind of out-of-place. And I had originally had this with a dotted line going up to a plateau where he's in the car and yells "stop" finding Charlie, but I decided instead it should only be more of a hill because it's only a temporary high. And he slides right back down where it levels off again, where there's other children.

Then there's only Leo and Charlie. Then I had a small step up when he gives the class presentation because he was excited about that. And it made him feel good. He wasn't real thrilled with what the other kids were saying, but I'm pretty sure he liked what he was saying.

And then, finally there's the principal and Leo and he's holding Charlie in his hand and that's a big step up because I think for once he feels faster.

And then, at the end I had little arrows going up because I think that this is just the beginning to where things are going to start moving faster and better for him as he gains more self-confidence.

Figure 2

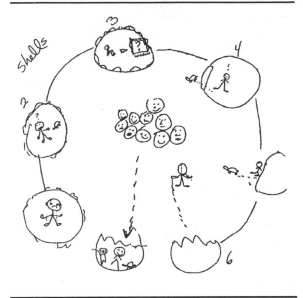

Here [in Figure 2] I have Charlie inside of a shell himself and he's isolated, that's what the shell represents, and he's isolated from the people in the middle, okay?

And in the second shell, that's where he's met Charlie, you know, he's wondering "What is this?" And how do I relate to this animal in a shell also?

And then we have him up in the third shell and that's a window outside the shell and this is kind of like Charlie is looking out of the window also and he's observing things and he's getting Leo to look outside also.

Now there's Charlie walking outside the shell and he's showing Leo there's a way out. And Leo is real surprised and saying, "Maybe I can do that also."

And in #5 he follows Leo toward the group of people so Leo has a lot of curiosity and he wants to explore the world and things like that, and he's showing Charlie that there's no harm in going outside his shell.

In #6 of course he's outside his shell, it's shattered and he goes toward the crowd and he interacts with them like when he interacts with them like when he shares his experiences and his thoughts about the fire and his experiences with Leo.

And the arrow and the dots show him having returned to his shell again, he's got his little first prize award with him to the left and he's a happy little boy there in his shell. But the shell is now shattered and he can go in and out now and interact with people. So that's how I saw it.

I've represented both Charlie and Leo as turtles [see Figure 3]. I didn't use any people and I made the rest of the people hares, rabbits. At the beginning Charlie was behind the rabbits, he was very slow and then he meets another turtle and they're both sort of moving along at the same pace. Then they start to fall in love with each other, they're just really fond of each other. Then he moves over and gives his presentation. And then all the hares fall in love with him and the turtle too and then they receive the award and all the hares are just sitting around looking at him and they're satisfied. Then at the end they're sort of in the same place as the hares.

Figure 3

Saul

I was very pleased. These interpretations were surely literary; students had struggled, productively, to say something significant about the story. And they knew that they had done well. Moreover, they had talked to one another and profited from the suggestions of their peers. Smugly I again asked them to list a few questions for children, now that they better understood the nature of literary conversation.

With one exception (the woman who did the diagram about the shell) nothing changed. The second batch of questions was every bit as mechanical and uncritical and uninspired as the first.

I was puzzled. My only explanation was that they needed more time, that old habits die hard. But the students had been really impressed with one another's work. Why hadn't they, minimally, used the metaphors set up by their peers? Why had no one, for example, asked the children to compare the turtle in this story to the one in "The Tortoise and the Hare"?

Six Months Later

I took the problem, such as you see it, to yet another group of students. I began with a discussion of the importance of literary conversation, and we examined questions from last term's class. This year's group, too, saw these queries as boring, mechanical, not the stuff from which literary understanding is born.

Then we moved to the three renderings cited above. My idea was that the points where the three interpretations differed might serve as a well from which to dip better questions. This happened before I anticipated it. One student, just after hearing the second explanation noted, "Isn't it interesting how they all confuse Leo and Charlie? That might be a good question...Why?" Others agreed. "Why did Rylant give them these names?"

I had a definite sense that this class, composed largely of English majors, clearly understood what an interpretive move looked like. They were even able to generalize some of the characteristics of a literary question:

> "It goes beyond what is in the text, but always comes back to it."

> "The answer to the question could be argued intelligently either way."

> "There are at least two good answers, either of which could help us with the story."

> "The question should help us better understand the story."

> "The question should view the work as a human construction and take seriously issues of craft."

Moreover, the questions asked in last term's class were clearly familiar to this year's group. One student commented:

> My son, he's in ninth grade, loves English this year, for the first time ever. But he tells me that it isn't really English, it's philosophy. His teacher asks what you are calling literary questions, but my son was so used to the other kind he doesn't even recognize this class as English.

The discussion began to shift. Their explanations suggested that the basal-type questions may have to do with some other, more powerful notion of curriculum:

> "Teachers are looking for things they can correct."

> "Teachers want to make sure that the kids have really read the book. We assume they can't be trusted. It also seems that we can't ask something significant until after we've...it's like we've got to separate out the tasks. Like in math, one kind of thing has to come before another."

It became clear that issues of teacher power and powerlessness may also complicate the issue of literary study.

But the influence of nonliterary concerns on literary matters is nowhere more clearly felt than in this statement, which elicited much head nodding:

> But I can see that there's a safety net in those crummy questions. What happens if you get really introspective and very literary-minded and produce children who love English and love books, even in the lower grades, and then their achievement tests aren't great? And then you have everyone, parents and administrators, to contend with, and they all see it as your fault because your questions weren't like the ones on the test. Doing something different is a lot riskier.

They were right. Although one needs the conceptual understanding and experience to write literary questions, the politics of schooling cannot be ignored. Was that threat to their perceived welfare what, in fact, made my previous group of students, usually so anxious to please, hold fast to the safety net of skill-driven questions? Again, a student summarizes this point:

> Maybe we just don't trust our own interpretations. Instead we rely on our ideas of what teachers are supposed to do. We're afraid to play in school, and literary discussion is fun.... Teaching is supposed to be serious business.

I thought we had it all figured out. Just to prove the point, and so that we could all congratulate ourselves, I asked them to write good, literary questions about the Cynthia Voigt novels we had just read.

They began to work. They looked frustrated. And then Dine, in a state of utter agitation, raised her hand. "I want to know why they became friends, but can I say it that simply, or do

I want to say, 'What qualities did Izzy possess that attracted Rosamond to her?'"

There it was, the piece I was looking for. My students had taught me where the inadequate questions came from—the problem was conceptual, yes, and political, yes, but it was also rhetorical.

"Let's try it both ways," I suggested. We did. Stilted lists did not compare favorably to even a rambling struggle to articulate meaning.

Other students jumped in. "If I were talking to a friend, I'd say, 'Why are they friends? Why did it work?' but I want to know if the second question might give kids some help in clearly listing traits."

I felt "M." catch herself falling: "I preferred the question about what qualities because I thought it gave students a framework. If you're trying to move them in a literary direction, maybe we should give them some literary jargon."

Barbara disagreed, "What 'qualities,' what 'personality traits,' makes it sound more psychological than literary." Many nodded in agreement.

We talked a bit longer about how jargon is not jargon when the idea is a part of you and about the importance of authentic language in eliciting authentic responses. Students volunteered, one after another: "I have a really good example of a bad question: 'What is the significance of Patrice's nationality in the story?' What I really want to ask is, 'Why is Patrice French when the story is set on the Eastern Shore?'" There were many more examples— translations of formal language into teacher-owned language, or "comfortable talk." An unusually quiet student summed it up: "If you asked someone your age these [stilted] questions, you'd be embarrassed. Why not be embarrassed asking them to kids?"

I thanked the students. The students thanked me. And we all walked out of class grateful to be engaged in a field that at least, on occasion, celebrates such exchanges.

Conclusion

I knew where to go from here—to the library for further conversation, for a lengthier and more disciplined discussion of the issues raised by my students. The ideas my students and I developed were not exactly new, but through our classroom discoveries they became "ours." This classroom research made scholarship once again fresh—philosophy and research had to be tested against experience, rather than vice versa.

Again, this year I find my students asking questions from basal land, but I understand their impulses more clearly and can, at least, help them practice an alternative: "How is the answer to the question you ask informed by the text?" and "Why does that question interest you?" and "Is that the way you would speak to someone whose ideas you respect?"

I wish to learn with my class, to see ourselves as a community with genuine, bothersome curiosities that drive us to conversations *and* books. Again, my student Mary says it best:

> I worry that I won't, that teachers don't, identify themselves as learners. You go through the educational system and you think you've collected all your credentials and you assume, or you've been invited to assume, I think quite erroneously, that you have the answers. And then you put yourself in the position of a teacher or a parent, and you think you should share this knowledge or wisdom with children. Whereas, if you put yourself in the position of learning, continuous learning, learning from them and learning something about yourself, you're in a better position to teach.

Reference

Rylant, C. (1985). *Every living thing*. New York: Bradbury.

CHAPTER 4

The Books Make a Difference in Story Talk

Miriam G. Martinez and Nancy L. Roser

I
T IS SPRING, and Ms. González's second grade class has begun to move from picture book read-aloud units to reading and talking about chapter books. Their first chapter book was *The Castle in the Attic* by Elizabeth Winthrop. In this fantasy the young hero, William, through a magical gift from his nanny, Mrs. Phillips, travels back in time to medieval England. There he confronts the wicked wizard, Alastor, who has conquered the kingdom and turned much of the populace to stone. Now they are reading Phyllis Reynolds Naylor's *Shiloh*, the Newbery award–winning story of Marty, a boy who secretly harbors a dog to protect it from further abuse by its owner—the surly Judd Travers. Marty struggles with a moral dilemma: whether it is better to lie and shelter a dog that is not legally his or to give Shiloh back to certain cruelty from Judd. The second graders stop to talk after the second chapter of *Shiloh*:

Ms. G: Kind of rethinking on chapters one and two and what you had written

in your journals, what were your thoughts and wonderings? Matthew?

Matthew: William reminds me of Marty.

Anna: Marty *is* sorta like William because he's so nice to the dog and stuff.

Ms. G: Paul, did you want to bring up somebody else you're reminded of?

Paul: William and Marty both found something wonderful. Marty found a dog, and in *Castle in the Attic* William found the half of the token.

Ben: He didn't *find* it.

Paul: I mean when the soldier [knight] dropped it, he was looking at William, and he found it.

Albert: Judd is like Alastor.

Ms. G: How is he like him?

Albert: Because Judd was mean to everybody just like him. And Alastor didn't like anybody either. He froze them. And Judd hurts them.

Adam: Judd's like Alastor. The dogs are [like] the people and get turned to stone. The dogs are sort of like that.

32

Ms. G: Why do you see them like that?

Adam: Cause he...instead of turning them into stone, he [Judd] is mean to them.

Paul: I disagree. I think Marty is like Tolliver.

Ms. G: You're saying he's more like Tolliver, the young boy in *Castle*.

Lindsey: I think William and Marty are more alike because they each had to make a choice in the story.

Alex: Yeah, because Shiloh has to leave and Mrs. Phillips.... He [William] don't want Mrs. Phillips to go [to return to England], and Marty don't want Shiloh to go. So, it's kind of like the other.

Amanda: When William didn't want Mrs. Phillips to go and Marty didn't want Shiloh to go, because there's two different reasons....

Children have much to say about stories. At times their talk is remarkably insightful, as in this instance. As we watch and listen in classrooms, we find even very young children sharing wonderful ideas in response to books. Like the other authors in this volume, we are convinced that book talk can serve to promote deeper insights, tap into and build children's literary and language experiences, and bring life experiences to the surface. Book talk gives children a chance to say what they think, to share their connections with text, and to collaborate in group-constructed meanings.

Rich book talk has some distinctive features. It is diverse talk that explores the story world, the messages that emerge from that world, and the crafting of the story. Good book talk is recognizable when children grapple with core issues, compare insightfully, observe closely, question profoundly, and relate life experiences to story situations. When talk with these kinds of features occurs, we often find

that the "book talkers" are members of a community of readers (and writers) who collaborate to build meanings.

The best book talk is not launched when a teacher fires a set of questions designed to monitor readers' grasp of the storyline, as noted in the previous chapter; rather, it occurs when the story itself and children's honest, spontaneous reactions are central to the discussion. If we look closely at the practices of teachers who effectively lead literary discussion, we can find commonality in what teachers do to preserve literature (and children's ideas) as they initiate and receive rich talk:

Good book talk happens when books are drawn together into instructional units that share a focus, topic, or theme. When books are linked, their interrelationships can elicit insightful comparisons and literary talk.

Better book talk is fueled by writing opportunities. After reading or listening to a story, giving children an opportunity to write (or scribble or draw) their thoughts or feelings before group discussion allows them time to formulate their thoughts. This type of personal writing before story talk enriches the talk and ensures wider participation and genuine exchange.

Many teachers are finding that better book talk is a result of having a plan for book talk. The plan is shaped by the story itself and its possibilities but can be abandoned or modified as the conversation changes.

Good book talk seems to depend on a conversational setting. Book talkers who gather face-to-face simulate conversational (rather than traditional classroom) style—facilitating the free flow of ideas.

Book talk is sometimes dependent on returning to the story. For young children, this may mean rereading. For older children, returning to the text means finding support for thoughts and is desirable for literature study.

Good book talk depends on having experienced models who offer genuine responses to the story. Most often, that model is a teacher who has read the story, has noted her or his own responses, and comes to the book discussion prepared to share those insights.

Story as Experience, Message, and Object

Teachers have clearly discovered a great deal about promoting literary discussion in elementary classrooms. Nonetheless, some classrooms have effective practices in place, and even then the *nature* of the talk varies considerably. Sometimes, for example, children appear to be caught up in exploring the world of the story as they talk through the characters' obstacles and operate within the web of story events. At other times, children spend more time exploring the messages or meanings (metaphors) of stories. More rarely, the children's talk delves into the author's crafting of the story.

To understand some of the diversity of story talk, we have referred to Cianciolo's (1982) article "Responding to Literature as a Work of Art," which explains that readers consider story as *experience*, as *message*, and as *object*. Talk about story as experience is talk about the world of the story—about its characters, their motivations, tensions, and triumphs—as a "lived-through experience." When story is construed and talked about as *message*, readers explore the central truths or themes that the story holds for each of them. When story is considered as *object*, readers look at how the story works, how it is crafted, how the author establishes tension, determines the point of view, helps characters grow and change, establishes mood, or uses symbols. As we have worked with teachers from kindergarten through fifth grade, we have noticed that story talk moves in all these different directions and that the story itself helps to shape the story talk.

Stories Shape Book Talk

We have selected excerpts from story discussions in three classrooms to illustrate the directions story talk takes and the characteristics of the stories that seem to move the talk in certain ways. The experienced teachers we work with read aloud daily to their students and give them time to talk about what they are reading. In these daily discussions, teachers like Ms. Fry, Ms. González, and Ms. Lopez invite children's talk about the book features and events they notice, wonder about, or connect with. They see their role in classroom book discussion as participants who share their insights, support their students' meaning making, and follow conversational leads. But with teachers and children who are experienced with book talk, conversations naturally shift emphasis depending on *what* story is being talked about.

Stories that Stimulate Talk Within the Story World

When children become engaged in lengthy discussions about the story world, they "step into the story," as Judith Langer (1992) describes it. Once inside this world, they reason logically (and sometimes vehemently), weaving ideas from across the text to support their positions. They build on and challenge the stances their peers have assumed, as they conscientiously defend their interpretations of characters and events. This involvement in the world of the story was apparent when Ms. Fry's fourth graders dis-

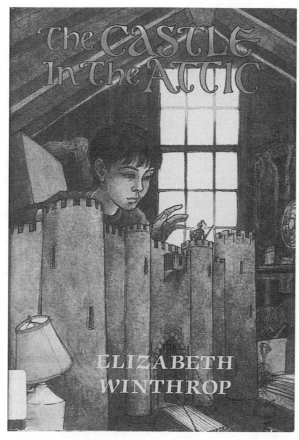

Cover illustration from The Castle in the Attic *by* Elizabeth Winthrop, *jacket by* Trina Schart Hyman. ©1985 *by* Elizabeth Winthrop. *Reprinted by permission of* Holiday House.

cussed *The Castle in the Attic*: they speculated about whether the aged Calendar, once caregiver to the brave knight, Sir Simon, knew how to restore the people of the kingdom (who had been turned into lead by the wicked Alastor) to their natural state:

> Gina: I wonder if Calendar knew how to save the lead people.
>
> Ms. Fry: Suppose Calendar may have a clue to all this, do you think? Anybody want to respond to anything Gina just said?

> Carol: I think Calendar does know the antidote because Calendar never got to finish because Alastor started coming in the room [and talking] about the mirror and everything. There may have been more she wanted to say, but there may not have been enough time.
>
> Ms. Fry: Okay, that's a possibility.
>
> Mark: I think Calendar knows because when William was fixing to look in the mirror Alastor said, "You don't know what the mirror does, do you?" And then he said, "Right Calendar?" still looking at William because Calendar knows most of the stuff 'cause she's been there for awhile.
>
> Laura: I agree with Alisa and Gina and Mark because Calendar's been there for a long, long time, and earlier in the book the apple man said, "Alastor won't let my mom come out of the castle." And so there is a spell that she'll probably know about because she knows about the mirror, and she knows how to turn people into lead. She probably knows how to turn people back into human beings.
>
> Allison: I agree with them because in the beginning of the book it said she heard a lot of the spells that Alastor had been saying, and she was in there. She peeked in the castle.
>
> Alisa: Well, my question for Laura is why if she [Calendar] knows the spell, then why wouldn't she just use it when Alastor was gone? I mean, like a tiny one that he might not notice right away.
>
> Thomas: Well, I know she really hates Alastor and everything, but maybe she really didn't have the strength to do it because she saw what happened to all those other people. And then she saw all the strength

in William and she said, "I can do it; I can do it."

Ms. Fry: She's feeding on William's courage.

Alisa: Then why, when she heard that Sir Simon was coming with a boy, why did she think that that little boy that doesn't have any weapons or anything [unintelligible] who doesn't even have a simple dagger....

Ms. Fry: Who wants to respond over here to what Alisa's talking about?

Chris: I think that [the reason] she didn't want to use the spells that turned the lead people into humans again is because all the guards would probably tell Alastor and *she'd* be turned into lead.

Like these fourth graders, other elementary school students also become immersed in the world of the story. Yet, this type and degree of involvement occur only with some of the stories the children talk about. What is it about particular texts that focuses and sustains such "grand" book conversations (Eeds & Wells, 1989)? What kinds of text engage, support, or lead children into this lived-through experience?

Perhaps stories with dramatic plot structures have the greatest power to propel children into the world of the story. Stories with a *problem* with which children can identify—and to which a solution is not immediately evident—invite them to live a little longer under the spell of a good story, as Galda, Cullinan, and Strickland (1993) contend. Stories such as *Cloudy with a Chance of Meatballs* by Judi Barrett make children giggle, then guffaw, and finally really chatter about what will become of the town of Chewandswallow when the weather goes out of control and giant pancakes cover the school. *Two Bad Ants* by Chris Van Allsburg and William Joyce's *George Shrinks* cause children to think about their world from different perspectives. And when a character that children have taken to their heart stumbles, the children climb right into the story to pose fix-up plans, as they do for *Maniac Magee* by Jerry Spinelli.

Stories that Cause Children to Tussle with Story Theme

As children express and try to support what they are thinking and feeling, they trust the other members of their "interpretive community" (see Chapter 10 by McGee) to receive their naive, imperfectly formed impressions of what the story offers. Children's discussion of themes or story messages can take different forms. Sometimes students talk about characters' dilemmas and the lessons characters learn; sometimes they talk about what authors are saying to readers. One thing is certain: although children's expressions of story messages are not offered with adult precision, they can be fresh, graceful, and wise. Children of all ages *can* reach to express their understanding at the level adults call "thematic" (Lehr, 1991), and some stories seem to result in greater proportions of this thematic talk, as in the following examples.

Ms. González's second graders raised questions about Marty, the boy who wanted the dog Shiloh so much that he built a hidden pen and told no one the dog's whereabouts—neither his parents who forbade him to keep the dog nor Judd Travers, the dog's abusive owner. Enclosed in the pen, Shiloh is savagely attacked by a German shepherd. Marty's intentions to protect Shiloh have gone awry, and the second graders struggle with the moral and ethical dimensions of the problem:

Sabrina: I wish Marty told the whole truth in the beginning.

Ms. G: What do you mean by the whole truth?

Sabrina: If he would have told the whole truth, then it would have been a lot gooder.

Tishia: Because if he lied the rest of his life, then...

Chris: He could lie sometimes because...

Tishia: He lied to Judd Travers because he didn't want to give up Shiloh, and Shiloh didn't want to go back.

Ms. G: So should Marty tell the truth?

Anna: He had a good reason!

Ms. G: What's a good reason that Marty had for lying?

Albert: He doesn't want another dog to get hurt...

Even young children work toward understanding theme as it reveals itself through character dilemmas. When Ms. Lopez introduced her kindergarten class to their first chapter book, the conversation was lively and sustained. The children thought long and hard about William and his problem throughout the daily chapters of *The Castle in the Attic*. When the main character, William, selfishly used a magic talisman to shrink his beloved nanny just to keep her from leaving him, five-year-old Uri tried to express one of life's and literature's most poignant insights:

Ms. L: Do you he think he [William] feels bad now when he looks back at having done all this [having made Mrs. Phillips small in order to keep her]? How do you think he feels about that now?

Children: Bad.

Uri: Better.

Ms. L: Why do you think he feels better?

Uri: Because he can help her get back to normal size, and she can go and do whatever she wants because even if you love them, you always have to let somebody go.

Children seem to talk about thematic issues when they read and listen to multilayered stories in which characters deal with dilemmas that call values into play. Perhaps that is why the students that Eeds and Wells (1989) observed producing "grand conversations" about books had the grandest of all about *Tuck Everlasting* by Natalie Babbitt—a story worth turning over in the mind and talking meaningfully about. Even when the same teachers and children talked together, the children's ideas were more perceptive and carefully weighed when *Tuck Everlasting* was the conversational focus rather than, for example, *Harriet the Spy* by Louise Fitzhugh. While *Harriet the Spy* is a book that is rich in character development and adventure, it does not address the kinds of life and death issues that are central to *Tuck Everlasting*. Just as *Tuck Everlasting* is a prime example of a novel worth savoring, so are Mary Hoffman's *Amazing Grace* and *The Wednesday Surprise* by Eve Bunting picture books to consider deeply. Teachers count on Cynthia Voigt, Katherine Paterson, Susan Cooper, Virginia Hamilton, Lloyd Alexander, Cynthia Rylant, and Mildred Taylor as just a few authors who consistently give readers stories to ponder.

Stories that Cause Children to Notice Author and Illustrator Craft

In general, children are not as likely to launch into talk about the crafting of a story as they are about the story experience. Even so, we have noted that when young children do try to view the story as a creation, it may be because the book has some distinctive, easily discernible structural, design, or language features. Kindergartners immediately noticed the page design of *Up and Down on the Merry-Go-Round* by Bill Martin Jr and John Archambault, and made the following comments:

"I think the words are real neat, because when you read the last part, one was on one side and the other was on the other side!"

"The other part of the horse is on the back."

"The tail's on the other side."

Kindergartners also recognize the styles of favorite artists:

"Leo Lionni draws good mouses."

"His mouses are as good as Jose Aruego."

And, they pay attention to the patterns of language, as did these five-year-olds who were invited to talk about *Up and Down on the Merry-Go-Round*:

Ms. L: What did you think of the book?

Child: That made me go ummm, ummm, ummm.

Ms. L: It made you feel like you were going up and down.

Child: Yes, I got dizzy by it.

Ms. L: Why did you get dizzy?

Child: Because my head, remember my head's going ummm, ummm, ummm.

Books with pages and patterns to talk about, with language that tumbles or dances rhythmically or with design features that cannot be ignored, lead the youngest book talkers to say what they see and appreciate. *I Am Eyes Ni Macho* by Leila Ward causes young readers to find patterns in color; Eric Carle's *The Very*

Books that Entice Students to Respond to Story as Experience

Picture Books

Blueberries for Sal by Robert McCloskey (1963). New York: Viking.
A Chair for My Mother by Vera Williams (1982). New York: Greenwillow.
Chrysanthemum by Kevin Henkes (1991). New York: Greenwillow.
Doctor DeSoto by William Steig (1982). New York: Farrar, Straus & Giroux.
Flossie and the Fox by Patricia McKissack (1986). New York: Dial.
Jimmy Lee Did It by Pat Cummings (1985). New York: Lothrop, Lee & Shepard.
The Mysterious Tadpole by Steven Kellogg (1977). New York: Dial.
Sylvester and the Magic Pebble by William Steig (1979). New York: Windmill.
The Wreck of the Zephyr by Chris Van Allsburg (1983). Boston, MA: Houghton Mifflin.

Chapter Books

The Boggart by Susan Cooper (1993). New York: Margaret K. McElderry.
Charlotte's Web by E.B. White, illustrated by G. Williams (1952). New York: HarperCollins.
From the Mixed Up Files of Mrs. Basil E. Frankweiler by E.L. Konigsburg (1987). New York: Dell.
Hatchet by Gary Paulsen (1987). New York: Bradbury.
The Hideout by Eve Bunting (1991). San Diego, CA: Harcourt Brace.
James and the Giant Peach by Roald Dahl, illustrated by N.E. Burkert (1961). New York: Knopf.
Jeremy Thatcher, Dragon Hatcher by Bruce Coville (1991). San Diego, CA: Harcourt Brace.
Ramona Quimby, Age Eight by Beverly Cleary, illustrated by A. Tiegreen (1981). New York: Morrow.
The Stories Julian Tells by Ann Cameron, illustrated by A. Strugnell (1981). New York: Knopf.
Trumpet of the Swan by E.B. White, illustrated by E. Frascino (1970). New York: HarperCollins.
The Whipping Boy by Sid Fleischman, illustrated by P. Sis (1986). New York: Greenwillow.

Books that Entice Students to Respond to Story as Message

Picture Books

Chicken Sunday by Patricia Polacco (1992). New York: Philomel.
Drylongso by Virginia Hamilton, illustrated by J. Pinkney (1992). San Diego, CA: Harcourt Brace.
Faithful Elephants by Yukio Tsuchiya, translated by T. Dykes, illustrated by T. Lewin (1988). Boston, MA: Houghton Mifflin.
Frederick by Leo Lionni (1967). New York: Pantheon.
The Lotus Seed by Sherry Garland, illustrated by T. Kiuchi (1993). San Diego, CA: Harcourt Brace.
Nana Upstairs, Nana Downstairs by Tomie dePaola (1978). New York: Penguin.
Summer Wheels by Eve Bunting, illustrated by T.B. Allen (1992). San Diego, CA: Harcourt Brace.
The Tenth Good Thing about Barney by Judith Viorst, illustrated by E. Blegvad (1971). New York: Atheneum.
William's Doll by Charlotte Zolotow, illustrated by W.P. duBois (1972). New York: HarperCollins.
Working Cotton by Shirley Anne Williams, illustrated by C. Byard (1992). San Diego, CA: Harcourt Brace.

Chapter Books

Bridge to Terabithia by Katherine Paterson (1977). New York: Crowell.
The Lion, the Witch and the Wardrobe by C.S. Lewis, illustrated by P. Baynes (1961). New York: Macmillan.
Missing May by Cynthia Rylant (1992). New York: Orchard.
Mississippi Bridge by Mildred Taylor, illustrated by M. Ginsburg (1990). New York: Dial.
Number the Stars by Lois Lowry (1989). New York: Dell.
Sadako and the Thousand Paper Cranes by Eleanor Coerr, illustrated by R. Himler (1977). New York: Dell.
Sarah, Plain and Tall by Patricia MacLachlan (1985). New York: HarperCollins.
The Shimmershine Queens by Camille Yarbrough (1989). New York: Putnam.
A Wrinkle in Time by Madeline L'Engle (1962). New York: Farrar, Straus & Giroux.

Busy Spider is just one of this author's books worth touching and noting patterns in text. Lois Ehlert lets children discover special features in perspective and color, and Dr. Seuss and Bill Martin Jr are two of the most appreciated masters of craft who cause books to be viewed as works of art.

Stepping back from text also allows older children and their teachers to inspect the way stories work and appreciate the skilled crafting that has created the art form. When fifth grader, Yoshio, talked about *Shiloh*, she said of Phyllis Reynolds Naylor:

> I know why the author wrote a boy instead of a girl. I think that because a boy or man proves their manhood by killing or abusing animals. So she wrote a soft boy instead of a soft girl. So she was trying to say that just 'cause you're a boy or man does not mean you have to abuse animals to prove your manhood.

If they are given the best of carefully crafted books and the guidance of perceptive teachers, children will respond readily to many of the "literary arrows" (as Eeds and Peterson call them) that teachers loft. However, if older students who read these finely crafted books choose to talk about "the story as object," it may be necessary for the teacher to first be knowledgeable about the art of literature (see also Chapter 2).

Titles that Invite Lively Talk

Carefully choosing books for read-alouds is a prerequisite for ensuring lively book discussions. We asked experienced teachers to recommend titles they have found to be especially evocative of rich responses to the story as experience, message, or object. Here in the figures on pages 38 to 40 is a sampling of these titles.

Picture Books

Black and White by David Macaulay (1990). Boston, MA: Houghton Mifflin.

Chicka-Chicka-Boom-Boom by Bill Martin Jr & John Archambault, illustrated by T. Rand (1988). New York: Henry Holt.

The Day of Ahmed's Secret by Florence Parry Heide & Julie Heide Gilliland, illustrated by T. Lewin (1990). New York: Lothrop, Lee & Shepard.

Fortunately by Remy Charlip (1971). New York: Parents Magazine Press.

The Great Kapok Tree by Lynne Cherry (1990). San Diego, CA: Harcourt Brace.

Jumanji by Chris Van Allsburg (1981). Boston, MA: Houghton Mifflin.

The Napping House by Audrey Wood, illustrated by D. Wood. (1989). San Diego, CA: Harcourt Brace.

Pish, Posh, Said Hieronymus Bosch by Nancy Willard, illustrated by L. & D. Dillon (1991). San Diego, CA: Harcourt Brace.

The Stinky Cheese Man by Jon Scieszka, illustrated by L. Smith (1992). New York: Viking.

Tuesday by David Wiesner (1991). New York: Clarion.

Chapter Books (and Poetry Collections)

Journey by Patricia MacLachlan (1991). New York: Delacorte.

Joyful Noise by Paul Fleischman, illustrated by E. Beddows (1988). New York: HarperCollins.

Maniac Magee by Jerry Spinelli (1990). Boston, MA: Little, Brown.

My Side of the Mountain by Jean Craighead George (1959). New York: Dutton.

On Meeting Witches at Wells by Judith Gorog (1991). New York: Philomel.

The Phantom Tollbooth by Norton Juster, illustrated by J. Feiffer (1961). New York: Random House.

Tuck Everlasting by Natalie Babbitt (1975). New York: Farrar, Straus & Giroux.

Illustration from Nancy Willard's Pish, Posh, Said Hieronymus Bosch. *Illustrated by the Dillons.* ©1991 *by Nancy Willard. Reprinted by permission of Harcourt Brace & Company.*

Different Books = Different Invitations to Talk

Children have much to say when they read the right books, and particular types of books appear to move talk in different directions. To ensure that children respond to literature in diverse ways, teachers must share a rich array of books. The range of book experience should include multilayered stories that challenge children to think deeply about important issues, books in which characters are caught up in problematic situations that are not readily resolved, and distinctly crafted stories that are truly memorable for their artistry. Teachers who use such a profusion of literature, as well as instructional strategies that invite children to share their thoughts, will find (given time and patience) that rich talk will flourish in their classrooms.

Notes

We wish to thank Debbie Price for her help in gathering and compiling teachers' recommendations for books that lead talk and Martha Garcia for letting us preserve her children's thoughts.

References

Cianciolo, P. (1982). Responding to literature as a work of art—An aesthetic literary experience. *Language Arts*, 59, 259–264.

Eeds, M., & Wells, D. (1989). Grand conversations: An exploration of meaning construction in literature study groups. *Research in the Teaching of English*, 23, 4–29.

Galda, L., Cullinan, B.E., & Strickland, D.S. (1993). *Language, literacy and the child*. Fort Worth, TX: Harcourt Brace.

Langer, J. (1992). Rethinking literature instruction. In J.A. Langer (Ed.), *Literature instruction: A focus on student response* (pp. 35–53). Urbana, IL: National Council of Teachers of English.

Lehr, S.S. (1991). *The child's developing sense of theme: Responses to literature*. New York: Teachers College Press.

Children's Literature

Babbitt, N. (1975). *Tuck everlasting*. New York: Farrar, Straus & Giroux.

Barrett, J. (1978). *Cloudy with a chance of meatballs*. Ill. by R. Barrett. New York: Atheneum.

Bunting, E. (1989). *The Wednesday surprise*. New York: Clarion.

Carle, E. (1984). *The very busy spider*. New York: Philomel.

Fitzhugh, L. (1980). *Harriet the spy*. New York: Dell.

Hoffman, M. (1991). *Amazing Grace*. New York: Dial.

Joyce, W. (1985). *George shrinks*. New York: HarperCollins.

Martin, B. Jr, & Archambault, J. (1988). *Up and down on the merry-go-round*. Ill. by T. Rand. New York: Holt.

Naylor, P.R. (1991). *Shiloh*. New York: Atheneum.

Spinelli, J. (1990). *Maniac Magee*. Boston, MA: Little, Brown.

Van Allsburg, C. (1988). *Two bad ants*. Boston, MA: Houghton Mifflin.

Ward, L. (1978). *I am eyes Ni macho*. Ill. by N. Hogrogian. New York: Greenwillow.

Winthrop, E. (1985). *The castle in the attic*. New York: Holiday House.

CHAPTER 5

Teacher Book Clubs: Making Multicultural Connections

Diane Lapp, James Flood, Carol Kibildis, Mary Ann Jones, and Juel Moore

"IF YOU DON'T do something about her language, I'm going to beat her up!" There they stood, glowering at one another in front of the principal's desk—three African American girls and one white girl, Shannon, from a fifth grade class. In anger, Shannon had used racial slurs. The other girls had made it clear they were restraining themselves from pummeling Shannon, and something had to be done. The principal had several options, but she chose education; she chose to involve all the girls in a multicultural book club to help promote understanding among cultures. Where did this idea come from?

Creating Multicultural Book Clubs

A year before this incident, Shannon's principal was involved in establishing and participating in a multicultural book club for teachers at her elementary school. She learned about faculty book clubs from two professors from the local university who had established a teacher preparation program at her school. Together she and the professors set up the book club, which was similar to one the professors had helped found at a local high school in the same district. The high school book clubs began when an English teacher talked with her principal about feeling unprepared to understand the many cultures that were represented in her classroom. Her principal, a doctoral student of the professors, initiated a group conversation from which grew the idea of creating a multicultural literature discussion group comprised of teachers who would read and reflect on issues of multiculturalism in U.S. society. They wanted to see if fiction by authors from various ethnic backgrounds would help them better understand themselves and their students from diverse backgrounds. This book club—teachers of different subjects and ethnic groups as well as the principal and the two university education professors—met at a large urban, multiethnic, multilinguistic high school. The group's readings included short stories from *Woman Hollering Creek* and *House on Mango Street* by Sandra Cisneros, *The Bluest Eye* by Toni Morrison, Zora Neale Hurston's *Their Eyes Were Watching God*, and *The Joy Luck Club* by Amy Tan. The educators met once a month at lunchtime for literature discussion. (For a more complete description, see Flood et al.,1992.)

Shannon's principal's student population was similar to this high school—multicultural and multilingual. When she and the professors introduced the idea to her faculty, a group also decided to form a book club. The teachers came from different grade levels, represented different ethnic groups, and read some of the same works as did the high school teachers in their book club.

The teachers, the principal, vice principal, and the same two university education professors met together after school once a month. In addition, the elementary principal also organized a book club for a small group of students. Currently, an ethnically diverse group of six students meets with the principal once a week at lunchtime to discuss a book the principal reads aloud. The students also choose another book to read on their own and talk about in the weekly session. Their choices have included *Do Like Kyla* by Angela Johnson, *Sami and the Time of the Trouble* by Florence Heide and Judith Heide Gilliland, Eloise Greenfield's book *Sister*, *Molly's Pilgrim* by Barbara Cohen, Judith Vigna's *Black Like Kyra*, *White Like Me*, and *Three Strong Women* by Claus Stamm. It was a club like this that Shannon joined.

Developing Multicultural Understanding from One Another and from Text

In teacher and student book clubs, readers look at similarities among people, despite their cultural differences. The awakening insights of the members become most apparent when they make a personal connection with a text written by an author who represents an ethnic group other than their own, as illustrated in the following comment by an African American male English teacher:

> When she talks about the sweater it reminded me of my cousin and me. We grew up together. We got sweaters from my aunt and my mom, and they were really ugly sweaters. And we had to put them on and go to school. We had to walk a little distance out in the country from our home to the road, so we hid them in the woods and got on the school bus and picked them up on the way home (Flood et al.,1992, p. 4).

As another illustration of crosscultural empathy, an African American female elementary teacher said:

> This story really touched on my struggle for education. Like the Jimenezs', I'm pursuing education when I could be earning a living for my family.... It is scary to go beyond the known. It's scary to leave your own world, your own culture (Flood et al., 1992, p. 5).

When participants are the same ethnicity as the focus author, they often share insights from their personal experiences to clarify and enrich aspects of the story for other members of the group, as the following exchange illustrates. Lydia is Hispanic and teaches English; Jeff is Euro-American and teaches math.

> Lydia: Can I...um...interject just one little
> thing about those candies that are cone

shaped? I don't know how many of you have ever seen those...

Jeff: I've never seen those.

Lydia: ...but they're rainbow colored, and in Spanish they're called pidoleans.

Jeff: Pidoleans?

Lydia: They were always sold in my neighborhood. There would be this man with this cardboard thing with holes in 'em, and the pidoleans would be for sale. And so that would be.... Talk about a familiar image, just like you mentioned. I can just see that hard candy. You could never chew it. It was to be licked (Lapp et al., in press).

Teachers in many school districts are joining literary discussion groups and being exposed to new multicultural insights. One teacher said, "I gained a broader understanding of other cultures" and "a respect for other life styles" (Bealor, 1992, p. 23); another revealed, "I need to realize and deal with the fact that my students may be coming from a completely different place than I am. I must see that in order to teach them effectively" (Hansen-Krening, 1992, p. 14).

Discussing the Text: Shared Voices

Many teachers admit to not having had much experience in literary discussions. Rather, their personal reading is a solitary activity (Bealor, 1992). They recall that in their own school experience they learned about literature through various experiences, many of which did not stress reader response. Book clubs provide them an outlet through which they can express their responses and understandings. Teachers who have had experience in literary discussion have opportunity to model responsive reading for others (Fisher & Shapiro, 1991; Hansen-Krening, 1992). All participants in a book club can progress at their

own rate; for example, in a book club of preservice teachers in San Diego, California, two members had had little to say during their first semester of participation. During their second semester, though, they joined a newly formed book club, found themselves to be its most experienced members, and became discussion leaders.

As teachers participate in book clubs that focus on multicultural literature, they share ideas, thoughts, feelings, and reactions. Often, these discussions begin with teachers offering their personal responses to literature. As trusting connections develop among the conversants, they develop awareness of other cultures through the books' characters and their interactions. Also, over time, book club participants seem to move from talking more about personal experience to talking equally about text and personal experience (Flood et al., 1992), as the following quote from a Euro-American male social studies teacher demonstrates:

People would say this is Hispanic. But I think it transcended all that. It was almost a parallel. I was reading the story as a story, fascinating and well done, but I was...I was living along with some of the things that brought back memories of a kid. I was telling this girl, I was living with my grandma who was Yugoslavian. The similarities with almost the classic grandma were just incredible.... That's the beauty of reading; we can stop and go back (p. 4).

Building a Team

When teachers work together over time and share their thoughts, bonds begin to form, and trust grows. Teachers see one another in a different light, which may lead to collaboration on curriculum issues. As teachers begin to use literary discussion in the classroom, they feel more connected to others. One teacher summarized, "This group has helped

If you are thinking of starting a teacher book club, here are some tips:

• Start with short stories to accommodate teachers' busy schedules, and move to short novels later. Ask members to suggest works they know.

• Vary the represented ethnicity of works after two or three sessions.

• Seek out staff members representative of the ethnic groups at the school to be involved in the book club.

• Ask participants to respond to their reading in a journal. Journal entries can be used to begin discussion or referred to during discussion.

• Begin discussion with broad questions such as, "What did you think about the book?" If the discussion lags, use prompts such as, "What feelings did you have as you were reading the book?" or "Did the story cause you to think about other experiences you've had?" or "What questions did you have as you were reading?" With experience, once the discussion begins, it flows easily, and there is very little need for additional questions.

• The transfer from teacher book club to classroom practice does not happen immediately; teachers need plenty of time to experience the literature and literary discussion involving personal response.

• Team building will happen without any preplanning on your part.

its members find a forum where all thoughts and opinions were welcomed and respected. It also helped the participants come to know one another better. These new relationships have carried over into other areas of the education program" (Bealor, 1992, p. 23).

Taking Book Clubs into the Classroom

So what happens when teachers who are book club members take the book club idea into their classrooms? After teachers have participated in these book clubs, they demonstrate an enthusiasm for multicultural literature. They carry this enthusiasm back to the classroom as they adapt and implement book club procedures with their students. We noticed that when teachers used book club discussion with their classes, their students were increasingly able to explain aspects of the literature to one another; they developed a deeper understanding of both the text and

their classmates, and they developed stronger ties with their peers (Lapp et al., in press). As one teacher explained, "The students seem to be much more involved and inspired to read books with characters and situations with which they can identify or at least recognize. The characters in these books represent them or their friends" (Bealor, 1992, p. 23). Samway and her student colleagues (1991) report that students' interpretations of the text, reactions, insights, and impressions are not only considered worthy to bring to discussion, but are regarded as essential.

When teachers have become more familiar and comfortable with multicultural literature and literary discussion through their own book clubs, they begin to add to the contents of their library shelves and broaden the choices within their text sets and reading lists. The most evident change is their active introduction of more multicultural titles into their classrooms (Hansing-Krening, 1992). Some teachers also present this literature to their students differently than before; because teachers have been experiencing their own vital book club conversations, classroom talk begins to take on richer textures. One Hispanic female elementary teacher explained it this way:

> I got so much out of participation in these discussions, and they were so much fun. I decided to try the same thing out with my students.... They really enjoyed it. Well, I had to work at it, but I think my students got a lot more out of the book this way [discussion groups] than they would if I had taught this book like I usually do (Flood, 1992, p. 5).

Along with the discussion group format, many teachers who are in book clubs bring more responsive writing opportunities to their classrooms, modeled on the response journal format of their book club experiences. Students also seem to write more first drafts of responses to bring to discussion group.

Book Clubs in Action

In Carol Kibildis's seventh grade reading class, groups of 8 to 18 students participate in literature discussion circles while Carol acts as mediator and facilitator. Carol's students are first either read to or read for themselves. The literature she selects for discussion represents diversity and may be humorous, serious, or thought provoking. An important aspect of literature sharing in her class is listening to book language and getting a sense of how an author's choice of words serves the story. In this third period, Wednesday class, the 10 students are Mexican American, Filipino, and African-Mexican American.

Carol has just completed reading "Seventh Grade," a short story from *Baseball in April* by Gary Soto. The hero, Victor Rodriguez, has experienced his first day of seventh grade in his Fresno, California, school. Victor is madly in love with a beautiful, intelligent girl named Teresa, who does not even notice he is alive. He is overjoyed to discover they share some classes together, including French. When the teacher asks who can speak French, Victor raises his hand, hoping to impress Teresa. But when the teacher addresses Victor with "Parlez-vous Français?" Victor, who speaks no French, bluffs his way through. Speaking no French herself, Teresa is impressed by Victor's performance, and the teacher is sensitive enough not to disclose Victor's "secret." Determined to continue impressing Teresa, Victor races to the library after school to check out French textbooks.

Carol asks her students to write a question about the story to bring to discussion. She uses either student questions or their journal responses to provide a lead-in to discussion. The students eagerly ask their questions of one another.

Felipe: Why did Victor say he knew how to speak French?

Latisa: That's easy! He wants to impress Teresa! Why didn't Mr. Bueller (the French teacher) let on that Victor couldn't really speak French?

Juan: Mr. Bueller remembered when he was in college and couldn't afford a car. His friends let him borrow theirs, and his girlfriend thought he was all rich and everything. He got in trouble when he ran out of money and had to call his parents for more!

Michelle: He's [Victor's] such a macho boy! He wants to be so cool, but he knows he's really a fool! I went out with a boy like that. He acted so wild just to get my attention, but I thought he was stupid.

Josh: Yeah, but if we don't act like Victor, you don't look at us. The only guys you like are the ones who act all slick!

Alicia: (addressing Josh) It's like Victor's friend. He was all cool with that "scowling" thing and kicking back and expecting the girls to just come to him. And all these girls kept looking at him and stuff. I don't understand why some girls fall for that. It's so fake!

The spirited discussion continued for another 20 minutes until the bell rang for fourth period. The students were still discussing the story as they exited the classroom.

Carol's students know what kinds of questions stimulate discussion: those that are based on the reading of the text, but require personal experience, analysis, and evaluation to formulate defensible answers. As discussion begins, a student poses his or her question to the group and then indicates another student to address the question. The question poser can probe for additional responses. When there are no more responses, a new volunteer poses a question. From time to time, Carol injects her own question, such as, "How would you feel if you were in Robert Suarez's situation?" or "Have you ever been in a situation like Robert's?" (from discussion of "The School Play" by Soto). She also offers personal anecdotes to stimulate conversation: "I remember when I wrote the play for sixth grade graduation. There was a girl in my class who reminded me of Belinda, and she was one tough girl! I knew if she didn't get the lead in the play, she would beat me up. I wasn't sure what to do!"

It seems reasonable that Carol can best serve as the classroom's first discussion leader. Over time, we can assume that she can relinquish aspects of control of the discussion to the students as their capabilities develop (O'Flahavan et al., 1992).

Connecting Personal and Text Experiences

The personal anecdote usually prods even Carol's most reluctant students to open up. Everyone has a story to share, and personal stories may be a discussion's most honest beginning. Sometimes Carol finds it difficult to keep the personal narrative on target and related to the story; she must gently steer the discussion back on track, feeling for ways in which students' personal experiences link with that of the story characters. Personal and text experiences become symbiotic; personal experiences aid in understanding the text, and the text enlightens the personal experience.

During a discussion of "The 11:59," a story from a collection of African American stories called *The Dark Thirty* by Patricia C.

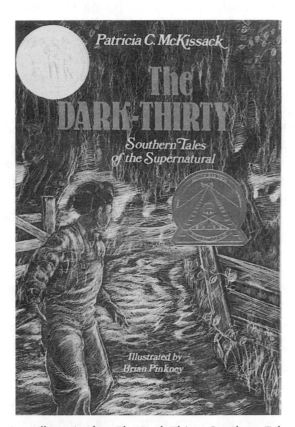

Cover illustration from The Dark-Thirty: Southern Tales of the Supernatural *by Patricia C. McKissack, illustrated by Brian Pinkney. Illustrations ©1992 by Brian Pinkney. Reprinted by permission of Alfred A. Knopf, Inc.*

McKissack, told originally on front porches during the last 30 minutes of daylight, a Mexican American student was prompted to tell "La Llorona," the story of the ghost of a woman who roams border towns from Texas to Southern California looking for her children, scaring to death those who encounter her. Another student, a Filipino child, told of "The Lady in White" who comes to take people away to death. Yet another student, a Caucasian boy from the southern United States, talked about conjuring up "Bloody Mary" by looking in a mirror, where her visage is supposed to scare the viewer to death. Everyone had a ghost story from his or her culture to share, and similarities and differences among the stories were noted. The students then discussed the characters in "The 11:59," the historical background and setting, and how personified death is a theme that appears in the literature of all cultures. Again, the book club succeeded in stimulating the participants to lively, animated conversation.

Students in Carol's grade seven reading class, however, were not nearly as successful with the book club at the beginning of the year as they grew to be. Like all good classroom practices, book clubs take thought, planning, and patience.

Considerations for Classroom Book Clubs

Teachers stimulate an appreciation of literature among their students when they express enthusiasm as they read and discuss books, regard each student as an able reader and capable respondent to literature, and plan ways for their students to respond to and discuss shared literature (Koeller, 1981). Through their enthusiasm, teachers encourage participation, which leads to increased understanding of the text and of one another. The atmosphere of the literature discussion circle should be positive. The idea is to get students to share their ideas about the literature. To feel comfortable enough to do this, the literature discussion circle must be a "safe" zone: rules for the circle need to be posted, explained, and discussed before it is established. Carol and her class established these rules: (1) only one person speaks at a time, (2) no one is to be interrupted while speaking, (3) no speaker or response is to be labeled as "stupid" or "dumb," and (4) the discussion circle is to be kept free of racial, ethnic, or gender slurs.

> "Teachers and students who come together to read multicultural literature feel more of a connection with one another."

Enjoying the Process of Learning

Some teachers are drawn to a book club for themselves and their students for the sheer enjoyment of reading and the excitement of trying new authors. A new member of a teacher book club said after the first meeting, "I haven't had any time to read since the beginning of the [school] year. It felt so good to read something adult and discuss it!" When Toni Morrison was named the Nobel prize winner for literature, the teachers at one school who had read *The Bluest Eye* the year before talked about the book and how glad they were to have read it.

Even more important, teachers and students who come together to read multicultural literature feel more of a connection with one another. They feel more confident in their own literary discussion ability, more knowledgeable of multicultural literature, and more collegial with other members of the book club. As Soto's character Victor Rodriguez put it, "Yeah, well, I picked up a few things from movies and books and stuff like that." Maybe Shannon and her perceived adversaries mentioned in the beginning of this chapter will pick up valuable understandings, too.

References

Bealor, S. (1992). Minority literature book groups for teachers. *Reading in Virginia*, 17, 17–21.

Fisher, P., & Shapiro, S. (1991, May). *Teachers' exploration of historical fiction in literature discussion groups*. Paper presented at the 36th Annual Convention of the International Reading Association, Las Vegas, NV.

Flood, J., Lapp, D., Alvarez, D., Romero, A., & Ranck-Buhr, W. (1992, December). *A teacher book club: A study of teachers' participation in a contemporary multicultural fiction literature discussion group*. Paper presented at the 42nd Annual Meeting of the National Reading Conference, San Antonio, TX.

Hansing-Krening, N. (1992). Authors of color: A multicultural perspective. *Journal of Reading*, 36, 124–129.

Koeller, S. (1981, November). *A neglected essential*. Paper presented at the 71st Annual Meeting of the National Council of Teachers of English, Boston, MA.

Lapp, D., Flood, J., Ranck-Buhr, W., & Moore, J. (in press). What happens when teachers get together to talk about books?: Looking at teacher book clubs. *The Reading Teacher*.

O'Flahavan, J., Erting, L.C., Marks, T.A., Mintz, A.W., & Wiencek, J. (1992, December). *At the intersection of mind and society: Synthesis of research on school-based peer group discussion about text from a sociocultural perspective*. Paper presented at the 42nd Annual Meeting of the National Reading Conference, San Antonio, TX.

Samway, K.D., Whang, G., Cade, C., Gamil, M., Lubandina, M.A., & Phommachanh, K. (1991). Reading the skeleton, the heart and the brain of a book: Students' perspectives on literature study circles. *The Reading Teacher*, 45(3), 196–205.

Literature

Cisneros, S. (1991). *House on Mango Street*. New York: Vintage.

Cisneros, S. (1991). *Woman Hollering Creek and other stories*. New York: Random House.

Cohen, B. (1983). *Molly's pilgrim*. New York: Lothrop, Lee & Shepard.

Greenfield, E. (1974). *Sister*. New York: HarperCollins.

Heide, F.P., & Gilliland, J.H. (1992). *Sami and the time of the trouble*. New York: Clarion.

Hurston, Z. (1978). *Their eyes were watching God*. Urbana, IL: University of Illinois Press.

Johnson, A. (1990). *Do like Kyla*. New York: Orchard.

McKissack, P.C. (1992). *The dark-thirty: Southern tales of the supernatural*. New York: Knopf.

Morrison, T. (1972). *The bluest eye*. New York: Washington Square.

Soto, G. (1990). *Baseball in April and other stories*. San Diego, CA: Harcourt Brace.

Soto, G. (1993). The school play. In *Local news* (pp. 60–68). San Diego, CA: Harcourt Brace.

Stamm, C. (1990). *Three strong women*. New York: Viking.

Tan, A. (1989). *The joy luck club*. New York: Putnam.

Vigna, J. (1992). *Black like Kyra, white like me*. Morton Grove, IL: Albert Whitman.

The Tools of
Story Talk

CHAPTER 6

Preparing Focus Units with Literature: Crafty Foxes and Authors' Craft

Joy F. Moss

MORE THAN 20 YEARS ago, I developed the Focus Unit as a framework for providing my elementary students with opportunities to experience a wide variety of literature: traditional and modern, prose and poetry, fantasy and science fiction, contemporary and historical realism, and nonfiction (Moss, 1984, 1990). A "Focus Unit" is a series of literary experiences organized around a central focus (a literary theme, genre, author, topic, or narrative element or device) and designed to integrate the language arts. Each unit provides an organizational framework for read-aloud experiences through which students explore a group of related books in terms of their literary content and craft and the connections among them. Participating in these read-aloud experiences prepares students to engage in independent and collaborative reading and writing and various creative extension activities.

Why Focus Units?

The Focus Unit is based on theories of literacy and literary response that emphasize the active role of the reader. Louise Rosenblatt (1993) distinguishes between reading to gain information (efferent reading) and reading as an aesthetic experience. While *efferent* refers to the stance of the reader who focuses on what is to be carried away at the end of the text, *aesthetic* reading means that the reader enters into the story and the story characters' world. Aesthetic reading is a personal and emotional experience in which readers create their own stories from personal memories, literary experiences, feelings, beliefs, and expectations.

The more children read, the more knowledge about language, literature, and the world they can bring to new texts. The literature program as a whole, comprising a series of Focus Units, provides opportunities for the wide reading necessary to build a rich background of literary knowledge. Each Focus Unit is designed as a cumulative experience in which children listen to or read related texts and search for connections among them. Harste, Short and Burke (1988) have observed that "learning and understanding are processes of making connections. We are able to understand what we read only because of the connections we make between the current books and our past experiences, which include books we have read or written" (p. 358). In the context of the Focus Unit, reading one text serves as preparation for reading subsequent texts, and students generate meaning in each new literary experience by drawing on their own literary histories.

In a Focus Unit, children are invited to "live through" the stories selected and to share their experiences as aesthetic readers in the ongoing dialogue that is a central feature of the unit. Children have opportunities to respond to literature in large and small groups and with the teacher in conferences and in dialogue journals (Staton, 1980, 1989). The discussion time built into the literature program enables the teacher and students to respond to and study literature together. The term "community of readers" describes children working together to explore and build meanings (Hepler & Hickman, 1982). The teacher is also a participant in this community of readers and writers.

During the Focus Unit, then, children encounter quality literary texts, expand and revise their "theory of the world" (Smith, 1988, p. 7), generate their own ideas, and react to those of others. A Focus Unit featuring "fox tales" is presented here to translate these theories of literary experience into practice and to illustrate this particular thematic approach to exploring literature. (This "Fox Tales" Focus Unit was originally developed for and with first and second graders. However, it can be revised and adapted for use in classrooms with younger or older children.)

Fox Tales: Steps in Building a Focus Unit

It should come as no surprise that the first step in developing a Focus Unit is to choose the focus. It is essential to consider students' interests in planning literature experiences that will be enjoyable, relevant, and meaningful. For example, my observations of children's responses to literature have provided me with ample evidence of the general appeal of diverse traditional and contemporary stories featuring fox characters. The choice of a focus is also determined by the availability of quality literature that shares a feature of interest to children—such as crafty foxes. For this unit, excellent examples of diverse genres featuring foxes were available in school and public libraries.

In addition to exposing children to a variety of interesting and enjoyable literary selections, the Focus Unit should be designed to provide children with opportunities to learn about literature and authors' craft and to extend and enrich their transactions with and response to literary texts. A survey of the selected literature featuring foxes suggested rich possibilities for exploring genre characteristics and recurring themes as well as character types and development, point of view, folktale motifs, literary devices, and illustrators' techniques. In addition, these selections promised to engage children in comparative analysis of diverse tales linked by their focus on the fox. The collection of fox tales also suggested interesting possibilities for extending children's insights about the fox from the story world to the natural world.

The second step in building a Focus Unit is to collect the related literature and display it in the classroom. Encourage children to add to the collection as they discover new titles in local or home libraries during the unit. (The bibliography for the Fox Tales Focus Unit is included at the end of this chapter.)

The last step is to plan the procedures for implementing the basic components of this instructional unit.

Components of the Focus Unit

The Read-Aloud Experience

A central component of the Focus Unit is the read-aloud experience in which children are invited to respond to a selected text before, during, and after listening to the story unfold. The teacher introduces questions to stretch and enrich children's explorations of the books read and asks students to search for connections among them. Key ideas and insights are recorded by the teacher on a chart during each read-aloud session.

This series of read-aloud experiences is designed to build a literary background so that children can respond to each new text in light of previous ones. The dialogue that extends from one literary session to the next is cumulative so that children can draw from their growing store of literary knowledge to make predictions, raise questions, develop understandings, and generate meanings as they listen to selected stories.

Self-Selected Literary Experiences

After the first read-aloud session, children are introduced to the Focus Unit story collection and invited to select books they would like to read independently or with a partner. To prepare the children for self-selected reading, the teacher talks about the books in the collection and asks children to recommend titles they have already read and enjoyed. For example, the fox books by James Marshall are very popular among beginning readers who tend to recommend them with great enthusiasm to their classmates. Many children select books already read aloud by the teacher before moving to unfamiliar titles for independent reading. At least 15 minutes each day is set aside for reading self-selected fox tales independently or with a partner.

A list of the titles in the Focus Unit collection is posted on the wall so that children can record their names next to the titles they have selected. This information is used to identify children who read the same book or books by a single author so they can form small groups to share their personal responses to the books. Time is set aside each week for these dialogue groups to meet. Some groups may have only two or three participants; others may include six or eight children who have selected a particular title. Several children may plan together to read the same title if they want to work in the same dialogue group. To suggest ways to discuss self-selected books in these small groups, the teacher posts a list of questions that have been introduced during the read-aloud sessions. The questions stimulate children's reactions to characters, setting, conflict, theme, language, illustrations, or connections to the read-aloud books (see sample questions in the next section). The children are also encouraged to create their own questions to initiate dialogue. The teacher moves from one group to another and joins in as a visitor; the children are encouraged to assume responsibility for the content and direction of their discussions.

Story Journals

During the unit each child keeps a journal (a notebook) to fill with personal responses both to the stories read aloud and to his or her self-selected books. Several questions are introduced to suggest other ways to think about the books for this exercise. Some children may choose to begin their journal writing with drawings accompanied by brief captions, but generally, over time, text begins to dominate their journal entries, and drawings are used to amplify or decorate the text. After recording the date, title, author, and response, the children are asked to choose one or more of the questions to expand their responses:

1. Who was your favorite character? Why?

2. Was there a character you did not like? Why?

3. What was your favorite part of the story? Why?

4. Who was the hero or heroine? How do you know?

5. Who was the villain? How do you know?

6. Was there a helper? What did this character do?

7. What was the problem in the story? How was it solved?

8. What do you think is the most important thing to remember about this story? What do you think was the author's message?

9. Does this story remind you of any other story you have read or heard? Explain.

10. What did you think of the illustrations? Did you find anything in the pictures that was not included in the words?

11. How did you feel about what the central character did in this story? What would you have done differently?

12. Would you recommend this book to a friend? Why or why not?

Once their writing is complete, members of each dialogue group may choose to read aloud entries from their journals to initiate conversation about a particular book.

As children's writing skills improve, they gradually focus more attention on the content of their journal entries, which, in turn, becomes increasingly expressive of their thoughts and experiences. In the meantime, they are developing the habit of literary response.

The story journal can also be used as a dialogue journal in which the teacher responds in writing to the child's entries and generates a written conversation about literature and literary response (see Staton 1980, 1989; and Chapters 20 and 21 in this volume). These written conversations reinforce the notion that reading and writing are complementary processes of meaning making and help children discover the value of these skills for communication. In the dialogue journal, a teacher can encourage more written expression by responding to each child's comments and questions, by introducing questions and comments that support and extend the child's topic, by offering new or related topics, by expressing appreciation, empathy, or understanding in response to a child's entry, and by sharing personal thoughts, feelings, and experiences.

Time for writing in journals is scheduled into the daily routine after the read-aloud sessions, after the self-selected reading experience, or, in some classrooms, during the time set aside for writing. However, the amount of time spent on journal writing varies from one day to the next. Some children may choose to respond to a self-selected book as they experience the unfolding story. Other children may prefer to wait until they have completed the book before writing about it in their journal. After discussing their books in the dialogue groups, some children may have new ideas to add to previous entries.

Planning the Unit Projects

Another component of the Focus Unit involves projects that extend the literary experiences. Participants in each dialogue group work together on a special project related to the book or books they discuss. They meet with the teacher to explore possibilities before deciding what kind of project would be of interest to them. They may choose to create murals to portray major characters and scenes in their books, construct dioramas, re-create a story through drama, dance, or puppetry, or write a sequel about the characters in a favorite story. For the Fox Tale Focus Unit, some children may choose nonfiction sources to create illustrated booklets about foxes in the natural world; others may collect poems about foxes to create a book. Still others may choose to create a mobile with origami animal characters or make the seven tangram pieces used by Grandfather Tang to tell the tale of the shape-changing fox-fairies and the hunter in *Grandfather Tang's Story* by Ann Tompert. When the projects are completed, time is scheduled to allow each group to share their literary extensions.

Writing an Original Text

The final component of the Focus Unit is a writing experience in which children draw from their experiences with the books in the unit collection to compose an original narrative.

Into the Classroom with Fox Tales

Session One

In the introductory read-aloud session, the teacher asked first and second graders to rely on their prior knowledge to respond to questions such as, "What do you know about foxes?" and "What stories with fox characters do you know?" As children shared their knowledge about foxes in the natural world and in the story world, the teacher recorded key ideas on two wall charts: Fox Facts and Fox Tales. During the Focus Unit, new entries were added to these charts, and corrections were made as children acquired new information and insights.

Roland the Minstrel Pig by William Steig was selected for reading aloud in the first group session to introduce the Fox Focus Unit. The children examined the front cover, title page, and dedication, and then they responded with comments, predictions, and questions. Some of the children were able to name other Steig stories, and one child noted: "Mr. Steig likes to write stories about animals." When a child asked about the meaning of the word "minstrel," the teacher suggested that they all try to figure it out from the picture on the front cover. The cover and title page also elicited predictions about the story:

> "It's going to be a story about a pig. He's the important one."
>
> "I think it's going to be about how he gets to *be* a minstrel pig."
>
> "Maybe the banjo—is that a guitar?—maybe it's magic like in *Sylvester and the Magic Pebble.*"

As the story was read aloud, the children revised their original predictions in response to new information in the unfolding text. Many children discovered that their understandings changed, and they created new meanings as they moved through the story. For example, when Sebastian the fox first appears in the story, some children predicted he would be a friend for Roland, but others disagreed:

> "Roland is lonely. He *needs* a friend."
>
> "But look at his face here: he looks sly!"
>
> "What is that word 'scheming'? It doesn't sound good."

Before helping with the word meaning, the teacher reread the last line that contained the word "scheming" to gather more conjectures: "So they started out with brisk steps—Roland dreaming and the fox scheming" (p. 13).

The children were also asked to respond spontaneously to the story and to share thoughts and feelings about the characters, illustrations, language, and ending. Excerpts from this segment of dialogue reveal the diversity of students' responses:

> "I thought it was so funny that Roland didn't even know the fox was trying to kill him!"
>
> "He was sort of stupid—but he was nice and he made good songs."
>
> "It was scary when he put that...when he was strangling him."
>
> "I like the end when all his [Roland's] friends come. See—in this picture—these animals look like his friends from before!"
>
> "It's like Sylvester—when he got back with his mom and dad. That's a good ending."

After these individual responses, the teacher asked three questions to focus attention on the distinguishing features of specific characters and the nature of the conflict:

1. Who were the most important characters? Why were they important in the story?

2. What words would you use to describe each one?

3. What was the problem in the story?

The children identified Roland as the hero, Sebastian as the villain, and the king as "the one who helps the hero"; they listed qualities of each character and explained how these qualities fit their labels. Several children noted that the title page contains pictures of the five main characters: two of them are the friends who encourage Roland to go out and pursue his dream; the other portraits are of Roland, Sebastian, and the king. The third question generated a discussion about the conflict between Roland's "dream" and Sebastian's "scheme."

At the end of this discussion, the teacher recorded the children's responses on a chart: the three main characters were identified as "hero," "villain," and "helper," respectively; and the problem was identified as "The fox wanted to eat Roland." With each subsequent read-aloud session, relevant information was listed under the three major headings on the chart: title, characters, and problem. (For a detailed explanation of other Language Charts, see Chapter 8 by Roser and Hoffman in this volume.)

At the end of the read-aloud discussion, the children were introduced to the collection of fox tales in the classroom and were invited to select a book for independent reading. The teacher also explained the story journals and dialogue groups described earlier. During subsequent read-aloud sessions, the children were encouraged to make connections between their self-selected texts and the teacher-selected texts, which were read aloud to the group.

Sessions Two and Three

In the next two sessions, additional fox stories by William Steig—*Doctor DeSoto* and *The*

Amazing Bone—were read aloud. Again, the children examined the front covers and title pages for clues about the stories and made predictions and asked questions. As each story unfolded, they revised or confirmed original predictions and made new ones, engaging in the process of understanding and creating new meanings. At the end of each story, the children shared their reactions to the story, characters, illustrations, and language and identified the hero or heroine, villain, and helper, as well as the plot conflict and resolution. The teacher continued to record on the chart information about the characters and problem in each story. By the end of the third session, the children were asked to compare all three of Steig's stories. The following comments represent just some of their insights:

> "The fox is the villain in all three."

> "The mouse [Dr. DeSoto] was the smartest. He outfoxed the fox."

> "I just read a book like that! It's called *Fox Outfoxed*."

> "It's so funny when he gets tricked back."

> "The bone tricked the fox, too.... [The Amazing Bone]."

> "But he didn't plan it. The mice had a scheme!"

> "...like a fox!"

> "The problems are the same. The fox wants to eat them."

> "And they end the same. The villain doesn't get what he wants, but the others do."

> "And they get to be with their friends again and their mom and dad."

> "Mr. Steig likes to draw animals."

> "He makes big and little ones together."

> "He likes to do cartoons."

> "I like how he makes eyes. You can tell when they're [the characters are] mad, or mean, or scared."

These insights reflect the children's ability to move beyond the analysis of single texts to explore literary, linguistic, and artistic connections among multiple texts. Their comments suggest they internalized new word meanings, connected with the concepts of character types and plot patterns introduced in previous sessions, and figured out ways to use visual clues to explore implied meanings in picture books.

Session Four

On the fourth day, several traditional fox tales were read aloud to introduce two literary genres—the fable and the "pourquoi" or "why" tale, a folk tale genre that explains certain animal traits or natural phenomena. The children talked about the cover, title page, and dedication in Tom Paxton's *Aesop's Fables*. The words under the title—"retold in verse by"—were repeated to draw attention to writers who retell stories from the oral tradition. "The Fox and the Grapes" was read aloud and its "lesson" discussed. When the second fable, "The Fox and the Stork," was read aloud from *Twenty-Five Fables* by Norah Montgomerie, the children recognized the word "retold" on the front cover and reviewed its meaning. After listening to this fable and debating about the lesson, the children decided that "tricky" was the best way to describe this fox character:

> "He likes to play tricks."

> "But the stork was tricky, too. She taught him a lesson."

> "She outfoxed him!"

The third fable, "The Fox and the Crow," was read aloud from an unusual collection of fables called *Anno's Aesop* retold by Mitsumasa Anno. The children noted that this was a retold tale, too, and compared it with the other fables. When asked to create a definition for the fable as a special type of story, one child

The Fox and the Crow

Illustration from Anno's Aesop *retold and illustrated by Mitsumasa Anno. Illustrations © 1987 by Mitsumasa Anno; English text ©1989 by Orchard Books. Reprinted by permission of Orchard Books, New York.*

responded: "It's a little, short story that has an important lesson."

After this introduction to the fable as a literary genre, the children were introduced to an example of a pourquoi tale called "Why the Bear Is Stumpy-Tailed" by Virginia Haviland in which a fox plays an important role. Most of the children were familiar with other examples of this genre and named some of their favorites.

At the end of this session, a new heading, "genre," was added to the chart that had been started in the first session; relevant information about each of these stories was recorded under the appropriate head.

Session Five

When the word "trickster" was introduced to describe the fox characters in these old tales, several children were able to identify other literary tricksters: Anansi, Puss 'n Boots, Brer Rabbit, Coyote, and Iktomi. In this session, several examples of retellings of tales of the famous trickster, Reynard the Fox, were pulled from the collection for the children to examine (see the Fox Tales bibliography). Selina Hastings's retelling of *Reynard the Fox* was selected to read aloud, and children discussed Reynard's tricks and wit and narrow escapes as well as the characteristics of the other animals portrayed in words and pictures in this edition. Several children who had selected *Something Nasty in the Cabbages* by Diz Wallis for independent reading were delighted to report that it, too, was about Reynard the Fox. A boy who had read *Proud Rooster and the Fox* by Colin Threadgall noted that his story was "sort of like" Reynard and Chanticleer but "it doesn't have a 'retold' in it, and it has a surprise ending because the fox tricks the rooster and gets all the hens, but he doesn't eat them and he just wants fresh eggs for breakfast, and it's different because it doesn't have so many words." A girl who had read *Something Nasty in the Cabbages* responded: "My book had 'retold' on the title page. But they should of put it on the cover so you'd know right away it's an old, old story."

Session Six

In Yossi Abolafia's *Fox Tale*, Fox tricks Bear out of his honey, and Bear discovers that other animals have also been duped by the cunning Fox: Crow lost her cheese, Donkey did not get his share of chestnuts, and Rabbit traded sweet grapes for sour ones. So the four victims decide to collaborate on a scheme to outfox Fox and retrieve what he had stolen from them. As they listened to this humorous tale unfold, the children were delighted to recognize the author's allusions to fox fables read in an earlier session.

Session Seven

The cover of *The Fox's Egg* by Ikuyo Isami has a picture of a fox with a tiny chick on his head. Several children commented that this fox did not look as sly as the other fox characters they had encountered. One child said the picture reminded her of the cover of Graham Oakley's *The Church Mouse*: "The cat is talking to the mouse like friends instead of enemies like normal. Maybe the fox is friendly...with the chick."

The story is about a fox who finds an egg and decides to wait for it to hatch so he will have a more tasty meal. When it finally hatches, he cannot bear to eat the little chick and eventually decides to take care of this tiny creature who calls him "Mommy." At the end of the tale, the children engaged in comparative analysis:

> "He starts out like the other foxes—greedy and sly!"
>
> "But then he changes!"
>
> "He's not mean anymore because he has the chick. And the animals like him now."
>
> "I read about a fox that starts out a thief—but he changes and gives everything back. It's *so* good...it's called *Fox Under First Base*."
>
> "I thought Reynard was going to change—but then he didn't."
>
> "In the *old* stories, the foxes are villains."
>
> "But I read an old one about a fox that *helped* a horse. He was a trickster. He tricked the lion to help the horse [*The Horse, the Fox, and the Lion*]."
>
> "Well, in a lot of the old ones they're villains."

At this point, the teacher read a note from the author on the front flap of the book: "In old times, foxes are described as bad and sly. I have always believed there must be a good, humorous fox somewhere in the world." The children were satisfied.

Session Eight

When the cover of *The Friendly Fox* by Jenny Koralek was displayed, the first responses were as follows:

Cover illustration from Ikuyo Isami's The Fox's Egg. ©1986 by Ikuyo Isami. English edition first published in 1989 by Carolrhoda Books, Inc. Reprinted by permission of the publisher. All rights reserved.

> "If you didn't see the title, you'd expect the fox is the villain...."
>
> "It's not retold. It's a new one."
>
> "Maybe it's going to be a fox that changes—like the other story."
>
> "Look at the title page—he's got rabbits all around him—like friends."

The fox in this story wants to befriend the rabbits and chickens and eventually earns their trust. When the first page was read aloud beginning with the words, "Once upon a time there was a lonely fox...," one child commented: "That fox looks sad. He's lonely. Maybe this is about how he gets friends." The children's comments about the story also reflected their developing grasp of the fable as a literary genre:

> "It's sort of like a fable—to teach about friendship."

> "The fox got a bad reputation from the old stories."

> "The fox wanted friends, but they didn't know he was nice."

> "They had to get to know him."

> "See—it's like a fable—it teaches you to try to get to know a person before you decide about her."

Session Nine

The picture on the front cover of Irina Korschunow's *The Foundling Fox* prompted comments about the realism of the illustration and predictions that this would be a realistic story instead of fantasy. One child noticed that it had been translated from German: "These fox tales are from so many different countries!" Several children who wondered about the word "foundling" used the title page to get the first clue about its meaning: the subtitle reads "How the Little Fox Got a Mother." The first page of the story provides further information that the fox's mother had been killed by a hunter. This is the story of an orphan fox who is adopted by a vixen with three kits of her own. The vixen risks her life to save the foundling from a hound dog and a badger as she carries him on the long journey home to her den.

The children were totally immersed in this story as it unfolded. They entered into the world of the courageous vixen, lived through her encounters with danger, and finally sighed with relief when she was home at last. After sharing their feelings about the story, the children talked about the differences between this story and other fox tales:

> "This one is real. The animals act like animals instead of humans."

> "This story is serious. You feel like you're in the story."

> "It isn't funny—but I liked it."

> "The fox is the heroine and the dog and badger are villains."

> "I think this story is really about adoption. It shows the mother can love the adopted one like the others." (This comment came from an adopted child. She was the only one who interpreted the story in this way, and she referred the class to the last part of the story in which the vixen's neighbor asks, "Are you going to bring up a stranger's kit?")

Many of the children expressed an interest in the factual information about the life of the fox. Those who had selected some of the realistic or nonfiction accounts for independent reading recommended such titles as *Gray Fox* by Jonathan London, Claudia Schnieper's *On the Trail of the Fox*, *Fox's Dream* by Keizaburo Tejima, *Reynard: The Story of a Fox Returned to the Wild* by Alice Mills Leighner, and Mary Ling's *Amazing Wolves, Dogs, and Foxes*.

Synthesis: Session Ten

During this session, the teacher asked the children to review the chart on which they had been recording key elements of the stories explored in the read-aloud experiences. They compared these stories in terms of character types, conflict, and genre. They also shared their analyses of self-selected stories and identified heroes or heroines, villains, helpers, conflicts, and genres. In their analysis of genre, the children distinguished between fables, "why" stories, and longer narratives with more complex plots and character development; between fantasy and realism; between fiction and nonfiction; between prose and poetry; and between "retold" or traditional tales and "new" or modern stories. During this Focus Unit these young children had learned to engage in comparative analysis as they considered each story in light of the others and discovered connections and contrasts. They talked easily about what authors and artists do to create stories: how they develop characters and conflict and mood and how they get the reader to feel sorry for one character and angry at another. The children looked at the complete Focus Unit collection and formulated their generalizations. For example, they concluded that in most of the traditional or older stories, the fox characters were portrayed as villains, but in the newer tales and realistic narratives, the fox is portrayed in a more positive light. They also concluded that many writers use old stories to create new ones and use facts about foxes to create fiction. Several children discovered that the tricksters in these fox tales were able to take advantage of other characters because of the weaknesses of their victims. One child noted: "These stories are really about people!"

This session, with its focus on the significance of the collection as a whole, prepared the children for a final assignment: to write their own fox tales. They could choose between realism and fantasy; create a fox character as villain, hero, victim, or helper; and decide on the nature of the conflict and how it would be resolved. Children who did not yet have adequate writing skills for this project worked in a group with the teacher or with another student and engaged in a collaborative production of a fox tale. When these original tales were completed and illustrated and bound into books, complete with cover, title page, and dedication, they were shared in a final session and discussed in terms of content, craft, and connections—just as the work of professional writers and illustrators who had been studied throughout the Focus Unit.

Reading About Foxes and Learning About Literature

During this cumulative literary experience, the children became aesthetic readers, and they were also able to critique the stories and explore literary elements, connections, contrasts, interesting patterns, and larger concepts. They moved from analyses of single texts to comparative analyses of multiple texts, and finally, toward synthesis. By pulling together ideas from the diverse texts in the collection, the children discovered unifying themes and concepts about content and craft. Teachers who decide to adapt this unit for their own classrooms should select read-aloud stories appropriate for their students. Each Focus Unit is unique in that it reflects the interests, needs, and goals of teachers and students in a particular time and setting. These crafty fox books are only one example of the many possibilities for thematic literature study in the classroom.

References

Harste, J., Short, K., & Burke, C. (1988). *Creating classrooms for authors: The reading–writing connection.* Portsmouth, NH: Heinemann.

Hepler, S., & Hickman, J. (1982). "The book was okay, I love you'": Social aspects of response to literature. *Theory into Practice, 21,* 278–283.

Moss, J.F. (1984). *Focus units in literature: A handbook for elementary school teachers.* Urbana, IL: National Council of Teachers of English.

Moss, J.F. (1990). *Focus on literature: A context for literacy learning.* Katonah, NY: Richard C. Owen.

Rosenblatt, L. (1993). The literacy transaction: Evocation and response. In K. Holland, R. Hungerford, & S. Ernst (Eds.), *Journeying: Children responding to literature* (pp. 5–23). Portsmouth, NH: Heinemann.

Smith, F. (1988). *Understanding reading: A psycholinguistic analysis of reading and learning to read.* Hillsdale, NJ: Erlbaum.

Staton, J. (1980). Writing and counseling: Using a dialogue journal. *Language Arts, 57,* 514–518.

Staton, J. (1989). An introduction to dialogue journal communication. In J. Staton, R. Shuy, & J. Peyton

(Eds.), *Dialogue journal communication: Classroom, linguistic, social and cognitive views* (pp. 1–32). Norwood, NJ: Ablex.

Children's Literature

Oakley, G. (1972). *The church mouse*. New York: Atheneum.

Steig, W. (1988). *Sylvester and the magic pebble*. New York: Simon & Schuster.

Fox Tales Bibliography

Abolafia, Y. (1991). *Fox tale*. New York: Greenwillow.

Anno, M. (1989). *Anno's Aesop: A book of fables by Aesop and Mr. Fox*. New York: Orchard.

Aronsky, J. (1985). *Watching foxes*. New York: Lothrop, Lee & Shepard.

Auch, M.J. (1993). *Peeping beauty*. New York: Holiday House.

Belpre, P. (1965). The wolf, the fox, and the jug of honey. In *The tiger and the rabbit and other tales* (pp. 43–47). New York: Lippincott.

Brown, R. (1969). *Reynard the fox*. New York: Abelard-Schuman.

Bunting, E. (1993). *Red fox running*. New York: Clarion.

Carey, B. (1973). *Baba Yaga's geese and other Russian stories*. Bloomington, IN: Indiana University Press.

Christelow, E. (1987). *Olive and the magic hat*. New York: Clarion.

Clifford, E. (1992). *Flatfoot fox and the case of the nosy otter*. Boston, MA: Houghton Mifflin.

Conover, C. (1989). *Mother Goose and the sly fox*. New York: Farrar, Straus & Giroux.

Dahl, R. (1970). *Fantastic Mr. Fox*. New York: Knopf.

Edmonds, I. (1966). Reynard and the fisherman's dream. In *Trickster tales* (pp. 99–102). New York: Lippincott.

Fillmore, P. (1958). Budulinek. In *The shepherd's nosegay: Stories from Finland and Czechoslovakia* (pp. 94–102). San Diego: Harcourt Brace.

Galdone, P. (1968). *The horse, the fox, and the lion*. New York: Seabury.

Galdone, P. (1971). *Three Aesop fox fables*. New York: Seabury.

Ginsburg, M. (1973). *One trick too many: Fox stories from Russia*. New York: Dial.

Ginsburg, M. (1976). *Two greedy bears*. New York: Macmillan.

Harris, J.C. Adapted by Parks, V.D., & Jones, M. (1986). *Jump! The adventures of Brer Rabbit*. San Diego, CA: Harcourt Brace.

Hastings, S. (1990). *Reynard the fox*. New York: Tambourine.

Haviland, V. (1953). The lark, the wolf, and the fox. In *Favorite fairy tales told in Poland* (pp. 39–54). New York: Little Brown.

Haviland, V. (1961). Why the bear is stumpy-tailed. In *Favorite fairy tales told in Norway* (pp. 65–66). New York: Little Brown.

Haviland, V. (1979). *North American legends*. New York: HarperCollins.

Hogrogian, N. (1971). *One fine day*. New York: Macmillan.

Hooks, W. (1989). *The three little pigs and the fox*. New York: Macmillan.

Isami, I. (1989). *The fox's egg*. Minneapolis, MN: Carolrhoda.

Koralek, J. (1982). *The friendly fox*. New York: Little Brown.

Korschunow, I. (1982). *The foundling fox*. New York: Harper-Collins.

Latimer, J. (1991). *Fox under first base*. New York: Scribner.

Leighner, A.M. (1986). *Reynard: The story of a fox returned to the wild*. New York: Atheneum.

Lester, J. (1987). *The tales of Uncle Remus: The adventures of Brer Rabbit*. New York: Dial.

Levine, D. (1975). *The fables of Aesop*. Ipswich, England: Gambit.

Ling, M. (1991). *Amazing wolves, dogs, and foxes*. New York: Knopf.

Littledale, F. (1971). *King fox and other old tales*. New York: Doubleday.

Livermore, E. (1981). *Follow the fox*. Boston, MA: Houghton Mifflin.

London, J. (1993). *Gray fox*. New York: Viking.

Manning-Sanders, R. (1970). King fox. In *Gianni and the ogre* (pp. 76–102). New York: Dutton.

Manning-Sanders, R. (1970). *A book of magical beasts*. Camden, NJ: P. Nelson.

Marshall, E. (1982). *Fox and his friends*. New York: Dial.

Marshall, J. (1983). *Rapscallion Jones*. New York: Viking.

Marshall, J. (1988). *Fox on the job*. New York: Dial.

Marshall, J. (1990). *Fox be nimble*. New York: Dial.

Marshall, J. (1992). *Fox outfoxed*. New York: Dial.

Marshall, J. (1993). *Fox on stage*. New York: Dial.

McKissack, P. (1986). *Flossie and the fox*. New York: Dial.

Montgomerie, N. (1961). *Twenty-five fables*. New York: Abelard-Schuman.

Parker, A. (1970). *Skunny wundy: Seneca Indian tales*. New York: Albert Whitman.

Paxton, T. (1988). *Aesop's fables*. New York: Morrow.

Preston, E.M. (1974). *Squawk to the moon, Little Goose*. New York: Viking.

Reeves, J. (1962). *Fables from Aesop*. New York: Henry Walck.

Rice, E. (1979). *Once in a wood*. New York: Greenwillow.

Riordan, J. (1976). Little sister fox and brother wolf. In *Tales from central Russia* (pp. 20–22). Harmondsworth, Middlesex: Kestrel.

Riordan, J. (1976). Liza the fox and Catafay the cat. In *Tales from central Russia* (pp. 91–95). Harmondsworth, Middlesex: Kestrel.

Riordan, J. (1976). The Fox and the Pitcher. In *Tales from central Russia* (p. 194). Harmondsworth, Middlesex: Kestrel.

Ross, T. (1986). *Foxy fables.* New York: Dial.

Schnieper, C. (1986). *On the trail of the fox.* Minneapolis, MN: Carolrhoda.

Steig, W. (1968). *Roland the minstrel pig.* New York: HarperCollins.

Steig, W. (1976). *The amazing bone.* New York: Farrar, Straus & Giroux.

Steig, W. (1982). *Doctor DeSoto.* New York: Farrar, Straus & Giroux.

Tejima, K. (1987). *Fox's dream.* New York: Philomel.

Threadgall, C. (1992). *Proud rooster and the fox.* New York: Tambourine.

Tompert, A. (1990). *Grandfather Tang's story.* New York: Crown.

Wallis, D. (1991). *Something nasty in the cabbages.* Honesdale, PA: Caroline House.

Westwood, J. (1985). *Going to Squintums: A foxy folktale.* New York: Dial.

Wilson, B.K. (1954). The adventures of Iain Direach. In *Scottish folktales and legends* (pp. 121–136). London: Oxford University Press.

CHAPTER 7

Promoting Meaningful Conversations in Student Book Clubs

*Taffy E. Raphael, Virginia J. Goatley, Susan I. McMahon,
and Deborah A. Woodman*

I T IS RARE to find an educator with an interest in literacy who does not look forward to talking about books. We read books and share them with our friends and colleagues. We find newspaper articles that make us think and photocopy them to send to friends and family. We check bestseller lists to see what others are reading. We belong to book discussion groups to ensure that we have people to talk with about books we read. We want to join in the conversation.

Think of the last time you read an interesting book. Did you encourage someone else to read it and did you look forward to talking about it? Did you bring up the book in conversation? We predict that most of you answer these questions positively. Now, think of what you asked your friend about the book. How many of you began the conversation with, "Tell me, who was the main character?" "What happened first?" or "Where and when did the story take place?" We predict that none of us start

our book conversations in this fashion, although many of us have led our students in just such interactions.

Our Book Club Project was designed to create opportunities for upper elementary students of all ability levels to engage in *real* conversations about books—not those designed only to ensure that comprehension has occurred. The project stresses students' extended engagement with books and personal responses, which we and the other authors in this work feel is necessary to students' literary development.

Enhancing Students' Talk About Books: Why and How?

Over time, educators have debated instructional methods and materials, underlying theories, classroom structures, and the relationship among literacy and all aspects of the classroom curriculum. More recently, the professional literature is filled with calls for thematic instruction (Altwerger & Flores, 1994; Lipson et al.,1993; Pearson, 1994), for meeting the literacy needs of diverse learners (Hiebert, 1993), and for greater attention to students' home, community, and school literacy experiences (Edwards, 1991; Heath, 1983; Moll, Tapia, & Whitmore, 1993). These perspectives support our belief in the need for reform in the methods we use to teach students to read and, specifically, talk about text.

> "Research supports our belief in the need for reform in the methods we use to teach students to read and, specifically, talk about text."

Researchers who have studied classroom talk have found that it has been traditionally dominated by teachers who ask a question, elicit one student's response, and then evaluate the response (see Cazden, 1988). This pattern holds for both large and small group interactions (McDermott & Aron, 1978) and reveals a frustrating situation in which students have little opportunity to raise topics of interest, pursue lines of thinking, or collaborate in critical problem solving—a situation even more pronounced for poor readers (Allington, 1991; McDermott & Aron, 1978). Yet, current theories suggest that language is fundamental to thinking (Gavelek, 1986; Vygotsky, 1978) and that through classroom talk, students come to experience the social, collaborative nature of literacy (Wells, Chang, & Maher, 1990). Thus, we must create classrooms in which students engage in meaningful talk if we are to promote higher level thinking important to success in and out of school.

Many university and school researchers have explored how literary and literacy talk can become part of the everyday classroom curriculum. Some have studied the role of the teacher in creating "grand conversations" about literature (see Chapters 2, 10, 12, and 13). Others have studied story discussion groups of nonmainstream youngsters (for example, Battle, 1993; Gilles, 1990; Goatley & Raphael, 1992; Raphael & Brock, 1993). Still others have explored issues related to age levels of discussion participants (Goatley, Bisesi, & Urba, 1992; Leal, 1992) or to the focus of the discussion (Wiseman, Many, & Altieri, 1992). There has perhaps been a greater focus on infusing talk about text into classrooms with readers of all ages than ever before.

From all this inspection of classroom talk, a range of formats for literary discussion groups has emerged. Variations occur in the roles teachers play, the size of the groups, whether the discussion occurs in response to text read by or to the students, how the books to be talked about are selected, and the role of writing in response to literature. For example, in the fifth grade "literature study groups" described by Eeds and Wells (1989) and the first grade groups described by McGee (1992), the teacher is present and helps to orchestrate conversations about books. Gilles's (1990) work with special education youngsters differs in that although the teacher is usually present, students conduct their own "literature study circles."

When students lead their own discussions, variations exist in the degree to which they explore topics of their own choosing (as in Gilles's classroom) or are given guidance by the teacher's specific prompts (see O'Flahavan, 1989). But provision of prompts is not limited to cases in which students conduct their own discussions; Wiseman, Many, and Altieri (1992) note that teachers can prompt students to share aesthetic responses through general discussion of thoughts and reactions and through more specific questions and comments that raise awareness of literary elements and authors' craft.

Regardless of the variations in the names book discussion groups assume (literature study groups, literature study circles, book clubs, or story floor), they share the overarching goal of enhancing students' talk about text. They also have in common some additional critical features: (1) high-quality literature in the form of trade books; (2) opportunities for all students to participate through interaction with their peers; (3) acceptance and valuing of personal responses as highly as traditional displays of comprehension; and (4) a natural approach to how students structure conversation about text and determine discussion topics.

It was within the spirit of promoting such talk about text that we formed the Book Club Project (see McMahon, Raphael, & Goatley, in press; Raphael et al.,1992). "We" are teachers, teacher educators, and teacher-researchers interested in identifying the kind of talk about text students engage in and how such talk can be enhanced through instruction. Our focus was on creating student-led discussion groups, so we began by closely examining students' initial abilities to hold such discussions and then designed instruction to meet the needs we found. At first, some groups of students did not engage easily in meaningful conversations about the books they read. Some, for example, drew on their previous school experience and used a restricted approach in discussions (for instance, responding round-robin fashion from their reading logs) but rarely engaging in unprompted exchange (Raphael & McMahon, 1994). Other groups were more spontaneous in their conversations, but often the talk bore little or no connection to the book the students

had read (McMahon, 1992; McMahon & Hauschildt, 1993; Raphael & McMahon, 1994). We felt that they could benefit from instructional support with both what to talk about and how to exchange responses during book discussions.

The Book Club Project

In the Book Club Project, we developed language and literacy components that supported students' participation in student-led book clubs. Three to five heterogeneously grouped students formed the book clubs, which met simultaneously each day during reading and language arts. We felt that daily opportunity to read and discuss their books was critical for students' literacy development. Thus, we felt the student-led groups and book clubs were a reasonable solution to a potential problem. Students would have less opportunity for such small group talk about books if we limited the experiences to when a teacher or other adult could be present. Further, we felt that such book clubs paralleled the world outside school in which mature readers engage in informal conversations about the books they read. Our Book Club Project, then, consisted of four interconnected components—reading, writing, community share, and instruction—designed to support the student-led book clubs.

Reading

The reading component reflected the range of opportunities each student had to read on his or her own, with a peer partner, or within small groups. We structured Book Club around thematic units: for example, for a unit on "Survival" students could read books such as Scott O'Dell's *Island of the Blue Dolphins*, *Sign of the Beaver* by Elizabeth Speare, or Gary Paulsen's

Hatchet. For each Book Club theme unit, students read the related books, listened to the teacher read a book aloud, and selected books for independent reading from the theme-related classroom collection or from the school library. This approach provided diverse students with books representing a range of difficulty and titles worthy of in-depth discussion. Less able readers could count on appropriate support (such as partner reading or taking books home to read with parents or siblings).

Reading instruction within this component included teaching students comprehension strategies as well as discussing difficult vocabulary. Students used this new knowledge during some of the writing component activities, particularly those using the reading log.

Writing

Students recorded individual responses to books they were reading in reading logs, which contained blank pages for representing ideas through pictures, charts, and maps and lined pages for written reflections. Students' logs included their responses to story events and characters, interesting words or language the author used, funny sections including dialogue and descriptions, and so forth. Students alternated among (1) relying on a prompt (provided by Deb, their teacher) to focus their writing and discussion related to the story (for example, "How do you think Annemarie is feeling?" or "What do you think you would do if you were in her situation?"); (2) generating and writing responses based on their own interests and issues related to the text; and (3) combining teacher-directed and self-initiated responses. Within their logs, students also practiced typical comprehension strategies such as creating a character map to better identify with the characters in the story, making a sequence chart to review story

events before a discussion, or generating questions to ask of peers. They reflected on their responses to the story as they focused on their upcoming book club discussion. Finally, students used their reading logs after their group meetings to summarize what they had talked about and to reflect on what they had gained from the discussion.

In addition to the reading log, writing was also promoted through the use of "think sheets"—individual prompts that encouraged particular ways of organizing or focusing on ideas related to book club units. For example, Figure 1 shows a think sheet that Jennifer used to synthesize ideas from three books in which war plays a significant role. This think sheet provided Jennifer opportunity to consider similarities among the books in preparation for additional synthesis activities.

During the school year, Deb encouraged multiple types of responses in the log, so that by the students' second year in the Book Club Project, they had many ways to respond and took responsibility for using their logs to record ideas in their own ways. Toward the end of their second year, Jean and Crystal wrote in their logs about Chapter 4 of *Park's Quest* by Katherine Paterson. Both students responded to the prompt for the day, "What is it like to meet someone you've never met before? How was it for Park?" But notice in Figure 2 that Crystal used several additional ideas, including title, a prompt she added to the classroom list because she found the chapter titles of the book interesting. Jean, a student receiving compensatory reading services, asked a question to prompt her group to identify Randy, one of the story characters (see Figure 3).

Community Share

Community share provided opportunity for whole class interactions, which were par-

Figure 1
Jennifer's Think Sheet

NAME _Jennifer_   DATE _November 5, 1990_

Stepping Out
BRINGING IDEAS TOGETHER

Topics that Sadako, Hiroshima No Pika, and Faithful Elephants make me think about are:

War, Japan, people dieing, people and animals, sadness, why peopl fight, bombs, Why did the US dropp the bomb on Japan, Whe did Japan and the US have a War, Why are they friends now after they had war.

The topic I want to share about is:

~~Why do people fight~~
War

because —I want to now why people have war —I dont thank that war is something to do. —I dont thank ~~it is~~ —I need ~~a~~ to grow up ~~old~~ ~~to~~ and see people fighting over somthing that can be solved by talking and communicating

Figure 2
Crystal's Response Log

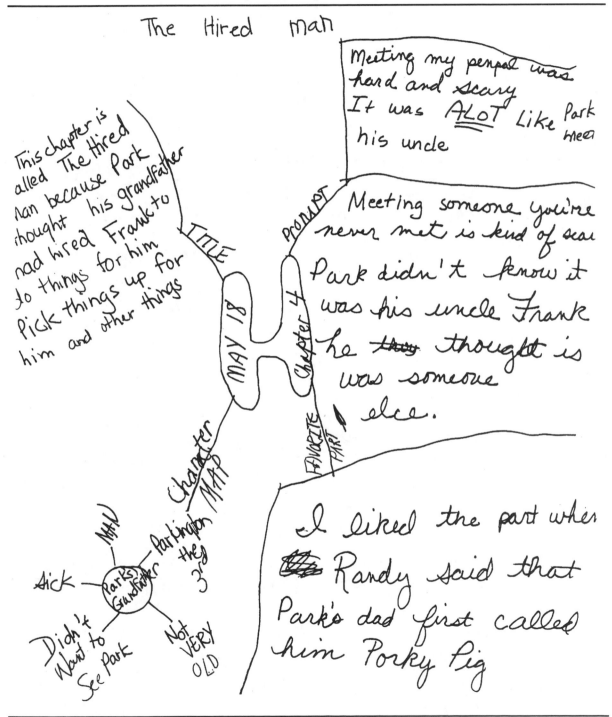

The Hired man

Meeting my penpal was
hard and scary
It was ALOT Like Park
his uncle meet

This chapter is
alled The hired
nan because Park
thought his grandfather
had hired Frank to
to things for him
Pick things up for
him and other things

TITLE

MAY 18

Chapter 4

PROMPT

Meeting someone you're
never met is kind of scar
Park didn't know it
was his uncle Frank
he thought is
was someone
else.

FAVORITE PART

Chapter MAP

MAN

sick — Parks Grandfather — Partington they 3rd

Didn't Want to See Park

Not VERY OLD

I liked the part when
Randy said that
Park's dad first called
him Porky Pig

Figure 3
Jean's Response Log

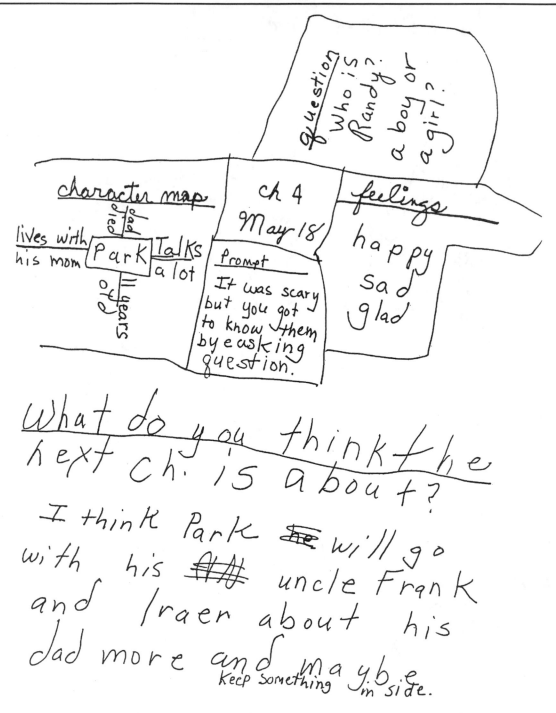

question
who is
Randy?
a boy or
a girl?

character map   ch 4   feelings
                     May 18

lives with   [Park] Talks   happy
his mom   dad died   a lot   sad
              11 years of   glad

                     Prompt
                     It was scary
                     but you got
                     to know them
                     by easking
                     question.

What do you think the
next ch. is about?

I think Park ~~He~~ will go
with his ~~####~~ uncle Frank
and lraen about his
dad more and maybe.
Keep Something in side.

ticularly important in building a classroom literacy community. Sharing occurred before and after book club meetings and served a different function at each of these times. Prior to meetings, community share helped prepare students for their discussions through reviewing the texts and highlighting important events or through students discussing their own experiences in relation to the upcoming reading. For example, before reading a chapter in Lois Lowry's *Number the Stars* in which Jews in Denmark are asked to wear identifying armbands, Deb used community share time to enlist students in a simulation in which all blue-eyed students were to be sent away from their homes solely because of their eye color. The ensuing discussion gave students some background to understand the fear the novel's characters experienced as they faced the cruel capriciousness of Nazi policies. When community share followed book club meetings, students from different book clubs told what they had talked about, raised questions that had not been clarified, and considered new ideas that had emerged from their peer groups.

Community share was also an important time for Deb to model conversation about text; she set an example through her questions, comments, and insights that pushed students to adopt supportive ways of talking about their books. For example, in a community share following the reading of Toshi Maruki's *Hiroshima, No Pika*, Deb modeled by asking for clarification or evidence ("What did the author say...?"), by encouraging identification with the characters' situation ("Can you imagine...?"), and by elaborating on a response ("Right, their eyelids....") during her orchestration of the conversation:

Cover illustration from Lois Lowry's Number the Stars. *©1989 by Lois Lowry. Reprinted by permission of Houghton Mifflin Company. All rights reserved.*

Deb: What did the author say the people who walked by looked like?

Ken: Ghosts.

Deb: Right, their eyelids were swollen and clothes burned away.

Mei: Why did they drop the bomb on the country?

Deb: Because they were at war—it was part of the war.

Jarrod: Why didn't she grow?

Deb: A result of the bomb. Can you imagine always staying the same size?

Landra: It was sad all those people dead or in hospital. Why can't people talk instead of wars, fights, and bombs? If everyone was nice to each other, everything would be all right.

Helena: The governments won't work probably saying that because they are not risking their own lives (Raphael & Goatley, 1994, p. 533).

The students in this example took control of the conversation as they offered clarifying questions and feelings prompted by the story. Community share allowed students to talk about responses to the book, ask questions, and understand their teacher's and peers' responses.

Instruction

Instruction for enhancing book club discussion was used during each of the reading, writing, and community share components. Deb indirectly supported students by (1) encouraging them to increase the range of reading log entries they wrote, (2) prompting conversations that promoted background knowledge, and (3) making efforts to clarify students' confusion. Direct support for improving talk about books included (1) asking students to listen to audiotapes of their book clubs and identify positive features, (2) having students dramatically reenact a book club from a transcript (using pseudonyms), with students assuming roles and then discussing their reactions, and (3) directing students to observe one another in book clubs and then talk about their observations. These teacher-led activities encouraged students to examine their own discussions, identify what they did well, and consider ways to improve.

Instruction focused on book talk as well as the other components of the book club project. For reading, Deb focused on fluency, vocabulary development, knowledge of genre, strategy use, and personal response. For writing, she concentrated on how ideas could be recorded, added, or changed over time and on ways to synthesize entries and texts. For community share, Deb highlighted both the content and process of interacting and the development of background knowledge. For book club meetings, she emphasized how to be a thoughtful contributor to the conversation.

Although a single Book Club period encompassed all the components (reading, writing, and sharing), every day was different. For example, one Book Club session began with community share when Deb explained to students "how to share," focusing on the difference between an authentic question for which the asker is curious about the answer and one for which the asker already knows the answer or does not really care about the response. The session then segued into a brief summary of what had happened in the story that day, with Deb asking for a volunteer to "fill Joshua in on what he missed when he was out yesterday." Following community share, students began reading the chapter from their book that would be discussed in their book club or revisiting it if they had already read it. While reading, the students wrote in their reading log, recording ideas they wanted to talk about in book club and questions they wished to ask. As students finished their reading and log entries, they moved into their book club meetings, where they used their reading logs as notes for discussion. As book clubs drew to a close, Deb pulled the groups together for a final community share to exchange ideas that had emerged in their discussions.

On certain days, Deb had students spend most of their time on only one component, such as writing (for example, doing a synthesis activity or producing narratives connected to the book), instruction (critiquing book club discussions using transcripts), or community share (learning the history and geography related to the book). As in many classrooms, Deb's time was affected by students' other school activities, so she remained flexible in her time allotments. It was clear to us that teachers have many decisions to make as they initiate and sustain classroom book clubs.

Teachers' Decisions in Implementing Book Clubs

Like any language arts program, the Book Club Project involves a range of decisions that teachers consider as they create their own adaptations and embed them in the larger context of their curriculum. Several teachers, including Deb Woodman, Laura Pardo, Kathy Highfield, and Julie Folkert, made decisions about initiating book clubs based on the needs of their students and the availability of resources. Other decisions about Book Club are related to decisions made in other areas of the curriculum; for example, decisions about the books students will read in their groups are related to decisions about the content areas with which Book Club will connect or the particular skills and strategies to be emphasized.

Decisions Within Book Club

Book selection. For each unit, Deb selects one to three book sets from those available in the district so that each student will have a personal copy. She also lets the students help decide on the focus during Book Club. Deb considers issues such as the difficulty of books, their thematic ties, and students' expressed interests. In addition, to form a classroom library, she selects books related to the unit theme from the school and public library. Laura was able to purchase sets of books after talking with her principal and requesting special funds; Kathy borrowed sets of books from other teachers when those she wanted to use were not available in her district. Each

teacher has been and remains innovative in obtaining the needed resources.

Grouping the students. Deb and Laura have both tried placing different numbers of students in the book club groups. Six seemed to be too many because some students rarely had a chance to talk. Groups of three worked well because all the students spoke for longer periods of time. However, even one absent student meant the end of a "group," so the teachers found themselves recombining groups daily. Thus, groups of four or five were best, as they provided all with access to the discussion and guaranteed enough participants if one was absent.

Another grouping decision related to *when* to reorganize the groups. Laura and Deb generally reconfigured groups after each unit so students could interact with many of their peers. Yet even this procedure varied, depending on the requests of the students and other instructional considerations: for example, during one unit, Deb's students enjoyed their interactions within their groups so much that they requested the same groupings for the next unit. Because the groups were working well together, Deb agreed to their request.

A third decision related to *how* to assign students to groups when considering options for student and teacher choice. Deb shifted groups to find a good balance based on the students' leadership, communication, and social skills. For example, when Crystal appeared to dominate the discussion or when Joshua needed extra support to become involved in the conversation, Deb was careful to place these students with others who could help them. She placed Crystal with Helena, who often took a leadership role herself, and Joshua with Jason because Jason worked to include everybody in book discussion. Deb also allowed students to select their own groups if classes appeared to be able to handle the choice wisely, with sensitivity to their peers' feelings. Kathy and Julie asked students to write names of two or three peers with whom they would like to be grouped. They used the students' requests and their own judgments to form groups. Laura (Pardo, 1992) described her grouping decisions as being based on ability, background knowledge, interpersonal skills, leadership, and interest.

Skill and strategy instruction. Instruction is a key component of student book clubs. Often working together, teachers identify skills and strategies they feel are important based on their knowledge of reading, district guidelines, and the scope and sequence of the district-adopted basal reading program. To help the students with their book clubs, decisions are made about *how to share* and *what to share.* These decisions are based on the teachers' observations (during community share and book club meetings) and students' analyses of their own book clubs (on video- or audiotape). For example, Deb wanted her students to ask questions that were challenging. In early fall, when she noticed the students were asking only basic questions, Deb taught them strategies during community share for thinking about more complex questions. Because Laura wanted her students to use a variety of responses in their reading logs, she introduced a range of strategies (such as mapping and critiquing). Over time the students took control of their strategy use, created their own variations in written responses, and taught them to peers (Pardo, 1992).

The research team and other teachers who have worked with the Book Club Project feel it is important students learn specific strategies to use while reading, so they have included instruction related to language conventions, comprehension, literary elements, and response to literature. For example, Laura provides writing prompts that encourage stu-

dents to think about specific events in stories and their own reactions to those events. She talks about the type of genre they are reading and encourages strategies such as predicting, comparing and contrasting, and summarizing—especially when the text is difficult and students need a tool to help them understand the story. This type of instruction also supports the book clubs when they need a common topic from which to begin their discussion. (Eventually, however, as students become more confident, they rely less frequently on instructional prompts.)

Providing appropriate levels of support. As the school year progressed, Deb, like other teachers, found that her students did not need as much support as they had earlier. Further, the type of support they needed changed as the students took more control of their book club groups and written responses. So her instructional decisions related to students' knowledge about the topic, content goals for the lesson, and activities within the lesson. Decisions to use explicit instruction often occurred when the teachers were introducing new concepts or ways of thinking about an activity. Modeling and scaffolding allowed the teachers to guide students and were used more often when the class had some knowledge of an activity or concept but still needed support to make progress. Further, teachers helped students communicate with one another in a whole group setting: for example, when Jason invented "condition," a new form of written response, Laura made certain that Jason had time and access to the rest of the class to explain his idea.

Decisions Extending Beyond Book Club

Making connections with other subjects. Many of the Book Club theme units connected easily with other content areas, particularly social studies and science. Deb made the decision to use books during Book Club that related to her environmental science unit. Other teachers, such as Kathy and Julie, used literature related to social studies to integrate the two subjects. They included a two-week research unit on the U.S. Civil War before reading book club novels, which gave the students historical background for better understanding of the unit books. For Laura's students, *the literature* led to questions about related historical and geographical information and to students' searches for materials that would yield answers to their questions.

Deciding on an assessment program. Many teachers chose to use portfolios as an assessment tool to help report students' progress to others and encourage students to self-assess their own progress. The portfolios for Book Club include students' reading logs, stories, synthesis activities, records of progress, and other literacy projects such as original stories. By using the portfolio in other areas besides the Book Club Project, the teachers felt they could better see connections in students' performance across subjects.

Students are participants in their own assessment. They keep daily evaluation sheets, noting what happened in their book clubs, what went well, and what could be improved. For example, Deb noted:

> Douglas decided it was important for his group to make rules for discussion and write them in their reading logs. At the end of each discussion, his group discussed how they did—both with discussion and with meeting the expectations in the reading log. They discussed which rules they had followed and which still needed work. Then, they put their hands together and said, "Good job."

Both Deb and Laura occasionally audiotape students to determine who needs more guidance. In addition, all teachers keep a notebook to make entries about students during the book clubs. A report card designed to match the goals of the program contains extra space for writing specific notes.

Decisions for including special education students. Deb and the other teachers have special education students assigned to their classrooms during the Book Club period. Like all students, these students have specific needs, so the teachers made decisions about how best to support them. In Kathy's room, students reading below grade level and labeled "learning disabled" work on Book Club activities in the resource room, using a book with a similar theme but an easier reading level. Laura's special education students participate in Book Club but receive additional support from the resource room at another time of the day when they read the book or write in their logs with the special education teacher. Each teacher involved feels Book Club activities can be appropriately modified for all children.

Concluding Comments

The decisions teachers make throughout planning, implementing, and evaluating Book Club contribute to their students' enthusiasm and success in the program and in other aspects of their literacy life. Fourth grader Jean reported reading more books during the summer than she had ever read in the past (noting that, in fact, she had never gone to the library in the summer before). Jarrod was in the hospital with a broken leg and asked to have his book club group visit him and talk about books. Randy provided his own version of field notes when he recorded important things he thought his peers had said during book club discussions. The students in the book clubs learned to value literacy, learned to talk about books inside and outside of school, and were enriched in ways that may not have been possible with more traditional approaches to school reading.

Notes

This work was sponsored in part by the Center for the Learning and Teaching of Elementary Subjects, Institute for Research on Teaching, Michigan State University, which was funded primarily by the Office of Educational Research and Improvement, U.S. Department of Education. The opinions expressed in this publication do not necessarily reflect the position, policy, or endorsement of the office or department (Cooperative Agreement No. G0087C0226).

References

Altwerger, B., & Flores, B. (1994). Theme cycles: Creating communities of learners. *Primary Voices*, 2, 2–6.

Allington, R.L. (1991). The legacy of "slow it down and make it more concrete." In J. Zutell & S. McCormick (Eds.), *Learner factors/teacher factors: Issues in literacy research and instruction* (40th yearbook of the National Reading Conference, pp.19–29). Chicago, IL: National Reading Conference.

Battle, J. (1993). Mexican-American bilingual kindergartners' collaborations in meaning making. In D.J. Leu & C.K. Kinzer (Eds.), *Examining central issues in literacy research, theory, and practice* (42nd yearbook of the National Reading Conference, pp. 163–169). Chicago, IL: National Reading Conference.

Cazden, C. (1988). *Classroom discourse: The language of teaching and learning*. Portsmouth, NH: Heinemann.

Eeds, M., & Wells, D. (1989). Grand conversations: An explanation of meaning construction in literature study groups. *Research in the Teaching of English*, 23, 4–29.

Edwards, P.A. (1991). Fostering early literacy through parent coaching. In E.H. Hiebert (Ed.), *Literacy for a diverse society: Perspectives, practices, and policies* (pp. 199–214). New York: Teachers College Press.

Gavelek, J.R. (1986). The social context of literacy and schooling: A developmental perspective. In T.E. Raphael (Ed.), *The contexts of school-based literacy* (pp. 3–26). New York: Random House.

Gilles, C. (1990). Collaborative literacy strategies: "We don't need a circle to have a group." In K.G. Short & K.M. Pierce (Eds.), *Talking about books: Creating literature communities*. Portsmouth, NH: Heinemann.

Goatley, V.J., Bisesi, T.L., & Urba, J.A. (1992). *Development of response to literature: First grade to adult*. East Lansing, MI: Michigan State University.

Goatley, V.J., & Raphael, T.E. (1992). Non-traditional learners' written and dialogic response to literature. In C.K. Kinzer & D.J. Leu (Eds.), *Literacy research, theory and practice: Views from many perspectives* (41st yearbook of the National Reading Conference, pp. 312–322). Chicago, IL: National Reading Conference.

Heath, S.B. (1983). *Ways with words: Language, life, and work in communities and classrooms*. Cambridge, UK: Cambridge University Press.

Hiebert, E.H. (Ed.). (1993). *Literacy for a diverse society*. New York: Teachers College Press.

Leal, D.J. (1992). The nature of talk about three types of text during peer group discussions. *Journal of Reading Behavior*, 24, 313–338.

Lipson, M.Y., Valencia, S.W., Wixson, K.K., & Peters, C.W. (1993). Integration and thematic teaching: Integration to improve teaching and learning. *Language Arts*, 70, 252–263.

McDermott, R.P., & Aron, J. (1978). Pirandello in the classroom: On the possibility of equal educational opportunity in American culture. In M.C. Reynolds (Ed.), *Future of education for exceptional students: Emerging structures* (pp. 41–64). Reston, VA: Council for Exceptional Children.

McGee, L.M. (1992). An exploration of meaning construction in first graders' grand conversations. In C.K. Kinzer & D.J. Leu (Eds.), *Literacy research, theory, and practice: Views from many perspectives* (41st yearbook of the National Reading Conference, pp. 177–186). Chicago, IL: National Reading Conference.

McMahon, S.I. (1992). *A group of five students as they participate in their student-led book club*. Unpublished doctoral dissertation, Michigan State University, East Lansing.

McMahon, S.I., & Hauschildt, P. (1993, April). *What do we do now? Student struggles with talking about books*. Paper presented at the annual meeting of the American Educational Research Association.

McMahon, S.I., Raphael, T.E., & Goatley, V.J. (in press). Changing the context for classroom reading instruction: The Book Club Project. In J. Brophy (Eds.), *Advances in Research on Teaching*. Greenwich, CT: JAI Press.

Moll, L.C., Tapia, J., & Whitmore, K.F. (1993). Living knowledge: The social distribution of cultural resources for thinking. In G. Salomon (Ed.), *Distributed cognitions: Psychological and educational considerations* (pp. 139–163). Cambridge, UK: Cambridge University Press.

O'Flahavan, J. (1989). *Second graders' social, intellectual, and affective development in varied group discussions about narra-*

tive texts: An explanation of participation structures. Unpublished doctoral dissertation, University of Illinois, Urbana.

Pardo, L.S. (1992, December). *Accommodating diversity in the elementary classroom: A look at literature-based instruction in an inner city school.* Paper presented at the annual meeting of the National Reading Conference, San Antonio, TX.

Pearson, P.D. (1994). Integrated language arts: Sources of controversy and seeds of consensus. In L.M. Morrow, J.K. Smith, & L.C. Wilkinson (Eds.), *Integrated language arts: Controversy to consensus* (pp. 11–31). Boston, MA: Allyn & Bacon.

Raphael, T.E., & Brock, C.H. (1993). Mei: Learning the literacy culture in an urban elementary school. In D.J. Leu & C.K. Kinzer (Eds.), *Examining central issues in literacy research, theory, and practice* (42nd yearbook of the National Reading Conference, pp. 179–188). Chicago, IL: National Reading Conference.

Raphael, T.E., & Goatley, V.J. (1994). The teacher as "more knowledgeable other": Changing roles for teachers in alternative reading instruction programs. In C. Kinzer & D. Leu (Ed.), *Multidimensional aspects of literacy research, theory and practice* (Vol. 43, pp. 527–536). Chicago, IL: National Reading Conference.

Raphael, T.E., & McMahon, S.I. (1994). 'Book Club': An alternative framework for reading instruction. *The Reading Teacher, 48,* 102–116.

Raphael, T.E., McMahon, S.I., Goatley, V.J., Bentley, J.L.,

Boyd, F.B., Pardo, L.S., & Woodman, D.A. (1992). Research directions: Literature and discussion in the reading program. *Language Arts, 69,* 54–61.

Vygotsky, L.S. (1978). *Mind in society.* Cambridge, MA: Harvard Press.

Wells, G., Chang, G.L.M., & Maher, A. (1990). Creating classroom communities of literate thinkers. In S. Sharan (Eds.), *Cooperative learning* (pp. 95–121). New York: Praeger.

Wiseman, D.L., Many, J.E., & Altieri, J. (1992). Enabling complex aesthetic responses: An examination of three literary discussion approaches. In C.K. Kinzer & D.J. Leu (Eds.), *Literacy research, theory, and practice: Views from many perspectives* (41st yearbook of the National Reading Conference, pp. 283–290). Chicago, IL: National Reading Conference.

Children's Literature

Lowry, L. (1989). *Number the stars.* New York: Dell.

Maruki, T. (1980). *Hiroshima no pika.* New York: Lothrop, Lee & Shephard.

O'Dell, S. (1960). *Island of the blue dolphins.* Boston, MA: Houghton Mifflin.

Paterson, K. (1988). *Park's quest.* New York: Dutton.

Paulsen, G. (1987). *Hatchet.* New York: Puffin.

Speare, E.G. (1983). *The sign of the beaver.* Boston, MA: Houghton Mifflin.

CHAPTER 8

Language Charts: A Record of Story Time Talk

Nancy L. Roser and James V. Hoffman
with Linda D. Labbo and Cindy Farest

"I am sad at the very beginning and at the end I feel happy." —Mike

"The characters of Ezra Jack Keats feel the same way as we do; first they're sad and then they're happy. Their names are mostly Peter and Louis." —Joy

THESE ARE SOME of the responses of a class of kindergarten children to the works of Ezra Jack Keats—works that have been read aloud to them over a period of days, works that they have talked about and responded to in various ways. But these particular reflections have been *written* as well, recorded by their teacher on a large chart in the library center. They are words for keeping and returning to.

In a read-aloud program that we have called "Language to Literacy" (LtL), children's responses to stories are gathered systematically at the close of story time talk. It is then that teachers and students turn to their "Language Chart" as a place for saving their ideas.

They rely on the chart to help them recall other stories in their unit, and they use the chart to notice similarities and differences among stories. By its presence, the Language Chart announces that children in the classroom have important ideas about books.

For five years, we have been "borrowing" these charts from teachers in kindergarten through fifth grade, inspecting them for the types and extent of responses they invite, and then gathering the language from these charts to learn more about the functions that Language Charts seem to serve in classrooms. In the examples and discussion that follow, we share what we have learned from these "artifacts" about the reflections, extensions, and

From *Language Arts*, January 1992, Volume 69, pp. 44–52. Copyright 1992 by the National Council of Teachers of English. Reprinted with permission. Photos courtesy of Nancy L. Roser.

creations of meaning in classrooms in which children talked about books and then saved their ideas in a dominant spot—on a Language Chart.

Background

The LtL project was developed initially in collaboration with over 70 primary grade teachers in the Brownsville (Texas) Independent School District, with support provided by a grant from the Texas Education Agency (Roser, Hoffman, & Farest, 1990). The project focused on the literacy needs of students deemed "at risk." The teachers described themselves as interested in books and story time but reported they often neglected both because of the more pressing demands of their curriculum.

In the manner of Moss (1978; 1980; 1984); Huck, Hepler, and Hickman (1987); Cullinan (1987); and Western (1980), the project staff worked to develop literature units for use by the teachers during their classroom story time. These literature units are simply plans for sharing books with some common element (such as theme, topic, genre, or author/illustrator). Each unit consists of 10 children's books (providing for a one-a-day "read" during a two-week period) and a unit guide. The guides contain background information for the unit as well as suggestions to teachers for sharing the books, opening story talk, and offering children additional response opportunities, including writing, art, and drama. (See Figure 1 for a list of representative units.)

Each literature unit is organized to provide a framework for the children's discoveries of the connections among the literature selections. In a strategic place in each guide we suggest a format for a Language Chart; that format is intended to provoke an awareness of the links among stories. As Jane Yolen (1977) has said, we wanted children to notice that "stories lean on stories."

Language Charts: Form and Intentions

Physically, a Language Chart is constructed from a large piece of butcher paper ruled into a matrix. Along one axis the titles (and author/illustrators) of the books are recorded; for the second axis, the literature unit guide suggests ideas for questions, invitations for reflection, or additional prompts for book discussion. The suggested formats for the Language Chart vary for each unit, but most focus on a connecting thread that draws the books together.

For example, one of the LtL units is organized to let readers explore the theme "Being Different Is Being Special." Each of the books in the unit extols a character who is "different" in some way, and who, through the course of story events, comes to understand and accept this difference as a positive attribute. The format for the Language Chart for this unit is illustrated in Figure 2 (with some sample children's talk inserted).

Another of the LtL units is organized around the works of Eric Carle. A suggested prompt for that Language Chart encourages children to talk about (and to record) what makes Eric Carle's books (for example, *The Hungry Caterpillar* and *The Very Busy Spider*) special to touch, see, and read.

Teachers and children add to the Language Chart after the sharing of each book. In some classrooms, the teachers record what children say; in other classrooms, children themselves write on the chart. Typically, children fill the empty spaces on the chart with artwork and colorful cutouts of characters, scenes, and favorite spots in the books. This

Figure 1
Representative Language to Literacy Units

Themes

Being Afraid
Being Different Makes Us Special
Being Friends
Big and Small
Brothers and Sisters
Cleverness
Courage
Home, Sweet Home
Laughter in the Classroom*
Make a Wish
Make it From Scratch
Mischief Makers
Pioneer Days*
Sacrifices (Stone Fox)
Say Goodnight
Seasons of Life*
Solving Problems
Sounder*
Survival*
That's Entertainment
The Earth Turns 'Round
Tickle Your Funny Bone
Travel Through Time*
Watch It Grow!
We are Family
Write to Me
Write to Me, Too
You're My Friend

Genre

Books that Read Themselves
Books to Sing
Cumulative Tales
Folktales by Tomie de Paola
Modern Day Fables (Lionni)
Mystery and Adventure, Sincerely Harold X*
Pattern Books
Predictable Books
Read Together Books
Sing Along Books
Tales from Other Lands
Tales of the Southwest
This is Your Life, Ben Franklin!*
What's a Biography, Jean Fritz!*
What's the Secret, Mrs. Frankweiler!*
Wordless Picture Books

Author/Illustrator

Arnold Lobel
Beverly Cleary*
Bill Peet
Charlotte Zolotow
Cynthia Rylant*
Dr. Seuss
Eric Carle
Ezra Jack Keats
It's Me Again, Hank the Cowdog
James Marshall
Katherine Paterson*
Leo Lionni
Lynn Reid Banks*
Marc Brown (Adventures with Arthur)
Roald Dahl*
Steven Kellogg
Susan Jeffers
Tomie dePaola

Topics

Bears, Bears, Bears
Books to Chew
Cats, Cats, Cats
Curious George
Days with Frogs and Toads
Dinosaur Time
Dog Gone Fun! (Dogs)
Fly Away With Me!
Giants
Horses
Let's Go to the Beach
Mice are Nice
Mighty Monsters
My House, My Home
On the Go! (Vehicles)
Perfect Pets
Pig Tales
Please Bug Me! (Insects)
Rabbit Round-Up
Smile: All About Teeth
Special Toys
The Cat's Meow
The Royal Touch

*Indicates chapter book unit

Figure 2
Being Different Is Being Special

Title	Author	Who was different?	How were they different?	What made the character special?
Oliver Button Is a Sissy	Tomie dePaola	Oliver	Some kids thought Oliver liked the same things as girls.	Oliver had talent!
Horton Hatches the Egg	Dr. Seuss	Horton	Horton was an elephant but he sat on a nest!	Horton was a faithful friend to sit until the elephant-bird hatched.
William's Doll	etc.			

chart activity is not intended to replace the natural book talk that accompanies and follows book sharing with children; rather, it is intended to focus thinking *after* book conversations have ranged freely. The chart is a record of a group's response, a prompt for some connections among the stories, and a reminder of the books in the unit. But we noticed that the charts seemed to serve other functions, too.

Language Charts—Functions

Our experience with literature units and Language Charts has now stretched to school districts in several other Texas cities (for example, Austin and San Antonio) and has continued to increase our awareness of some of the specific ways in which these focusing charts serve instruction and learning. Based on our interactions with hundreds of teachers involved with the LtL project and our inspection and analysis of their Language Charts, we have identified eight recurring functions that these charts seem to serve.

As evidence of testimony to the importance of the sharing and study of literature in a classroom. A Language Chart in a classroom signals that children there read, talk about, and value books. Because the charts are large and appealing, they are noticeable to all who enter the classroom, and they become a topic of discussion and explanation (see Photo 1). In one school district, Language Charts filled with pictures and responses line the school halls, announcing the importance of children's responses to literature.

Photo 1

As an historical account of experience with literature in a classroom. We noticed that when Language Charts were not discarded at the close of a unit but rather stayed on display after new units were begun, there were some serendipitous results: previous Language Charts were revisited; children returned to them to recall favorites and to make story connections across units.

As a demonstration of oral to written language connections. For beginners, as in the language-experience approach, Language Charts enable seeing one's own words recorded for others to read and for reading on one's own. Children also begin to use the language of stories as they reflect and respond, incorporating some of the author's words into their own talk to be recorded.

As a stimulus for expression of personal responses to literature. Because Language Charts are the product of cooperative effort, they often represent group-constructed meanings. Yet Language Charts also give opportunity for the expression of individuals' thoughts and feelings (see Photo 2). We observed lively discussions in which teachers and children explored the similarities and differences in their responses to varied aspects of stories—events, characters, pivot points, and themes. Language Charts offer a place to collect these valued responses; the discussions that occur seem to deepen individual responders' thinking about books.

As an occasion for connecting the individual books to the linking elements that undergird the unit. Sharing a good piece of literature is a valuable experience in its own right. Even so, Language Charts stimulate added interest and interaction about books. The use of Language Charts encourages participants to notice the universals that books share, thus promoting the recognition of connections between and among books (see Pho-

Photo 2

to 3). For example, a kindergarten class read *The Legend of the Bluebonnet* and *The Legend of the Indian Paintbrush*, both by Tomie dePaola. Among the children's responses were these:

"The two flower books are alike!"

"They both have Indians in the story."

"They both have flowers that grow on the hills."

"Tomie dePaola did them."

"The Indians gave them both a different name because they did something helpful for the other Indians that they loved."

As an opportunity to reflect on a literary experience. Through the regular sharing of literature, children acquire the background

Roser et al.

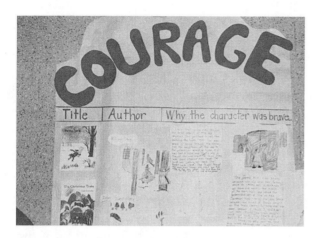

Photo 3

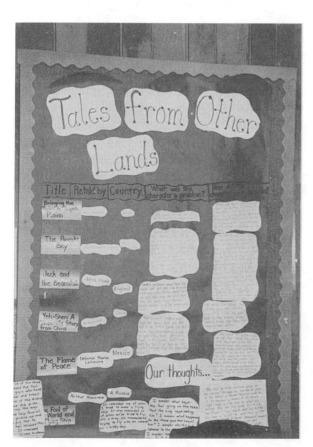

Photo 4

knowledge of those who study literature systematically—characterization, theme, point of view, style, mood, tone, and format. Children we observe seem to come to a better understanding of these notions and their labels through discussions focused by the Language Charts. Teachers and students converse about the characteristics that stories share (for example, characters, setting, problems, solutions, and outcomes) or reflect on the characteristics of a particular genre (tall tales, fables, myths, and historical fiction). (See Photo 4.) Teachers who use Language Charts with their literature units explained that the children became comfortable with the language of literature:

> "They developed an awareness of authorship, illustrators, and of themselves as writers."

> "They developed a more critical eye by comparison of styles."

> "They became familiar with various genres of literature.

> "They learned to appreciate literary devices."

As a bridge between trade books and content area study. Because Language Charts permit the collection and organization of ideas, they are also a means for collecting information from expository or nonfiction books in purposeful ways, thus initiating, framing, or extending content area studies (for example, social studies, science, or health). This integration of literature across the curriculum seems to enhance motivation for learning. One teacher described it like this: "My students seemed to discover the world."

As a springboard for other responses to literature. Because the space for recording language on a Language Chart is limited, children who are excited by their own ideas turn to writing for themselves in logs or response journals. In addition, the charts have been used as an initial step toward a variety of other valuable language extensions (such as debates, letter writing, storytelling, and dramatization).

Language Charts and Chapter Books

In our early work in Brownsville, Texas, we produced picture book units with the teachers. For the most part, the books were short enough so that they could be shared in a single story time session with primary grade readers and listeners. More recently, we have gathered works for older children and guided teachers to develop chapter book units. The organizational structure for these chapter book units is somewhat different from the picture book units, although the goals are the same. For example, in a unit that follows the adventures of Ramona Quimby, a character created by Beverly Cleary, the read-aloud book is *Ramona Quimby, Age 8*. It is read at a pace of one chapter per day. By gathering multiple copies of all the other Cleary books in which Ramona is a central character, each of the students in the class can choose a second *Ramona* book to read during the unit. The organization for free choice reading can vary across classrooms. For example, some teachers send the books home to be read aloud by a parent or together with another child; other teachers give time for independent reading of *Ramona* books in class; still other teachers allow students to form "book clubs" in which small groups read and talk about their independent choices.

In another chapter book unit, one that encourages exploration of the relations between people and their pets, teachers read aloud William Armstrong's *Sounder* and distribute class sets of the companion selection, *Where the Red Fern Grows* by Wilson Rawls. Again, teachers choose from among various plans for orchestrating the independent reading of the companion selection.

Some middle grade teachers in San Antonio are currently gathering books to prepare a unit on "Perspectives," which includes a combination of chapter and picture books used to explore the world's eye view of *Stuart Little* by E. B. White, *The Borrowers* by Mary Norton, Roald Dahl's *The BFG*, and Chris Van Allsburg's *Two Bad Ants*.

The role of the Language Charts seems to continue to be as central in working with chapter book units as it is in the teaching of the picture book units. Again, a large piece of butcher paper is often used to record the responses of the students; teachers have also used poster board, construction paper cutouts, and homemade "Big Books" to capture response. To prompt reflection and discovery, questions can be written across the top of the matrix, while the side column can be organized to reflect the chapter structure of just one book or the titles of all the texts that are in the unit. In the unit of Cleary books, we maintained a simple focus on the "into trouble and out of it again" humor in Ramona's adventures, following the problems and solutions chapter by chapter. In an author unit titled "Every Living Thing," focusing on the works of Cynthia Rylant, the Language Chart prompted discovery of the changes in lives that typify all of Rylant's works.

From Language Chart to Response Journal

Just as primary grade children were eager to see their thoughts and words recorded in a public place, so did middle graders seem eager to have their talk, discovery, reflection, comparison, and supporting ideas recorded. But, as suggested earlier, the charts sometimes overflowed as children's ideas and enthusiasm crowded the chart space. It was a simple and logical step to capture their eagerness to respond by introducing response logs for these children to record their own ideas about the units' books—not just to the read-aloud selection but to the books read independently, as well.

Sometimes, the Language Chart structures carry over into the journals and seem to help children shape their initial responses. But soon students let go of the frameworks for the Language Chart and respond entirely in their *own* ways with what *they* most want to write and connect with. For example, some students responding to *Sounder* and *Where the Red Fern Grows* preferred to weave in a stream of their own feelings about a pet in their lives.

Recently, we observed several teachers who were using response journals in combination with Language Charts in another way. These teachers asked their students to take a few minutes immediately following the story to record their personal responses in a log or journal. At the kindergarten level, these responses were illustrations or emergent writing. In the intermediate grades, the responses tended to be more extensive narratives, criticisms, and reactions. These teachers used the voluntary sharing of a few of these entries each day as a stimulus for group discussion. Not until this talk was fully explored were the group's collective responses recorded on the Language Chart.

Making It Work

Teachers who are using Language Charts as part of their classroom literature programs have described some struggles, adjustments, and adaptations of the process. First, as noted, they have reported they sometimes have difficulty recording as *much* as children want to say. Young students in particular are disappointed if their specific comments are not recorded on the Language Chart. Problems seemed less acute when more time was allotted to discussion before recording ideas on the chart—time for sharing many children's insights. Teachers discovered that if they rushed too quickly from the story to the chart, there was less chance for group-negotiated meaning, and more proprietary interest emerged in seeing one's own "quotes" on the chart. Other solutions to the limited space problem came in the form of the personal responses in the journal either before or after the Language Chart experience. Finally, and perhaps only as a last resort, some teachers planned a pattern of turn taking for recording on the chart. The best solution seemed to be more talking time, followed by negotiation and group decision making about the chart's entries.

Yet, the problem with Language Charts mentioned most frequently by teachers was the need for more wall space to hang them. We have seen some creative solutions to this problem: for example, hanging charts from the ceiling, working on only a section of the chart at a time and then attaching the separate section to the larger unit chart, or working on poster-sized boards and turning the charts into Big Books. The only solution that troubles us is one in which the teacher closets the Language Chart, rolling it out after read-aloud to record story talk, and then, after the recording is complete, rerolls the chart. We feel this strategy may detract from many of the important functions of Language Charts described earlier.

Turning Language Charts over to Children

The more comfortable children became with the unit format and with talking across books, the more they were able to discover for themselves how tales are bound. Students progressively took the lead in story discussion. Immediately, teachers began to follow the students' leads in book conversations and to participate in their explorations, which often included the talk of comparison. As a result, Language Charts came increasingly under the design of the users of the unit, taking shape as the unit progressed. Delightfully, they also became open-ended response charts, simply inviting children's "observations." Through the teacher's subtle guidance of the book talk, these observations were telling evidence of growth in children's pleasure, insights, and curiosity about books (see Photo 5).

Photo 5

Summary

The purpose of a Language Chart is realized when thinking is sparked. Language Charts seemed to give credence both to the thoughts and feelings of an individual responder (as in the example at the beginning of this article), as well as to group-constructed meanings and the products of cooperative effort. In both cases, we observed that when teachers and students explored similarities and differences in their responses across books, there were opportunities for more in-depth, thoughtful conversations. Although good stories (in and of themselves) evoke multiple levels of reader response, we observed that experience with Language Charts enriched and extended those responses to good stories.

Notes

Thanks especially to the teachers and Monica Sandoval and Becky Enloe of Brownsville, Texas; to the teachers and Nora Forester in Northside Independent School District, San Antonio, Texas; and to Cyndy Hoffman in Eanes Independent School District, Austin, Texas, for helping us learn in their schools.

References

Cullinan, B.E. (Ed.). (1987). *Children's literature in the reading program*. Newark, DE: International Reading Association.

Huck, C.S., Hepler, S., & Hickman, J. (1987). *Children's literature in the elementary school* (4th ed.). New York: Holt, Rinehart & Winston.

Moss, J.F. (1978). Using the "focus unit" to enhance children's response to literature. *Language Arts, 55,* 482–488.

Moss, J.F. (1980). The fable and critical thinking. *Language Arts, 57,* 21–29.

Moss, J.F. (1984). *Focus units in literature: A handbook for elementary school teachers*. Urbana, IL: National Council of Teachers of English.

Roser, N.L., Hoffman, J.V., & Farest, C. (1990). Language, literature, and at-risk children. *The Reading Teacher, 43,* 554–559.

Western, L.E. (1980). A comparative study of folktales. *Language Arts, 57,* 395–402, 439.

Yolen, J. (1977). How basic is SHAZAM? *Language Arts, 54,* 645–651.

Children's Literature

Armstrong, W.H. (1969). *Sounder.* New York: Harper-Collins.

Carle, E. (1969). *The hungry caterpillar.* New York: Philomel.

Carle, E. (1984). *The very busy spider.* New York: Philomel.

Cleary, B. (1981). *Ramona Quimby, age* 8. New York: Morrow.

Dahl, R. (1982). *The* BFG. New York: Farrar, Straus & Giroux.

dePaola, T. (1983). *The legend of the bluebonnet.* New York: Putnam.

dePaola, T. (1988). *The legend of the Indian paintbrush.* New York: Putnam.

Norton, M. (1952). *The borrowers.* New York: Harcourt Brace.

Rawls, W. (1961). *Where the red fern grows.* New York: Bantam.

Van Allsburg, C. (1988). *Two bad ants.* Boston, MA: Houghton Mifflin.

White, E.B. (1945). *Stuart Little.* New York: HarperCollins.

CHAPTER 9

Enriching Response to Literature with Webbing

Karen Bromley

THE RELATIONSHIP OF webbing to learning is clear. We know that learning occurs in an organized way (Novak & Gowin, 1984), so it is not surprising that graphic material such as semantic webs, used to illustrate the organization of ideas and information, aids comprehension and learning (Flood & Lapp, 1988; Heimlich & Pittelman, 1986; Pearson & Johnson, 1978). But fewer educators recognize the potential of webbing in promoting and supporting students' responses to literature. Webbing can provide an avenue for sharing and responding to literature; it can promote thinking and learning about stories and enhance students' enjoyment and appreciation of literature. Perhaps best of all, webbing is a way to connect students with stories and encourage their interaction around these stories.

Webbing is the process of constructing a visual display to represent organized relationships among those ideas or categories of information. Typically, webbing is used in the classroom as a planning tool to organize thematic instructional units. Some teachers also use webbing in reading or content area instruction to develop background knowledge or record brainstorming. But few teachers use webbing to foster and record responses to literature. Instead, many teachers attempt to evoke literary response through a question and answer format, unwittingly contributing to a classroom in which thinking is too often defined solely by the teacher. Too much questioning about literature can result in a minimum of student involvement and sharing and often discourage the genuine exchange that reveals rich response to literature.

What Is Webbing?

In the classroom, a web is a visual display of information a teacher and students create to structure ideas and aid learning.

Why Use Webbing?

Webbing serves as a tool for structuring classroom talk about stories and books—a tool that can broaden thinking and deepen response to literature. Its use is well established for building the critical relationship between collaborative talk and content area learning (Alvermann, Dillon, & O'Brien, 1987; Chambers, 1985; Wells & Chang-Wells, 1992). But teachers can also use webbing to promote talk about literature and help students construct shared meanings that extend their understandings, responses, and learning (Bromley, 1991; Norton, 1992). Webbing can

- provide a process for constructing meaning;
- organize and make literary insights visible;
- link reading, writing, and thinking;
- provide a stimulus and content for talk;
- foster understanding of characters, stories, and authors;
- allow for positive social interaction;
- encourage divergent thinking;
- foster the sharing of opinions and insights; and
- provide rehearsal and planning for writing.

Webbing promotes the sharing of ideas and information that helps students understand stories and books in ways they ordinarily might not. Webbing promotes interaction among students who construct story meanings together as they enjoy, appreciate, and respond to literature.

Creating Webs

In my work with children and teachers, I have discovered that modeling webbing for students helps them create their own story webs. When teachers "think aloud" while web-

bing, students see and hear the process used to respond to literature and organize ideas generated by a story. For example, when Brenda Myers read *Miss Rumphius* by Barbara Cooney to her third graders, she first encouraged them to talk about the story. As the children shared reactions, James said he liked the story because all Miss Rumphius's wishes came true. Brenda wanted to use Cooney's nonstereotypic portrait of a lively and determined elderly woman to help her students learn how writers develop characters in literature, so she used James's response to begin a web (see Figure 1). As she wrote the phrase "Miss Rumphius's 3 Wishes" on chart paper in the center, she said, "I want to explore the idea with you that James mentioned. It was one of the big ideas in the story for me, too. I think Miss Rumphius's entire life was guided by her wishes." Then she added, "Here are the three wishes I remember from the story," and she wrote each one at the end of a spoke drawn from the center of the web: to travel to faraway places, to grow old by the sea, and to make the world a more beautiful place. Brenda told her students what she was thinking as she did this by identifying story details that could serve to reveal the character, such as "First, she was a librarian in an inland city."

To show the children that character analysis is not always dependent on the order in which story events occur and that one idea often triggers others, Brenda randomly added observations to the web. She also showed her students how readers return to a story to verify an idea that needs support: for example, she said, "I think Miss Rumphius showed real gumption when she visited a tropical island and made some other daring treks, but I'm not sure I remember all of them...yes, here's one...." Then she read aloud the part of the story in which Miss Rumphius climbs a mountain. By doing this, she showed her students

Figure 1
Beginning a Character Study of *Miss Rumphius*

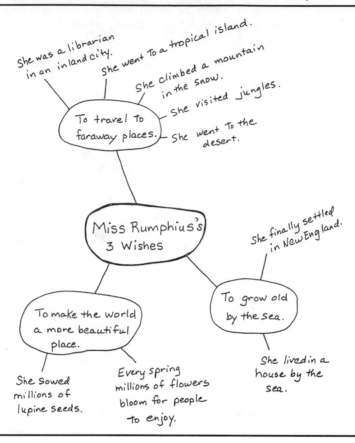

how important the story text is for supporting what they think.

When the web was finished, Brenda read it aloud to her students and remarked: "Reviewing the story like this reminds me that Miss Rumphius, her grandfather, and little Alice all had the same three wishes for their lives." Then she said, "I think Miss Rumphius's grandfather made the world a more beautiful place with his art and sculptures. We know that Miss Rumphius's lupines brought beauty. But I wonder what little Alice, her grandniece, will decide to do to make the world a more beautiful place." This genuine query (with no definite answer) prompted several students to offer ideas.

Looking at the web, Brenda said, "When I look at Miss Rumphius's wishes and accomplishments, I see a person to admire. She set goals early in her life, worked to achieve them, and was a caring, creative, independent, daring, and happy person...." Through her model of responsive reading, Brenda extended her students' responses to the story and helped them appreciate this sensitive portrayal of aging and the full life of this special character.

Brenda related the story to her own life by telling her students about her goals as a young girl and how she had worked to achieve them. She encouraged her students to create personal webs in which they identified their own life goals and speculated about ways to accomplish them.

Brenda and other teachers use chart paper, butcher paper, the chalkboard, or the overhead projector to model webbing for students. The chalkboard and chart paper are large enough to include lots of information in large print for easy reading. Even so, it is easier to maintain eye contact with students when using the overhead projector.

If you try webbing in your classroom, do not overlook the possibility of using colored pens, pencils, and chalk to create webs. Seeing "big ideas" in one color and "little ideas" in another may help students differentiate between major categories of information and their supporting details. For example, after you introduce webbing and your students understand the process, you can arrange students in small groups to create webs together. Giving children colored pens or pencils and chart paper for webbing in small groups motivates them and helps reveal important insights into their story interpretations. When each member of the group signs his or her name to the web, there is both tribute to and record of each student's ideas.

Two cautions are worth noting here: first, when you use children's literature to teach, it is important to remember that your students' enjoyment and appreciation of stories is paramount. Everything you do should foster personal response from which students can learn about literature; second, teaching students literary elements does not ensure their comprehension of or personal response to children's literature. Even young children who have no explicit knowledge of story elements or story

structure can recall, understand, and respond to stories. But better understanding of literary elements can promote comprehension and deepen response. Webbing can lend structure to readers' story experiences and responses and help them think about literary elements as they untangle the plot, connect related ideas, track character traits, consider the influence of setting, recall the creation of mood, or visualize aspects of the story in myriad ways.

Webbing to Elicit Response

When webs are generated *before* reading, students share their experiences related to some aspect of the story, which prepares them to respond more fully to literature. Webbing before reading also provides a forum for making predictions and establishing purposes for reading. For instance, Michele Mele, a second grade teacher, created a word web before reading *Thunder Cake*, a story by Patricia Polacco in which a young girl's Russian grandmother helps her overcome her fear of thunder as they anticipate an approaching storm. Michele wanted to organize her students' experiences and understandings of thunderstorms and establish what they already knew. She first wrote "thunderstorms" and then "thunder," "lightning," and "rain" and asked her students to describe each (see Figure 2). Michele then wrote her students' words in black on chart paper and added the author's vocabulary in blue. Creating this web showed Michele what her students knew and introduced the children to new language and concepts of "thunderstorms." In this way, Michele prepared her students to be involved in the story, understand the young girl's fear, and make predictions about what might happen. She found that organizing thoughts graphically enhanced her students' responses to the story.

Figure 2
Building Language and Concepts for Thunderstorms with *Thunder Cake*

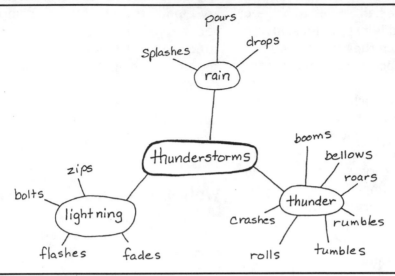

Figure 3
Setting the Stage to Read *Gorilla*

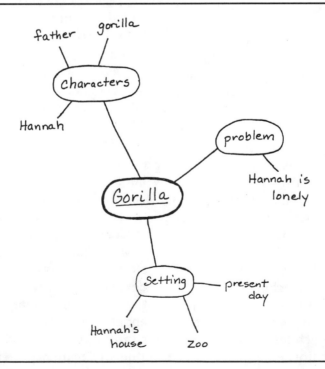

Teachers also use webs to introduce setting or character in a story, establish motivation for reading, and prepare students to become deeply involved in a story world. Presenting a partially constructed web gives students a frame of reference for what they will read or hear, while piquing their interest in the story. For example, before reading *Gorilla* by Anthony Browne, a story about a young girl who is neglected by her busy father, Kerri Schlimmer introduced it to her second graders by making a web on the chalkboard containing the story elements of "setting," "characters," and "problem" (see Figure 3). With the web, Kerri set the stage for the story and showed her students that Hannah was lonely; then the children talked about their own experiences with loneliness and discussed its causes and feelings. Kerri wanted her students to relate to Hannah's feelings and become part of her world so they could appreciate her fantasy.

Illustration from Patricia Polacco's Thunder Cake. *©1990 by Patricia Polacco. Reprinted by permission of The Putnam Publishing Group.*

Webbing to Extend Response

Generally, it is a good idea to read first and create webs afterward (as opposed to during reading), so that images, reverie, and personal meanings are not disrupted as students read or listen. Even so, webs created *during* reading can clarify an otherwise confusing story. *After* story reading, webs have a variety of uses, including sorting the important events, details, and relationships that aid understanding and prompt more insightful response.

Stefan Stowell, a sixth grade teacher, began reading to his class a chapter a day from *Let the Circle Be Unbroken* by Mildred Taylor, a story about racism in the 1930s in the central United States. After reading the first three chapters, Stefan found that his students were losing track of characters and their relationships. He and his students created a character web on a bulletin board to show relationships among the families in the story (see Figure 4), and each day these students added new characters to the web as the story progressed. The web also provided raw material for the later writing of personal reactions to characters.

Teachers sometimes use a web to record the sequence of events in an action-filled plot. Or, they use a web when they read a chapter book over a long period of time to chronicle changes in a character or to review the story. When students create a character web to show relationships between feelings and actions and then review it at the story's conclusion, they gain insight into a character's growth.

Fran Bose read daily to her third grade class from *The Flunking of Joshua T. Bates* by Susan Shreve, the story about a boy who is retained in third grade because he cannot read. After Fran read each day, she and her students recorded Joshua's feelings and actions on a web she put on a bulletin board (see Figure 5). Using this web, Fran illustrated to her stu-

Figure 4
Showing Relationships Among Characters in *Let the Circle Be Unbroken*

dents how an author develops a character such as Joshua. She also showed them how Joshua changed during the story as his teacher, Mrs. Goodwin, tutored him every day after school for three months until he could do well enough to be promoted to fourth grade.

A character or event web needs to be readily accessible for students to refer to during reading. Putting one on a bulletin board as Stefan and Fran did is a good idea. You can also give students a copy of a partially completed web so each can add his or her feelings about a character or record important events at will. For some students, interim graphing is an aid to comprehension and response, but for other students, stopping to write during reading (as mentioned earlier) disrupts the meaning they make and the responses they have. It is important to know your students' strengths and needs and use webbing accordingly.

As students share their responses to and meanings for stories, webs can become a place for collecting those responses. In one example of webbing used in such a way after reading, Chuck Hall, a fourth grade teacher, had his students add information to the story elements web he had used to introduce *A River Ran Wild* by Lynne Cherry, an environmental history of the Nashua River (see Figure 6). Before reading, Chuck told his students he wanted them to have important background

Figure 5
Showing Relationships Between Feelings and Actions in *The Flunking of Joshua T. Bates*

Illustration from The Wretched Stone *written and illustrated by Chris Van Allsburg. ©1991 by Chris Van Allsburg. Reprinted by permission of Houghton Mifflin Company. All rights reserved.*

information, and he gave them each a web containing the story elements of "setting," "characters," and "problem." This web provided a structure for better understanding the actions of Marion Stoddart, the woman who organized the Nashua River Cleanup Committee and was responsible for the river's restoration.

In discussion after reading, students shared their admiration for Marion Stoddart and her commitment to the cause of cleaning up the Nashua River. They worked together in small groups to record information on their webs for "solution" and "theme" to support these feelings, which helped them identify events leading to the restoration of the river.

Then groups discussed their webs with one another to outline Marion Stoddart's actions and the resulting changes in the river. When the students shared their webs with the class, Chuck helped them make comparisons between the Nashua River and their local river.

Chuck's class also read *Come Back, Salmon* by Molly Cone, in which a group of children adopt a polluted stream and bring it back to life. His students were impressed with what other children had accomplished, and they created a web that included information to support their feelings and tell the children's story. When they compared this web to the previous one, they had a clearer idea of how to get involved in similar civic activism. As a result of reading these two stories, Chuck's students decided to study pollution in their local river.

Webs can also be used to develop awareness of perspective in writing. Barbara Worobey's fourth graders read Chris Van Allsburg's *Two Bad Ants* and responded with delight to the illustrations and the ants' view of the world. She and her students completed a web by supplying information from the story about what the ants thought they saw (see Figure 7). Then Barbara paired students and had them create descriptions of classroom objects from an ant's viewpoint. Students enjoyed reading their descriptions aloud for their classmates to guess what giant object they were describing. This webbing activity grew from response to the story and was practice for writing about the story as well.

Webs can even be used to explore the extended metaphor of a story (see Chapter 2 by Eeds and Peterson in this volume). Barbara's students enjoyed *The Wretched Stone* by Chris Van Allsburg, a story told in journal format about a ship's crew that takes a strange glowing stone aboard and suffers dire consequences. In the discussion following reading,

Figure 6
Depicting Story Elements for A *River Ran Wild*

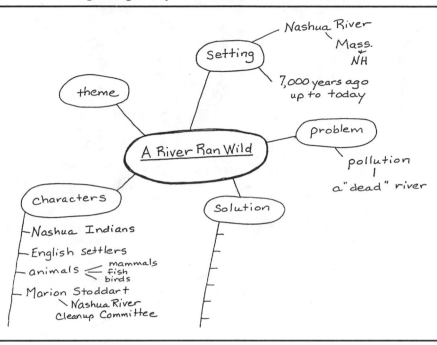

Figure 7
Developing Awareness of Perspective in *Two Bad Ants*

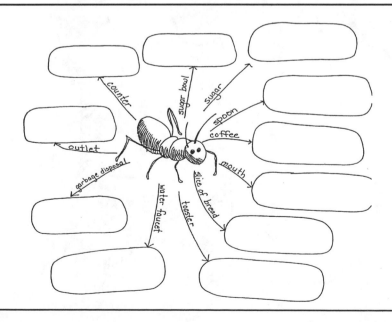

Figure 8
Interpreting *The Wretched Stone* as an Allegory

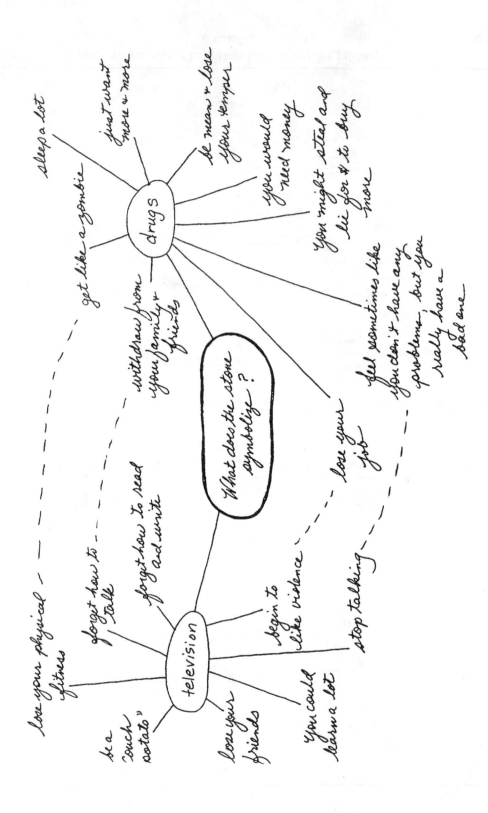

many students had questions about what the story meant. Barbara extended their responses through webbing and discussion; she asked what the students thought the stone might symbolize and used this as the core question for a web (see Figure 8). Some students felt it was a symbol for television, and Barbara encouraged them to describe the effects of watching too much TV as she added their ideas as supporting information to the web. During this discussion, one student observed that the stone could also symbolize drugs because they affect people in similar ways as watching TV does. So Barbara added drugs to the web while students supplied descriptions of the effects of drugs. They also pointed out similarities between the effects of watching TV and taking drugs, which Barbara showed on the web with dotted lines.

Concluding Comments

These are just a few examples of ways to use webbing before reading to elicit response and after reading to extend response. As you use webbing with literature, you will discover new ways to promote discussion among your students that will help them really understand stories and books. As your students interact to create webs, they will share ideas, learn to appreciate the perspectives that others bring to a story, and recognize that a particular text can not only have many meanings but also evoke various emotions. Finally, as students web together, they will structure their talk, broaden their thinking, and deepen their responses to literature.

References

Alvermann, D.E., Dillon, D.R., & O'Brien, D.G. (1987). *Using discussion to promote reading comprehension*. Newark, DE: International Reading Association.

Bromley, K. (1991). *Webbing with literature: Creating story maps with children's books*. Boston, MA: Allyn & Bacon.

Chambers, A. (1985). *Booktalk*. New York: HarperCollins.

Flood, J., & Lapp, D. (1988). Conceptual mapping strategies for understanding information texts. *The Reading Teacher, 41*, 780–783.

Heimlich, J.E., & Pittelman, S.D. (1986). *Semantic mapping: Classroom applications*. Newark, DE: International Reading Association.

Norton, D.E. (1992). *The impact of literature-based reading*. New York: Macmillan.

Novak, J.D., & Gowin, D.B. (1984). *Learning how to learn*. Cambridge, UK: Cambridge University Press.

Pearson, P.D., & Johnson, D.D. (1978). *Teaching reading comprehension*. New York: Henry Holt.

Wells, G., & Chang-Wells, G.L. (1992). *Constructing knowledge together: Classrooms as centers of inquiry and literacy*. Portsmouth, NH: Heinemann.

Children's Literature

Browne, A. (1983). *Gorilla*. New York: Knopf.

Cherry, L. (1992). *A river ran wild*. San Diego, CA: Harcourt Brace.

Cone, M. (1992). *Come back salmon*. New York: Sierra Club, Scribner.

Cooney, B. (1982). *Miss Rumphius*. New York: Dell.

Polacco, P. (1990). *Thunder cake*. New York: Scholastic.

Shreve, S. (1984). *The flunking of Joshua T. Bates*. New York: Scholastic.

Taylor, M. (1981). *Let the circle be unbroken*. New York: Dial.

Van Allsburg, C. (1988). *Two bad ants*. Boston, MA: Houghton Mifflin.

Van Allsburg, C. (1991). *The wretched stone*. Boston, MA: Houghton Mifflin.

Guiding Book Talk

CHAPTER 10

Talking About Books with Young Children

Lea M. McGee

A GROUP OF SEVEN first graders listen to their teacher, Karen King, as she reads aloud *The Pain and the Great One* by Judy Blume. After reading, Ms. King asks, "Who has something to say about the story?" Deanna responds, "I have a slobby old dog that jumps on my bed, and my mother blames me because she thinks I jump on the bed." Many other children tell their stories about catching undeserved blame. Then Jarrold says, "I really like when he, when he, he like rooooom, rooooom (makes motions and sounds as if driving a car), kapooooow (jerks as if hitting something in a car)." Stephen replies, "Yeah, when he knocked down the buildings." Later in the conversation the children wonder which child, The Pain or The Great One, the parents love best. Lakisha says, "Hey, look here at the end of this page (points to book) and on this page (turns to another page and points). It says the same, 'Yuck. I think they like her and (turns to another page) him better than me.'"

Many teachers such as Karen King are quite skilled in engaging young children in conversation about good books, as many authors in this volume illustrate. They know that after listening to a book read aloud, children enjoy talking about parts they liked best, wondering about characters and events, and even adding dialogue to act like a character. As children talk about books, they think deeply about their reading experiences, listen to one another, and together construct a richer understanding of the book.

Having good conversations about books may be particularly important during the early childhood years. Over stories, parents and other adults show children ways of making meaning (Baghban, 1984; Ninio & Bruner, 1978). In turn, children's ways of responding to literature seem to be influenced by their early involvement in story talk—meaning making. However, as many children enter school, their literacy experiences often narrow to focus almost exclusively on learning to read. Too often children spend more time practicing reading skills than they do reading, listening, and talking about stories. It is critical that young chil-

Cover illustration from Judy Blume's The Pain and the Great One. *Illustration ©1984 by Irene Trivas. Reprinted by permission of Macmillan Books for Young Readers, an imprint of Simon & Schuster Children's Publishing Division.*

dren, including those beginning to read conventionally, continue to have opportunities to respond to quality literature through talk, drama, art, and other expressive activities. Talking about stories and poems stretches and strengthens children's language and cognitive development and provides them with a pool of implicit literary understandings to use in their own reading and writing.

What Are Reader Response Theories Doing in Early Childhood Classrooms?

There are many good reasons for talking about literature with young children. Certainly, teachers who listen carefully to children as they talk about a story or poem can learn much about the children's enjoyment and un-

derstandings. The purposes for talking about literature have been amplified by reader response theorists such as Louise Rosenblatt (1978) and Stanley Fish (1980), who suggest that this practice provides readers and listeners with space to explore and expand their own unique and personal responses to literature. Reader response theorists give suitable recognition to the notion that all of us—including children—have unique responses, ones that only we are capable of having.

Rosenblatt's (1978) theories have been particularly important in suggesting directions and purposes for talking about literature. She argues that as readers are reading (or listeners are listening), they carry on a "shaping" activity in which they actually construct the meaning of literary works for themselves, guided by the blueprint of the text. Rosenblatt differentiates between two kinds of reading stances—efferent and aesthetic—which serve different purposes for readers. When taking an efferent stance, readers focus on remembering information that will be carried away after reading. For the most part, a recipe reader who is baking a cake is assuming an efferent stance as is a school child rereading to identify the "main idea" and three supporting details. In contrast, readers who assume an aesthetic stance focus on their inner experiences when reading. They savor the personal images, ideas, feelings, questions, and connections that are evoked during reading (such as when readers recall a nostalgic childhood incident or feel anxious about the plight of a character or outcome of an event). These feelings, images, and ideas —what Rosenblatt calls the lived-through experience—constitute the meaning of the story or poem for the reader. Rosenblatt argues that during the reading of text, readers naturally move along a continuum, sometimes with more of an aesthetic stance and sometimes with more of an efferent stance. However, stories and poems primarily invite an aesthetic stance. She further argues that all readers, but especially children, should have many opportunities to discover that reading stories and poems can be intense personal experiences. Taking an aesthetic stance allows readers and listeners to have these intense experiences.

Rosenblatt further differentiates between two reading processes—"the lived-through ex-perience" and "response." In the *lived-through experience*, mentioned earlier in this work, readers focus their attention inward, selecting and savoring a variety of images, feelings, and thoughts called to mind by the text. For example, a first grader described her lived-through experience with *Where the Wild Things Are* by Maurice Sendak: "I kept thinking about my little brother and how bad he can be and how

Illustration from Maurice Sendak's Where the Wild Things Are. *©1963 by Maurice Sendak. Reprinted by permission of HarperCollins.*

Talking About Books with Young Children

mad he makes me." Readers also *respond* to these images and associations that stories evoke; they stand back from the lived-through experience to interpret it. For example, readers may be aware of the contrast between what they expected to happen in a story and the actual events, or they may notice that their attitude toward a character is shifting. One second grader responded to the contrast between her experiences with punishment and what happened to Max in *Where the Wild Things Are*: "Hey, Max is supposed to get punished for being bad. How come he gets to eat? I don't get any snack when I'm punished." Responses do not stop when reading is finished; readers continue to respond to their experienced meanings long after reading is over, as did two first graders who acted out the "wild rumpus" scene from *Wild Things* for nearly two weeks after Max was safely back in his room.

Creating Meaning-Space

Although the purpose of conversations about books is to establish a forum for children's sharing of their lived-through experiences and responses, young children's initial responses are often a mixture of unarticulated feelings and global evaluations of liking or disliking. Because they may be uncertain of what feelings or personal connections are stirred by the text, young children often benefit from opportunities to talk about the hazy feelings, ideas, and images they have during reading. Teachers need to provide plenty of time for children to talk about what they are thinking during reading. Through this talk, children can discover what they actually *do* think.

Corcoran (1987) argues that conversations about literature in which children are encouraged to explore their tentative ideas provide them with much needed "meaning-space." Teachers who provide meaning-space give children time and opportunity to talk about what a story or poem calls to mind. Meaning-space is not a time for teachers to ask questions about a story or poem; rather, it is a time for free expression of thoughts and ideas. Good conversations about books encourage children to explore ideas of personal importance and meaning long before engaging in the process of analyzing or interpreting literature. For example, in the book conversation about *The Pain and the Great One*, Deanna and several other children talked about their personal experiences getting undeserved blame. Their teacher knows that protecting time for talking about just such personal experiences that can be linked back to the story can deepen children's understandings.

Using Interpretive Communities

Book conversations do more than provide meaning-space for children to explore and expand their initial responses to literature. Children who talk together about books create what Fish (1980) calls an interpretive community—a group of readers who both share their idiosyncratic interpretations and negotiate a group-constructed view of a story or poem.

Interpretive communities solve one of the criticisms related to the reader response theory. According to the theory, all readers construct different meanings from a literary text. But are all responses equally viable? How is the quality of an interpretation to be determined? Fish (1980) argues that interpretations become accepted and acknowledged as having merit through the persuasive acts of readers and "book talkers" who work within specific literary communities. Readers in interpretive communities persuade one another of the value of their responses and interpretations as they talk together about literature. They often rely on connections to other literature, related personal experiences, or the text to support their ideas. So, good conversations about books involve more than sharing individual responses. Through talking together, children may propose, defend, negotiate, become aware of, and accept multiple interpretations.

Guiding Book Conversations

Good book conversations are the product of teachers' careful planning and thoughtful interaction with children. They are not "gentle inquisitions" (Eeds & Wells, 1989) guided by well-meaning teachers who rely only on planned questions to engage children in talk about stories. Rather, they are more similar to the lively and natural exchanges that occur during the best possible dinner conversations. Eeds and Wells call such talks "grand conversations" to distinguish them from the type of comprehension-focused discussions more typical of school discussions (see Chapter 12 by Wells).

Before the Conversation

Selecting the literature. Good book conversations are stimulated by high-quality literature. One way to identify quality literature is to use the criteria for selecting picture books and poetry found in children's literature textbooks (for example, Cullinan & Galda, 1994; Norton, 1993). Another way to identify quality literature is to select books and poems that have been touted by experts, including "expert children," and review sources (*Horn Book*, *The School Library Journal*, and review columns in *The Reading Teacher*, *Language Arts*, and other journals). Media specialists and their myriad selection aids can offer recommendations, and teachers can be alert for books that have received special

awards. Any quality literature can be used to stimulate book conversations, including information books, picture story books, illustrated poetry, and individual poems.

Two additional criteria are particularly important to keep in mind when selecting books and poetry for book conversations. First, the literature should appeal to the particular audience or group of children. Some books and poems are favorites with young children; they ask for them to be read again and again. Second, books and poetry used in book discussions must be particularly rich in meanings, so that readers have room to work. Iser (1978) suggests that literature has "gaps" or holes for readers to fill in as they read. Perhaps the more enticing the gap, the harder readers and listeners will work to fill it. In any case, gaps leave room for young children to construct interpretations. For example, I have

Jacket design from Arthur Yorinks's Hey, Al. *Text ©1986 by Arthur Yorinks. Pictures ©1986 by Richard Egielski. Reprinted by permission of Farrar, Straus & Giroux, Inc.*

found that *Hey, Al* by Arthur Yorinks stimulates rich conversations with first graders because it leaves just enough room for readers' speculations. In this story Al and his dog Eddie are invited by a gigantic bird to a lush tropical island in the sky where they will no longer have to work or worry. On the island, they begin to turn into birds, but they use their newly formed wings to escape before the transformation is complete. Although first graders often mention these story details in book conversations, they also present hypotheses about aspects of the story the author does not directly address: They speculate about how the island got in the sky and why the bird wanted Al and Eddie in the first place; they wonder who all the birds on the island really are and who will be taken there next.

Other examples of books that both appeal to young children and are rich in meanings (both overt and subtle) include *The Pain and the Great One*, mentioned earlier, and *Rosie's Walk* by Pat Hutchins. *The Pain and the Great One* is really two stories in one: it tells the daily events of a brother and sister from each of their perspectives. By presenting each of the children's stories about the same events, the book offers an invitation to judge the characters from still another perspective. Similarly, *Rosie's Walk* allows readers to flesh out important details in the story. In this book, Rosie the hen takes a walk around a farmyard. She is followed by a fox who tries to catch her but is continually foiled by his own ineptness. The story is told primarily though its illustrations that depict the simple action sequence, but readers are left to speculate on the thoughts and motivations of the characters.

Identifying the composition of the group. Book conversations work with whole classes, but I have found them to be more effective in small groups of five to eight children. With that size group, I find that all children, and especially those who do not often volunteer to share ideas, are more comfortable. Children seem to listen more attentively to one another in small groups and to comment more on other participants' ideas. Teachers may choose to read a picture book or poem to the whole class but hold a conversation with only a small group, or they may choose to read aloud only to a small group of children who will be talking together. One first grade teacher holds book conversations during "center time" so that while one group of children is talking about a book, the other children are busy at other centers. During the course of a week, all the children rotate into the book conversation center.

I find that the best conversation groups are composed of children of different abilities. Children who have more difficulty expressing their ideas, or who are hesitant to speak, benefit greatly from participating in a conversation with children who express a wide variety of thoughts more easily. Conversely, highly verbal children who operate intuitively with stories benefit from demands for more precise explanations of their thoughts. I have also found that children who are struggling to learn to read are sometimes the ones who contribute the most thoughtful responses during book conversations. Many teachers have successfully included regular education, bilingual, and special education children in book conversation groups.

Keeping children in the same conversation group for several weeks may also be beneficial in helping children learn to listen to one another. More mature conversations seem to emerge over time as children get to know and trust one another and come to recognize the value of each participant's contributions.

Prereading the literature. In preparation for a book conversation, teachers are advised to read thoughtfully the selected picture book or poem. While reading, teachers should be attuned to their feelings, thoughts, images, and personal connections stirred by the literature, and then they should select which of these they might share with children during the conversation. Previewing also helps teachers identify places in the text appropriate for stopping to invite children's predictions or comments.

One way to select personal responses to share with children is to reflect on the kinds of responses that children are already making and the kinds of responses they seem to make infrequently. For example, teachers might notice that few children are seeing connections and patterns among the books they are reading. To encourage these linkages, teachers may plan to share a connection they noticed between characters or events in the read-aloud story with those in a familiar book. For example, when Karen, the first grade teacher highlighted at the beginning of this chapter, read *The Pain and the Great One*, she commented that the children in this story reminded her of the children in *I'll Fix Anthony* by Judith Viorst. This observation prompted a discussion about how the children in these two stories were alike. Over time, teachers will stretch children's response repertoire by sharing various ways to think and talk about literature.

After previewing the book or poem, teachers construct one or two interpretive questions they may use to prompt book conversation. Interpretive questions help children focus on the significance of the story as a whole. They go beyond the literal sequence of events and ask children to do more than make inferences or state opinions. They help children find personal significance in the story or poem, as revealed through the relationships among the characters, setting, dialogue, events, images, language, or other literary elements. Interpretive questions have more than one answer and encourage readers to go back to the text or their personal responses to support their po-

sitions. Sometimes teachers may want to use interpretive questions in conversations in which children's responses seem stuck on "The part I liked best was..." statements. At other times, children's responses are so rich with inferential and interpretive meanings that teachers may not need to ask questions.

Teachers craft interpretive questions by carefully noting the conclusions they draw from the story or by paying attention to noteworthy elements. For example, the literary element that I noticed first in *The Pain and the Great One* is that the story is presented from two points of view and with repeating language. I also noticed that I took yet a third perspective as I read—a perspective that allowed me to simultaneously take into account the views of both children, as mentioned earlier. Therefore, I developed an interpretive question that may help children notice this literary element: "How do you think the parents *really* feel about 'The Pain' and 'The Great One'?" As I read *Rosie's Walk*, I was especially aware of the repetitive plot structure in which the fox is continually bopped, while Rosie the hen nonchalantly continues her walk. Because I found myself asking, "Does Rosie know what's happening?" I decided to encourage children to explore this idea. In *Hey, Al* I noticed the drab colors used to illustrate Al and Eddie's home at the beginning of the story in contrast with the bright, cheery colors used at the end—a change that appeared to parallel the change in Al's attitude about his life. The interpretive questions I constructed to draw children's attention to this element were, "What do you think Al learned from being at the island? How did the illustrator help us understand Al's change?"

During the Conversation

Establishing guidelines. It is particularly important for teachers to set guidelines for group interaction during book conversations because these interactions may differ from children's expectations for school discussions. Most school discussions start with a teacher question, followed by the teacher calling on a student to answer the question, and finally the teacher's evaluation of the student's answer. This interaction pattern dominates teachers' and children's talk in many classrooms, and may be the pattern that children expect (see also Chapter 12). In these structured interactions, teachers talk every other turn and control the topic or content through the questions they pose. By contrast, in a good book conversation children talk directly with one another and introduce the topics of conversation. Teachers help children learn these new interaction patterns by setting clear guidelines for the conversation, which might include the following:

- Sit in a circle so that we can see one another.
- Only one person talks at a time.
- Listen to one another.
- Stay on the topic.
- Talk at least once but not more than three times before everyone has had a turn (Tompkins & McGee, 1993, p. 172).

Reading aloud. Teachers sit where all the children can see the book's illustrations and read the book aloud using interesting variations in voice and expression. Poems can be shown on the overhead projector, on charts, or in Big Books as the teacher reads. The important point is that teachers pause at selected places in the text to offer their own personal responses and encourage children's spontaneous talk—predictions, comments, and questions.

Guiding the conversation. Teachers may want every child in the group to have a copy of the book or poem. When there is only one copy of the book, it should be available for the children to look at during the conversation. Sometimes, children spontaneously begin the conversation by asking a question or making a comment after reading. If not, the teacher begins by extending an open-ended invitation to respond: "What do you think?" "Who has a comment about the story?" or "Who has something to say?"

During the conversation the teacher's role is partly one of stepping back and allowing children's ideas and comments to determine the direction in which the talk will move. As children talk, teachers may ask them to clarify or expand their comments by asking, "Why do you think that?" Or, they may help children respond to one another by asking, "Who would like to respond to what Jose said?" Most important, teachers act as participants in a real conversation; they respond and comment naturally, taking turns with the children. In the following conversation about *Rosie's Walk*, the teacher helps negotiate turn taking, encourages expanded responses, and adds her own opinion:

Joseph: I liked the part—it was awesome—when the sugar fell...

Lataoya: The flour!

Joseph: Yeah, when the flour fell on the fox.

Teacher: Why did you like that part?

Joseph: 'Cause the string got stuck on the chicken's foot. Like when she walked, it made the flour in the bag spill and the fox didn't know what was happening.

Dean: The fox is so stupid!

Teacher: I agree that the fox is dumb. Why do you think so?

Dean: 'Cause he's getting trapped all the time and he's always getting into trouble.

Sometimes, when teachers recognize a teachable moment, they may choose to step in and take a more directive role in the conversation. Teachable moments are opportunities for providing children with insights into genre, literary elements, or the roles of authors and illustrators. For example, during a conversation about *Hey, Al*, a first grader's comment about one of the illustrations signaled that he noticed a symbolic element in the story: "Look, he painted the sun in his room." Picking up on this opportunity, the teacher stepped into the conversation to help children notice and talk about symbols. She explained that in this story the yellow paint that Al used in his room showed that Al is painting his room a bright, cheerful color. However, the yellow color also stands for or symbolizes another meaning—it shows that Al has decided to make his life brighter and cheerier. She told the children that sometimes authors and illustrators communicate more than just one meaning through their words and illustrations; sometimes they communicate other, deeper meanings. Although this teacher did not expect her first graders to master the notion of symbolism, she knew that the children gained an appreciation of the significance of the color yellow in this particular story and perhaps the beginning of awareness that elements in other stories may have special meanings, too. In the following conversation about *Hey Al*, the teacher noticed that children were not sure about the role of fantasy. She stepped in to expand their understandings of the kinds of events and characters that could be expected in fantasies:

Shanna: I thought it was all a dream.

Eugene: I think it's all silly, all silly.

Rachael: Birds can't talk, except parrots.

Teacher: Right, birds can't talk in real life. Shanna said she thought it was a dream, and Eugene thought it was all silly. This kind of story is called a *fantasy*. A fantasy is a story about something that can't really be true. Now could some of the things in this story be really true?

Children: No.

Vivian: What if the pants he used to wear turned blue and fell off?

Teacher: That would be a fantasy. Anything like that can happen in a fantasy. I might put you in a story and the next thing you know, you might turn into a dragon!

Eugene: You might be a girl dragon (pointing to Vivian).

Vivian: You might be a boy dragon (pointing to Eugene).

Shanna: I don't think I would like to be a worm on that island. Then they would eat me!

Another reason that teachers step into conversations is to demonstrate and encourage more active listening. They do this by responding to a child's comments—as in, "I thought the same as Maryellen" or "I'm not sure I agree with Maria"—and then providing supporting evidence for their positions. Teachers might also synthesize what several children have been saying. For example, one teacher noticed that several children during a conversation about *Rosie's Walk* had taken different positions on Rosie's awareness of the fox. The teacher synthesized the positions by saying, "I heard Hector say that the fox was laying traps for the hen, but he kept getting caught in the traps instead. But John said the hen was laying traps for the fox. Who else would like to comment on who was laying traps—the fox or the hen?"

Another reason teachers step into conversations is to pose an interpretive question, as discussed in this chapter's section "Prereading the Literature." Of course, not all conversations need an interpretive question. However, even though children may eventually work to interpret the story without the teacher's asking a question, conversations may initially become mired in talk about story details or personal associations. At these times, a teacher's thoughtful question may nudge children's thinking. I have also found that posing only one interpretive question after children have had ample opportunity to contribute to the book conversation puts new energy into children's discussion and often doubles the amount of inferential, interpretive, and evaluative comments.

After the Conversation

After book conversations, children are often eager to continue thinking about and working with the story or poem. They may want to draw a picture, write in a response journal, compose an original story or poem, or participate in any number of response activities. Children can be encouraged to select and share response activities, or teachers may prepare activities that will continue children's exploration of the story. For example, after a conversation about *The Pain and the Great One*, children might be asked to recast the story from the parents' perspectives—first through telling and then through shared writing. After reading *Rosie's Walk*, they may pretend to be Rosie and act out how she might tell a friend about her day. (See the final section in this work "Other Responses to Literature.")

I have found that children's first conversations are sometimes quite brief and consist mainly of sharing favorite parts. Through planning opportunities for further explorations, teachers can enrich children's literature conversations. Teachers who place the book or poem on audiotape in the listening center or send a copy home with a letter encouraging a family member to read it aloud to the child report increased richness in children's talk (Short, 1993). Children can also be asked to plan for a second conversation about a story. With their teacher, they can brainstorm ideas to talk about. These ideas can be listed or placed on a web and used to prompt the next book conversation (Short, 1993). Children can further prepare for an upcoming book discussion by using sticky notes to mark places in the story they want to talk about.

Final Words

Talking about literature is often undervalued in early elementary classrooms, especially as young children begin reading instruction. However, all children are capable of making sophisticated responses to literature far beyond their reading ability, and conversations about quality literature should be a priority in the literacy program. Book talks provide children with space to explore their initial responses to literature, learn new strategies for evoking and responding to literature, and participate in constructing shared, enriched interpretations of literature. Book conversations not only captivate and challenge young children, they are also powerful tools for expanding children's responses to literature.

References

Baghban, M. (1984). *Our daughter learns to read and write*: A *case study from birth to three*. Newark, DE: International Reading Association.

Corcoran, B. (1987). Teachers creating readers. In B. Corcoran (Ed.), *Readers, texts, teachers* (pp. 41–74). Upper Montclair, NJ: Boynton/Cook.

Cullinan, B., & Galda, L. (1994). *Literature and the child* (3rd ed.). Fort Worth, TX: Harcourt Brace.

Eeds, M., & Wells, D. (1989). Grand conversations: An exploration of meaning construction in literature study groups. *Research in the Teaching of English, 23*, 4–29.

Fish, S. (1980). *Is there a text in this class? The authority of interpretive communities*. Cambridge, MA: Harvard University Press.

Iser, W. (1978). *The act of reading*. Baltimore, MD: Johns Hopkins University Press.

Ninio, A., & Bruner, J. (1978). The achievement and antecedents of labelling. *Journal of Child Language, 5,* 5–15.

Norton, D. (1993). *Through the eyes of a child: An introduction to children's literature* (4th ed.). New York: Merrill/Macmillan.

Rosenblatt, L. (1978). *The reader, the text, the poem: The transactional theory of the literary work*. Carbondale, IL: Southern Illinois University Press.

Short, K. (1993). *Literature circles: Talking with young children about books*. Presentation at the 38th Annual Convention of the International Reading Association, San Antonio, TX.

Tompkins, G., & McGee, L. (1993). *Teaching reading with literature: Case studies to action plans*. New York: Merrill.

Children's Literature

Blume, J. (1974). *The Pain and the Great One*. New York: Dell.

Hutchins, P. (1968). *Rosie's walk*. New York: Aladdin.

Sendak, M. (1963). *Where the wild things are*. New York: HarperCollins.

Viorst, J. (1969). *I'll fix Anthony*. New York: HarperCollins.

Yorinks, A. (1986). *Hey, Al*. New York: Farrar, Straus & Giroux.

CHAPTER 11

Fostering Talk About Poetry

Amy A. McClure

IT WAS EARLY May. The sixth grade children gathered as they usually did in the corner of the classroom. Many carried poetry books that looked well used—slips of paper between pages marked favorite parts, pages were turned down at the corners, and covers were ragged around the edges. The group looked up expectantly as their teacher sat down in her chair. She pulled out a book of poems she had been reading aloud for the past several days. "Now you are really going to have to think about this one," Sheryl Reed, the teacher, told the group. "It's very short, and there is a lot of meaning packed into it, so think about how this poem affects you."

> Daddy says the world
> Is a drum
> Tight and hard
> And I told him,
> I'm gonna beat out my own rhythm
> "The Drum" by Nikki Giovanni

As usual, a brief silence followed as the children thoughtfully considered the poem. "Sounds like a poem about how you're gonna live," said Carrie. "He's gonna find his own way," added Robin. Jim speculated aloud about the various possibilities he was considering. Although he was not articulate, he soon arrived at a definitive opinion:

> It sounds like the father is telling her what to do...or whatever...do what she...her father sounds like...but she is going to do what she wants to do.

Stacie cut in, "I don't agree with what Jim said because Jim said it sounds like she's doing what her father said, and then he switched to a completely different thing."

"No, I didn't say that," countered Jim. "What I said was her father was telling her what to do and how to do in the world, and the girl said that she didn't want to do that."

"Do you agree with that...that the father is telling her how to live?" asked Sheryl. "Let's listen." She read the poem aloud again.

"Like the world out there. It's hard when you don't have enough money or anything. It's just better to like make your own way," said Deon.

"How do you feel about that?" Sheryl addressed the rest of the group.

"I agree," said Jennifer.

"Do you think the dad is telling her how she has to live?" Sheryl asked again.

"No. Telling her what it's like. Like it's hard and everything," answered Jennifer.

"What do the rest of you think?" Sheryl questioned the group. Many agreed with Jennifer's comments.

"I think her father is trying to tell her what the world is going to be like—and she can't have her own way every time," said Mike.

"And then what?" asked Sheryl. She had noticed some children, particularly Jennifer, shaking their heads. "Well, disagree with him. Go ahead and talk back." Jennifer and Mike began a lively debate about each other's ideas and eventually realized that they essentially agreed about this point. The group listened quietly; such disagreements were not only allowed but encouraged because they frequently led to new insights. When Sheryl felt the issue had been resolved between the two, she turned to the group and asked, "Do you agree that the father is saying she can't have her own way all the time?"

"I think Mike's right about that because she goes, 'But I'm gonna beat my own rhythm,'" said Stacie.

"Is that always possible?" asked Sheryl. A chorus of "no" greeted her question. She continued, "Sometimes and sometimes not, maybe? Why isn't it? Why can't you always beat out your own rhythm?"

"Because if you do your work or something—the boss will tell you what to do, or the president or someone," answered Jim.

"Other people have higher rhythms, they have bigger jobs," added Robin.

"They have bigger drums," said Mandy.

"And harder rhythms," said Jimmy.

"What do you think about this poem?" Sheryl asked again.

"It has a lot of meaning to it," answered Angela.

"Like what?" Sheryl wanted to know. Aaron seemed eager to offer an opinion: "Well, when Mike said about when the father was telling what the world was going to be like— he said the world is a tight drum. He said it *is*, not it *will be*." Aaron seemed intent on examining each word carefully to understand the poet's message.

"Yes," agreed Sheryl. "Why did the father say the world is a drum, tight and hard. Why did he say it *is* instead of it *will be*?"

"Because it is right now," answered many voices.

"Because he is the one that has to pay all the taxes and make a living," said Stacie.

"Why does the father know that and the girl doesn't?" Sheryl asked again, determined to help them delve as far into the poem as they could.

Many voices again responded with "Because he's out in the world," "He knows about life," and "He's lived longer."

Discussions like this (from McClure, Harrison, & Reed, 1990, p. 61) are not common in elementary classrooms. Rather, research suggests that children usually dislike talking about poetry, often because they feel the need to construct a "right" interpretation. For example, Painter (1970) interviewed preservice education students to discover their attitudes toward the genre. Of all explanations for negative feelings, the one most frequently cited was an insistence on "correct" interpretation. One student commented,

> My interpretations were never the same or even close to what the teacher or some of my classmates found. Even after reading the poems over to myself several more times, I still missed the point. I used to dread poetry and cringed at the mention of the word (p. 15).

Verble (1973) in a study of elementary students, found similar attitudes. When he asked the children why they did not like poetry, the majority responded, "Because I can't understand it" and "Because my interpretation is never right."

When children do like poetry, their preferences are usually for the light, humorous pieces on topics such as animals, holidays, people, and familiar experiences. Narrative and limerick forms are enjoyed, while more abstract forms such as haiku and free verse are disliked (Bridge, 1966; Fisher & Natarella, 1982; Ingham, 1980; Simmons, 1980; Terry, 1972). The poetry that children prefer often lacks the subtle imagery, interesting rhythms, and clever plays on words that characterize the really good examples of this genre.

I have found this to be true in my own experience as well. In contrast to my two preschool children who love Mother Goose rhymes, playground chants, and advertising jingles and who make up their own poems, my undergraduate students almost universally dislike poetry. When I ask them to bring a poem to class that they remember from childhood, many arrive empty handed. And when I ask why they have such negative attitudes they, too, cite the necessity for interpreting a poem as well as requirements to memorize an assigned piece or copy poems from the chalkboard in "their best handwriting."

The discussion at the beginning of this chapter suggests that these attitudes are not inevitable: children can eagerly and knowledgably interpret poems together, and they can appreciate the subtle nuances of meaning and unique imagery that are the hallmarks of fine poetry. What makes the difference? What explains the discrepancy between the eager involvement in poetry conversations displayed by children such as Stacie, Jimmy, and Robin and the stilted, uninspired discus-sions generally seen in elementary classrooms? I think part of the problem comes from what we do with poetry in schools. Rather than stressing enjoyment and love of poetry, we tend to equate our task of teaching the genre to the teaching of biology: just as a class dissects a frog, we dissect poems. Usually we try to get children to come up with the only "right" interpretation, as if such a thing exists. Discussions are organized around the model of teacher questioning, one or two students responding, then teacher questioning again. Often teachers isolate poetry in a two-week unit, to be studied intensely then never referred to again. Or they require memorization for later recitation and testing. Most important, teachers often say they have no idea how to stimulate a poetry conversation. Thus, they tend to share poems that generate laughter and avoid the pieces that can offer rich rewards but initially may prompt blank stares and uncomfortable silences.

What a loss this is. Involvement with good poetry increases children's sensitivity and awareness. Poetry appeals to both thought and sense and can evoke rich sensory images for the reader. Through poetry children can become more aware of the world around them, seeing common, everyday things with fresh, wide-awake eyes. As Heard (1993) states,

> What poetry does is help me see, as if for the first time, those things which have become obscured by a film of familiarity. Part of a poet's job is to learn to pay attention to and love the things of the world and to find the poems hiding there (p. 119).

Poet Valerie Worth (1992) also affirms the value of poetry: "In evoking the unknown while also affirming the known, poetry can often reveal something quite unexpected in the midst of the familiar and ordinary" (p. 569). Poetry can cause children to look deeply within and beyond themselves to lead more examined lives.

Poetry also helps children pay more attention to language. Because poets are so attuned to language and so careful to craft their poems with precisely selected words and patterns, children who are exposed to much poetry develop a sensitivity to words, rhythms, and images. Their prose becomes more poetic, more fluent, and more to the point. They learn to say what they mean in well-chosen words (McClure, Harrison, & Reed, 1990).

Living Like a Poet

Before children can become informed, eager participants in conversations about poetry, they must see it as a vital and essential part of life. When poetry is experienced in a vacuum, it loses its vitality and appeal to the reader. It should not be presented as something separate, accessible only to the sophisticated reader, but rather as one additional interesting perspective on experience. This also means that poetry should not be confined to a two-week unit or used for handwriting exercises. Rather, it should be a natural part of children's daily life experience, shared both purposefully and spontaneously throughout the day.

Teachers accomplish this goal in many ways. Some hang poetry all over the classroom—in the science area, next to the gerbil cage, or under a colorful poster. For example, John Moffitt's "To Look at Anything" can be placed next to an interesting piece of driftwood, "Magnifying Glass" by Valerie Worth and Maxine Kumin's "The Microscope" can lie beside a magnifying glass and slides. Poems on observing the world such as Judith Viorst's "Just Before Springtime" or excerpts from Joanne Ryder's

Mockingbird Morning can be put next to a window so children can be encouraged to look out and observe their world with a fresh or deeper perspective. Teachers can then urge children to write their own observations or find related poems to add to the display.

Some teachers have special areas in their classrooms for poetry. A poetry center can be set up where children listen to poems on tape and also make tapes of their favorites. An art center can include examples of beautifully illustrated anthologies and picture book editions of poems to stimulate children's interest in illustrating their favorites. Teachers can establish a special classroom poetry book collection and encourage children to mark poems to recommend and share with friends.

Teachers can also integrate poetry with prose. For example, after reading Katherine Paterson's *Bridge to Terabithia*, one teacher read aloud Langston Hughes's "Poem," in which the poet mourns a friend's death. Another compared Judith Viorst's *Alexander and the Terrible, Horrible, No Good, Very Bad Day* with Karla Kuskin's similarly themed poem "I Woke Up This Morning." Children can then be encouraged to find poems on their own that they think relate to particular books. When Sheryl Reed's students read *Sounder* by William Armstrong, they were asked to find poems reflecting the mood, theme, or characters of the story; the children selected various poems, ranging from those about dogs such as Myra Livingston's "For Mugs" and James Tippett's "Sunning" to those about desire for a better life such as "Falling Stars" by Sara Teasdale (McClure, Harrison, & Reed, 1990). To find these poems, the children had to peruse many poetry books, conversing with friends as they made their choices.

Often children who have initial guidance from their teacher begin making spontaneous connections between books and poems on their own. One fifth grader casually confided to me her perceptions of the similarities between Randall Jarrell's *The Bat-Poet* and Leo Lionni's *Frederick*: "The bats all think the little bat's crazy, and Frederick has the same problem." In another instance, a fourth grader read *The Secret Garden* by Francis H. Burnett, then gathered poems she thought might appeal to Mary, the main character.

Teachers can also combine poetry reading and discussion with content area study, which provides an aesthetic perspective on a topic and can make such study more pleasurable. One teacher I have worked with stated:

> Poetry is the topping that makes it all worthwhile. Let's say we're doing a theme on turtles.

Illustration from The Secret Garden *by Frances Hodgson Burnett. Illustrations ©1987 by Random House, Inc. Reprinted by permission of Random House, Inc.*

You can read lots of nonfiction stuff on turtles...but a poem on turtles...is like that fudge topping or extra spoonful of sprinkles on your ice cream. It's special (McClure, 1992, p. 11).

For example, when Judy Markham's fifth grade class studied the American Revolution she had her children read narrative poems such as Henry W. Longfellow's "Paul Revere's Ride" that related to this era. Second grade teacher Peggy Oxley shared Walt Whitman's "Night on the Prairies" and Carl Sandburg's "Buffalo Dusk" during her theme study of pioneer life and settlements in the United States. During a study of time and after hearing many poems about time, one child wrote the following poetic observation about time passing:

> August
> August is a
> Child of July.
> Mother
> to September
> And a faded memory
> to November.
>
> *by Jennifer R., grade 6* (cited in McClure, Harrison, & Reed, 1990, p. 108)

Most important, children must have opportunities to browse through poems on their own and savor the sounds of the words, share enjoyable lines with a friend, or copy down a favorite for a later reading. They need time to be alone with a poem to choose what to linger over and what to skip and when to wonder and when to wander (Booth & Moore, 1988). Some teachers facilitate this by designating one sustained silent reading time per week as poetry day. During this session, students can read and mark their favorite poems with comments on why they liked them. This generates much talk as friends compare their favorites and share the excitement of discovering that someone else is also delighted with a poem. Other teachers who use small group literature studies in their reading programs have poetry as the focus for some groups. Children can read different poems on the same topic, for example, then meet for discussions on how poets interpret the same things quite differently.

Children may need some initial encouragement to read poetry on their own. Sometimes teachers make suggestions such as, "Find a poem you think might reflect the main character's feelings in the novel you're reading" or "It's a beautiful spring day; let's find some spring poems," which will help get children involved in browsing.

We want students to begin living their lives like poets—to find the unusual idea, bring it to light, and share it with others. Teachers can model this kind of living: if they communicate their love for poetry, showing how it enriches their lives, and admit they are continually growing in their understanding of it, they can nurture this same excitement and wonder in their students. Together they can search for the poetry to be found in life. As poet Naomi Nye says in her poem "Valentine for Earnest Mann,"

> I'll tell you a secret...
> poems hide. In the bottoms of our shoes
> they are sleeping. They are the shadows
> drifting across our ceilings the moment
> before we wake up. What we have to do
> is live in a way that lets us find them (cited in
> Heard, 1993, p. 119).

Discussing Poetry: Strategies to Encourage Conversation

It takes continual nurturing and scaffolding as well as carefully articulated questions to stimulate thoughtful talk about poetry. Most children do not know how they should participate in such discussions. Thus, they often fall back on bland phrases such as "it's fun-

ny" or "it's nice" or "kind of boring" because they lack a repertoire of phrases and ideas to use. They need experience with the kinds of comments people make about poetry and how discussions evolve. They also need many opportunities to engage in conversations about poetry and express genuine amazement and wonder about what is read. When teachers lead these conversations, they model the questioning and discussion behaviors they hope children will acquire. Eventually, as children gain confidence and competence, they are able to take an increasingly active role in these discussions.

Aesthetic response should always be the initial focus of any poetry discussion. Appreciating poetry means we negotiate what poets say about life in relation to our own experiences and perceptions. As children listen to poetry they should be encouraged to filter the language through their imaginations while opening their minds to multiple possibilities and asking, "How does the poem make me feel?" or "What are the images it conjures up for me?" or "What do I enjoy about the words?" These are the responses that must be accepted and valued first. Then children can explore what the poet did to craft the poem to evoke these feelings.

Establishing classroom procedures for poetry read-aloud sessions seems to be initially helpful. Many teachers like to gather the children close together; the proximity promotes a sense of community and intimacy, which leads to a willingness to take risks and voice partially formed ideas. Some teachers provide multiple copies of the poems to be read aloud. Others prefer to have the group just listen to the words.

Teachers often begin with an introductory sequence to develop the group's background. A typical session might begin with the teacher reading a poem's title and asking children to predict what it might be about. Children can also be asked to listen for something special in the poetry—how the poet uses words beautifully or creates an interesting image. Or teachers can suggest that children just listen and react to a particular poem. However, lengthy introductions and careful, specific directions on what children must learn from a poem should be avoided. As children become more experienced with these conversations, they can begin developing their own purposes and expectations for reading a poem.

The poem should then be read aloud slowly so children can construct their meanings and savor the words. After reading, the teacher can solicit initial responses from children, asking them to describe what moved them, suggesting they link it with their personal experiences, or encourage them to offer tentative thoughts about its meaning or purpose. Some have children write their initial impressions as the poem is read and share these with the group. However, it is important at this point to resist discussing a specific meaning and encourage students to listen completely to the poem.

Most teachers do not create detailed lesson plans with questions to ask students about poetry read. Rather, they usually feel their way along, preferring to guide the discussion in response to the children's questions, ideas, and impressions. Questions such as the following can be posed to facilitate this reflection process:

- What do you think?
- What did you like about this poem?
- Does this remind you of anything you know about?
- What is the poet saying here?
- What feelings did you have listening to this poem?

- Let's discuss what's going on here.
- What do you think this is all about?

Sometimes it helps to have children respond to just one aspect of a poem; each child can select the line or lines to which he or she wants to give more thought. The group can then pool their collected insights to gain a deeper appreciation of the total piece.

The teacher can reread the poem several times, stopping after each reading to ask for children's responses. The rereadings are usually needed to help children get beyond merely hearing the words to *listening* to and trying to make sense of them. The emphasis at this point is on inducing more thoughtful, complex responses, yet delight in and appreciation of the words and images should still be the main focus. Open-ended questions or comments that cause children to revisit the poem to examine how its crafting contributed to their enjoyment might include the following:

- Let's go back to the poem and think about it some more.
- Anything unusual you notice about this poem?
- What did the poet do to make you feel _____ as you read this poem?
- What do you think about _____? (the words, how the words fit what the poet's describing, how the rhythm makes you feel, the unique images the poet has created, and so forth)
- What in the poem makes you think that?
- Is this anything like your life?
- Does anybody have a different idea?

The following large group discussion, which emerged in response to the reading of Eve Merriam's "From the Japanese," shows

McClure

how more thoughtful comments evolve. The poem has subtle imagery and is not one I think teachers would use initially with children. Rather, it is the kind of poem that challenges a group that has had many previous experiences with poetry and figurative language. In this scenario, the poem has been read several times, and the teacher, Sheryl, is trying to stimulate more ideas:

"What do you think it means—'The summer night/Is a dark blue hammock/Slung between the white pillars of day'?"

"I think the poet is in a hammock, and she's writing about the night," said Johnny.

"Yeah...it's talking about how this poet is in a hammock at night," added Brandon.

Several children nodded, agreeing with Johnny and Brandon. Others looked puzzled, while still others looked downright skeptical. Sheryl noticed the looks and asked the group, "Well, what do you think? Does anybody have a different idea?"

Becky tentatively raised her hand, "I think it's talking about day against night."

"What do you mean?" asked Sheryl.

Stacie broke in, "Like it's between the end of one day and the beginning of another. You know, one day is one white pillar, and the next day is the other pillar. The hammock is like the night. You know, it's dark." Several children said, "Ohhh...yeah." Awareness dawned on their faces.

"Why do you think the poet called it a dark blue hammock?" asked Sheryl?

"Because dark blue is like the night's color. Lots of people say it's black but it really isn't always. White is for the day," answered Deon.

"That's a really different way to show it, isn't it? Would you have thought to show it like that? That's an interesting metaphor," Sheryl told the group (McClure, Harrison, & Reed, 1990, pp. 207–208).

An important premise that should underlie these discussions is that poetry makes sense. Poems should not be presented as mysterious puzzles that allude to obscure images discernible only to sophisticated readers; rather, the teacher should communicate that a viable meaning is accessible to any interested reader. In fact, a poem can have several meanings, depending on a person's perspective or expectation. At the same time, such flexibility should have limits: although it is appropriate to encourage the exploration of potential meanings, ideas that are clearly not supported by the text should be gently questioned or redirected.

Encouraging children to create anthologies of their favorites is another way to generate conversation about poetry. Choosing which poems to include and which to discard involves much discussion with trusted friends. This is particularly true if the anthology is a collaborative collection. Illustrating an anthology is another way to explore poems and ascertain the subtle nuances of meaning that lend themselves to design.

Allowing students time to think, ponder, and reflect is important in teaching poetry. Teachers must patiently give plenty of time to respond. They must encourage and accept responses from all students, weaving them into the general milieu of the conversation. And they should encourage children to take as much control as possible of their search for enjoyment and meaning in poetry. After hearing many poems, children become intuitively aware of the different kinds of poetry and develop an informed sense of its voice and music. Talking with others about what they have heard contributes to and expands this sense.

Developing Understandings About Poetry

Once teachers become comfortable with the general pattern for discussions, they often begin to explain to children the meaning and use of various poetic elements such as precise words, sound, shape, and figurative language. Many teachers also want their students to forge connections between poems and develop a sense of the unique style of various poets. This teaching should not be done formally through worksheets, multiple-choice tests, or specific lessons on poetic elements. Rather, it should be incidental as part of a general conversation about what makes a particular poem pleasing or enjoyable. Further, a poem should never be divided into discrete parts that are analyzed separately to determine meaning. Emphasis should always be on enjoying the poem as a whole and developing an appreciation for how the parts—rhyme, rhythm, imagery, or figurative language—contribute to this overall image.

One of the first things teachers often do is develop children's awareness of poetry as a genre—how it differs from prose. Although many children gain this knowledge intuitively as the result of much exposure to fine poetry, some children need more specific guidance. Thus, some teachers make lists of poetry characteristics, adding to the list as different poems are read. Others ask their students to write their own definitions of the genre or compare a prose piece with a poem on the same topic. Teachers also read aloud poems about poetry such as Eve Merriam's "Reply to the Question: How Can You Become a Poet" or "Unfolding Bud" by Naoshi Koriyama as a way to get children thinking about the unique qualities of this genre that distinguish it from others.

Teachers can also show children during discussions how poets pay particular attention to the way the words sound together as well as the particular form the words take on the page. Rhyme, in particular, is usually one of the first things children notice about poetry:

"If it rhymes, it's gotta be poetry," they invariably say. Conversely, it seems they think if it does not rhyme, it is not poetry. In poetry discussion sessions it is helpful to read aloud many examples of free verse to help children see that rhythm or unusual imagery can also make something a poem. Soon children begin making comments such as, "Sometimes poems rhyme, and then I tell myself that all poems don't have to rhyme. I know lots of famous poems that don't rhyme," as third grader Andrea told me.

Yet it is important to not overdo this. Rhyme, with its ability to weave lines into an integrated whole, is a pleasing aspect of poetry and is enjoyable to children. Teachers can help children appreciate rhyme even more by stimulating discussions on its more subtle aspects such as internal rhyming and assonance as well as other aspects of sound such as alliteration and repetition. This was what teacher Sheryl Reed did after reading John Ciardi's "The Cat Heard the Catbird." After reading the poem aloud once, she could tell the group had enjoyed the way the words rhymed. Many were repeating the words to themselves and to one another. She asked them,

> "Now, the author used common, everyday words but why are these words so effective?"
> "The place he put them and the way he used them, like 'a fat bird, a cat bird'," answered Johnny.
> "Yes, the way he used them," responded Sheryl. "If he'd just said, 'A fat bird was sitting on a stump'..."
> "It would be boring," said Stacie.
> "A fat bird, a cat bird, what is he doing with that?" Sheryl asked the group.
> "Rhyming," answered Bryan.
> "He's rhyming," Sheryl agreed. "That's called internal rhyme. It's not at the end of lines but inside, close together within a line" (McClure, Harrison, & Reed, 1990, p. 179).

Children also respond appreciatively to the rhythm of poems. When asked, "How is poetry different from other writing?" they often comment on rhythm as a critical element. For example, second grader Matt told me, "Poetry is like a song without music. But poetry has a beat," and his classmate Abbie said, "Poetry skips along." Teachers can encourage children to notice and comment on this element in discussions. For example, after reading Langston Hughes's "April Rain Song," discussion could center on how words are repeated to provide the effect of a soft rain. When reading Irene McLeod's "Lone Dog" children invariably comment on the compelling rhythm of this poem and how the words contribute to this rhythm.

Poets are word crafters. In no other genre do words mean so much because, due to poetry's concise nature, each word matters—where it is placed on the page, its shades of meaning and connotations, and its relationship to the adjacent word. It is poets who remind us that how something is said is as important as what is said. Poets are continually searching for the one special word that fits perfectly and conveys exactly what they mean. Teachers can attune children to this and help them become "word hunters." To do this, Booth and Moore (1988) suggest that a group discuss what they term "short sharp bits." With this technique, two or three lines in a poem are displayed to the children. After the teacher reads them aloud, general discussion takes place in which special words are pointed out and comments are made on interesting turns of phrase. Eventually, teachers ask children to notice the same things in longer poems as one fifth grade teacher did with Carl Sandburg's "Bubbles." Her students discussed how "flickered out" was such an unusual way to describe a bubble bursting and how Sandburg's reference to bubbles having "rainbows on their curves" was a unique comparison. After this

discussion, one girl commented, "I liked this poem...the words show you that something special can happen in only 30 seconds" (McClure, 1992). It is this sort of awareness of poetic language that we want children to become aware of.

It is also helpful to explain the meanings of words unfamiliar to children. Teachers should not be afraid to introduce poems with long words or unusual topics; many report amazement when children react enthusiastically to poems that are seemingly too difficult for them to understand. In these cases something has captured the children—and teachers should allow this experience to occur. If the poem is one that speaks to a child's experiences or perception of the world and has beautiful language, it is appropriate to use. Defining unknown words merely increases the poem's accessibility.

To further help children become more aware of words, teachers can read the class a line from a poem and have students fill in the missing word that they feel fits well. What is always interesting is that no group of students all picks the same word. Teachers can then ask them to tell why they chose particular words, compare words with one another, then compare their choices with that of the poet's (Booth & Moore, 1988).

Figurative language is another element teachers may want to point out to their students. Young children seem to create metaphor intuitively; in contrast, older children tend to dislike figurative language. The problem may be the way children are introduced to this element. Often, when the figurative language of a poem is discussed, emphasis is on discovering the "right" interpretation rather than allowing children to explore multiple interpretations of the images, as mentioned earlier. It is also counterproductive to have children memorize lists of similes and metaphors or fill in worksheets with statements such as "Love is _____" or "Happiness is _____." Instead, it is important to help children forge a connection between their own experience and the experience described by the poet. With this in mind, teachers should first encourage children to marvel at the unusual images in the poem being discussed. Comments and questions such as, "What do you like about this poem?" "What a way to describe that!" "Do you have a picture of _____ that you never had before?" or "How does this poem tell you about something you're familiar with but in a different way?" will encourage children to look more thoughtfully at the imagery.

Teachers can also help children make connections between poems by reading the same poet so they can develop a sense of the poet's body of literature and style. When reading poetry aloud, it is appropriate to select pieces by many different poets and a series of poems by one poet. Teachers can then challenge the group to make connections through questions such as the following:

- Does anybody know anything else by this poet?

- What kinds of poems does this person write?

- What about this poem reminds you of other poems we've read by this person?

- What did you think about when we read other works by this poet?

Once teachers begin initiating talk about various literary elements, they often find that children begin spontaneously noticing these techniques in poetry they read on their own and also begin using them in the poetry they write. Comstock (1992) recounts an incident in which, after discussing imagery in poetry, a child marveled at a poem with the line "blood red berries." "You could just picture the white snow and the red berries," she commented. Soon this child also began writing poetry that included vivid imagery.

Some teachers question the necessity of doing anything with poetry. "Shouldn't we just read it aloud and let them enjoy it?" is what I am constantly asked. Enjoyment is of course a foundation of any poetry reading experience. But enjoyment does not just happen. We have all had poetry read to us, and although we may have enjoyed the lilt and flow of the words, we may not have discovered the reason for our delight. Understanding can deepen enjoyment and lead to a more informed enjoyment. I think teachers are depriving children if they do not invite them to uncover the way poets choose just the right words or how poets forge an emotional connection with the reader. Such activities are infinitely rewarding because they open up new possibilities for enjoyment that go far beyond passive or superficial acceptance (McClure, Harrison, & Reed, 1990). Yet technique should not be taught out of context or without the child's desire and interest in knowing more about a poem. There is a subtle difference between imposing meaning on students and helping them discover meaning on their own; it is important to suggest possibilities rather than state probabilities.

Stimulating Talk: Selecting What to Read Aloud

If children do not like or cannot identify with the poems you choose to share, they will not be interested in talking about them. This applies to teachers as well. Teachers must like—no, love—the poems they read aloud. An enthusiastic teacher who views new poems as "unfamiliar territory in which one explores all the treasures the land might hold"

(Denman, 1988, p. 7) will create that same attitude in children. For this reason I think it is appropriate to begin with light, humorous, familiar pieces such as those in Shel Silverstein's two popular collections *Where the Sidewalk Ends* and *Light in the Attic*. Jack Prelutsky's *The New Kid on the Block*, William Cole's *Poem Stew*, and Jeff Moss's *The Butterfly Jar* are similar collections that also help children develop positive attitudes toward poetry as well as a thirst for more.

There are many poems that can serve as a bridge between children's initial preferences for the light, humorous pieces and those that require more thoughtful contemplation to enjoy. Balancing some simple pieces with those that are increasingly sophisticated can support developing tastes. Some excellent anthologies that include a balance of both types of poems are Jack Prelutsky's *Random House Book of Poetry*, Beatrice de Regniers's and others' *Sing a Song of Popcorn*, McGovern's *The Arrow Book of Poetry*, and *Reflections on a Gift of Watermelon Pickle* by Dunning and colleagues. Younger children respond positively to poems in collections such as X. J. and Dorothy Kennedy's *Talking Like the Rain*, Prelutsky's *Read Aloud Rhymes for the Very Young*, and Lee Hopkins' *Surprises*. These books are all easily accessible to teachers and can often be purchased inexpensively in multiple copies for whole class or small group use.

Specific poems selected for reading aloud should initially be on topics that are relative to the everyday experiences of children—pets, nature, sports, school, and so forth. Teachers should try to avoid poems with overly "sweet" topics or old-fashioned poems designed to teach moral lessons. Children need to see that poetry can be about anything in their lives—from a beautiful spring day to the experience of watching their pet die.

Reading several poems on the same topic or theme is particularly helpful because poems of differing complexity can be linked. Using the topic of "dogs," for example, McLeod's "Lone Dog," could initially be read aloud. This poem is popular with children because of its compelling rhythm and internal rhyme that convey the feel of a tough, stray dog on the run. This poem can then be contrasted with Worth's "Dog" or Tippett's "Sunning," poems that describe completely different kinds of dogs and use poetic language skillfully to create those images. Hopkins' *It's a Dog's Life* is a collection that would provide other excellent poems on this topic. Once children have heard many poems describing a topic from multiple perspectives, they are often ready for something more challenging and abstract such as Judith Thurman's "Flashlight," which presents a unique metaphor in which a flashlight is compared with a dog on a leash. After several poems are read, teachers can ask questions such as, "How did each poet describe dogs?" Or children can be encouraged to compare the images in their experience or the poems they have written themselves with those of professional poets.

Puzzle or riddle poems work particularly well in providing a bridge between simple and more sophisticated pieces. Reading Worth's "Safety Pin" or Deborah Chandra's "Balloons" causes children to look closely at words and how their meaning is conveyed. Much talk can be generated as a group tries to discern what is being described. Some helpful collections of puzzle poems are *Just Beyond Reach* by Bonnie Nims and *Complete Poems to Solve* by May Swenson.

Sensory poetry such as Worth's "Acorn" or "Seashell," in which something is being carefully and vividly described, can also capture children's attention, particularly if the object being described is something familiar to them. Having the object available for close examination while the poem is read will heighten the effect of the words and stimulate thoughtful discussion of how poets carefully select words to accurately yet creatively describe something. This close attention to language prepares children for more abstract pieces.

Teachers can also share poems that exemplify specific poetic elements as a way to introduce these elements before children encounter them in more complex poems. For instance, Merriam's "Summer Rain" or "Onomatopoeia" could be used to exemplify alliteration. Kuskin's "Spring" has a compelling rhythm that aptly illustrates this poetic element. Kaye Starbird's "December Leaves" includes a metaphor that young children can relate to, and Merriam's "From the Japanese" or Thurman's "The Night Wind" can provide an opportunity for older children to examine metaphor.

There are many beautiful picture book renditions of poems that often draw children into this genre. Some illustrate a single poem such as Susan Jeffers's version of Robert Frost's "Stopping By the Woods on a Snowy Evening," Diane Siebert's "Heartland," and W. Stafford's "The Animal Who Drank Up Sound." Others are beautifully illustrated anthologies, including Nancy Larrick's *Cats Are Cats* illustrated by Ed Young, Arnold Adoff's *In for Winter, Out for Spring*, illustrated by Jerry Pinkney, and Eric Carle's *Animals, Animals*. Young children enjoy illustrated versions of well-known rhymes such as Nadine Westcott's *The Lady with the Alligator Purse*, Eileen Christelow's *Five Little Monkeys* and Dennis Lee's *Alligator Pie*. Discussing how a picture book artist chose to use a particular medium or style to represent a poet's work or comparing children's own images of a poem with those of the artist can lead children to a deeper, more thoughtful response to the poem. Teachers could also encourage students to

Illustration from Eric Carle's Animals, Animals. ©1990 *by Eric Carle. Reprinted by permission of* The Putnam Publishing Group.

compare different illustrated versions of the same poem: for example, Ted Rand, Nancy Winslow Parker, and Paul Galdone have each depicted Longfellow's "Paul Revere's Ride" quite differently. Much talk could be generated as children compare the different visual interpretations.

Although some argue that we should be encouraging children to create their own images from a poem rather than creating those images for them, I think there is a place for sharing the beautiful and powerful images artists bring to the interpretation of poems. One way to circumvent this problem is to first read the poem, let children respond, show the illustrations, then encourage children to compare their own mental pictures with those created by the artist.

After children have been immersed in much poetry that is of high quality yet accessible to them, they are ready for poems that use subtle imagery, free-verse forms, and complex themes in ways that challenge the reader. Hughes's *The Dream Keeper*, Chandra's *Balloons* and *Rich Lizard*, Livingston's *Earth Songs*, Behn's *Crickets and Bullfrogs* and *Whispers of Thunder* and the more complex examples of Worth's *All the Small Poems* as well as the many fine collections done by Eve Merriam contain many excellent poems that help children discover themselves and their world.

The most important thing to remember, however, is not to worry about choosing the "right" poem. As your own tastes expand, you will naturally begin sharing the more challenging pieces while not abandoning those that are fun. Children seem to need both kinds—and isn't that true for adults as well? Sometimes we all pick up a book that is a quick read and serves as pure entertainment, but a steady diet of Shel Silverstein can get just as boring as too much Danielle Steel. We need our minds and souls nourished by something more substantial. As teachers become more knowledgeable about poetry, their enthusiasm for it will be contagious. It is a love for poetry that leads to a thirst to hear more.

Seeing the World Differently

In classrooms where poetry books are available and children have many opportunities to discuss poems, they develop a love for poetry as well as a sense of how poets fit words together. It is true that some poems are not meant to be discussed but rather should be left quietly in the back of one's mind to be pulled out at an opportune moment. However, there is much to be gained from children talking about selected poems and helping one another feel their way through as they test out their responses and ideas in a supportive atmosphere. In this way a poem will gradually

unfold to them, "revealing its rich inner self" (Koriyama, 1966, p. 13) and providing a new vision of the world.

References

Booth, D., & Moore, B. (1988). *Poems please! Sharing poetry with children.* Markham, ON: Pembroke.

Bridge, E. (1966). *Using children's choices of and reactions to poetry as determinants in enriching literary experience in the middle grades.* Unpublished doctoral dissertation, Temple University, Philadelphia, PA.

Comstock, M. (1992). Poetry and process: The reading/writing connection. *Language Arts, 69,* 261–267.

Denman, G. (1988). *When you've made it your own: Teaching poetry to young people.* Portsmouth, NH: Heinemann.

Fisher, C., & Natarella, M. (1982). Young children's preferences in poetry: A national survey of first, second and third graders. *Research in the Teaching of English, 16,* 339–355.

Heard, G. (1993). Living like a poet. *The New Advocate, 2,* 115–122.

Ingham, R. (1980). *The poetry preferences of fourth and fifth grade students in a suburban school setting in 1980.* Unpublished doctoral dissertation, University of Houston, TX.

McClure, A. (1992). *Second, third and fourth grade children's understandings of poetry in supportive literary contexts.* Final Research Report for the Elva Knight Research Grants Program. Newark, DE: International Reading Association.

McClure, A., Harrison, P., & Reed, S. (1990). *Sunrises and songs: Reading and writing poetry in an elementary classroom.* Portsmouth, NH: Heinemann.

Painter, H. (1970). *Poetry and children.* Newark, DE: International Reading Association.

Simmons, M. (1980). *Intermediate children's preferences in poetry.* Unpublished doctoral dissertation, University of Alabama, Mobile.

Terry, A. (1972). *A national survey of children's poetry preferences in the fourth, fifth and sixth grades.* Unpublished doctoral dissertation, Ohio State University, Columbus.

Verble, D. (1973). *A road not taken: An approach to teaching poetry.* Nashville, TN: Tennessee Arts Commission.

Worth, V. (1992). Capturing objects in words. *Hornbook, 68,* 568–569.

Children's Literature and Poems

Adoff, A. (1991). *In for winter, out for spring.* Ill. by J. Pinkney. San Diego, CA: Harcourt Brace.

Armstrong, W. (1969). *Sounder.* Ill. by J. Barkley. New York: HarperCollins.

Behn, H. (1984). *Crickets and bullfrogs and whispers of thunder*. Selected by L. Hopkins. San Diego, CA: Harcourt Brace.

Burnett, F.H. (1962). *The secret garden*. Ill. by T. Tudor. Philadelphia, PA: Lippincott.

Carle, E. (1989). *Animals, animals*. New York: Philomel.

Chandra, D. (1990). Balloons. In *Balloons and other poems*. Ill. by L. Bowman. New York: Farrar, Straus & Giroux.

Chandra, D. (1993). *Rich lizard*. Ill. by L. Bowman. New York: Farrar, Straus & Giroux.

Christelow, E. (1989). *Five little monkeys*. New York: Clarion.

Ciardi, J. (1977). The cat heard the cat-bird. In A. Hill, A. Perkins, & A. Helbig (Eds.), *Straight on till morning*. New York: Crowell.

Cole, W. (1981). *Poem stew*. Ill. by K. Weinhaus. New York: Lippincott.

de Regniers, B., et al. (1988). *Sing a song of popcorn: Every child's book of poems*. Ill. by nine Caldecott Medal artists. New York: Scholastic.

Dunning, S., Lueders, E., & Smith, H. (Comp.). (1966). *Reflections on a gift of watermelon pickle and other modern verse*. Glenview, IL: Scott, Foresman.

Frost, R. (1978). *Stopping by woods on a snowy evening*. Ill. by S. Jeffers. New York: Dutton.

Giovanni, N. (1985). The drum. In *Spin a soft black song: Poems for children*. Ill. by G. Martins. New York: Hill and Wang.

Hopkins, L. (Comp.). (1983). *It's a dog's life*. Ill. by L. Richards. San Diego, CA: Harcourt Brace.

Hopkins, L. (Comp.). (1984). *Surprises*. Ill. by M. Lloyd. New York: HarperCollins.

Hughes, L. (1969). April rain song. In *Don't you turn back: Poems by Langston Hughes*. Selected by L. Hopkins. Ill. by A. Grifalconi. New York: Knopf.

Hughes, L. (1969). Poem. In *Don't you turn back: Poems by Langston Hughes*. Selected by L. Hopkins. Ill. by A. Grifalconi. New York: Knopf.

Hughes, L. (1986). *The dream keeper and other poems*. New York: Knopf.

Jarrell, R. (1964). *The bat-poet*. Ill. by M. Sendak. New York: Macmillan.

Kennedy, X.J., & Kennedy, D. (Comp.). (1992). *Talking like the rain: A first book of poems*. Ill. by J. Dyer. Boston, MA: Little, Brown.

Koriyama, N. (1966). Unfolding bud. In *Reflections on a gift of watermelon pickle and other modern verse*. Comp. by S. Dunning, E. Lueders, & H. Smith. Glenview, IL: Scott, Foresman.

Kumin, M. (1966). The microscope. In *Reflections on a gift of watermelon pickle and other modern verse*. Comp. by S. Dunning, E. Lueders, & H. Smith. Glenview, IL: Scott, Foresman.

Kuskin, K. (1980). I woke up this morning. In *Dogs and dragons, trees and dreams*. New York: HarperCollins.

Kuskin, K. (1980). Spring. In *Dogs and dragons, trees and dreams*. New York: HarperCollins.

Larrick, N. (1988). *Cats are cats*. Ill. by E. Young. New York: Philomel.

Lee, D. (1983). *Alligator pie*. Boston, MA: Houghton Mifflin.

Lionni, L. (1967). *Frederick*. New York: Pantheon.

Livingston, M. (1976). For Mugs. In *4-way stop*. New York: Atheneum.

Livingston, M. (1986). *Earth songs*. Ill. by L. Fisher. New York: Holiday.

Longfellow, H.W. (1990). *Paul Revere's ride*. Ill. by T. Rand. New York: Dutton.

McGovern, A. (1965). *The arrow book of poetry*. Ill. by G. Dotzenko. New York: Scholastic.

McLeod, I. (1981). Lone dog. In *Good dog poems*. Comp. by W. Cole. New York: Scribner.

Merriam, E. (1976). From the Japanese. In *Rainbow writing*. New York: Atheneum.

Merriam, E. (1976). Reply to the question: How can you become a poet? In *Rainbow writing*. New York: Atheneum.

Merriam, E. (1977). Onomatopoeia. In *It doesn't always have to rhyme*. Ill. by M. Spooner. New York: Atheneum.

Merriam, E. (1984). Summer rain. In *Jamboree: Rhymes for all times*. Ill. by W. Gaffney-Kessell. New York: Dell.

Moffitt, J. (1966). To look at anything. In *Reflections on a gift of watermelon pickle and other modern verse*. Comp. by S. Dunning, E. Lueders, & H. Smith. Glenview, IL: Scott, Foresman.

Moss, J. (1989). *The butterfly jar*. Ill. by C. Demarest. New York: Bantam.

Nims, B. (1992). *Just beyond reach and other riddle poems*. Photographs by G. Ancona. New York: Scholastic.

Paterson, K. (1977). *Bridge to Terabithia*. Ill. by D. Diamond. New York: Crowell.

Prelutsky, J. (1983). *Random House book of poetry: A treasury of 572 poems for today's child*. Ill. by A. Lobel. New York: Random House.

Prelutsky, J. (1984). *The new kid on the block*. New York: Greenwillow.

Prelutsky, J. (1986). *Read aloud rhymes for the very young*. Ill. by M. Brown. New York: Knopf.

Ryder, J. (1989). *Mockingbird morning*. Ill. by D. Nolan. New York: Macmillan.

Sandburg, C. (1977). Buffalo dusk. In *The gift outright*. Ed. by H. Plotz. New York: Greenwillow.

McClure

Sandburg, C. (1987). Bubbles. In *This delicious day: 65 poems*. Selected by P. Janeczko. New York: Orchard.

Siebert, D. (1989). *Heartland*. Ill. by W. Minor. New York: Crowell.

Silverstein, S. (1974). *Where the sidewalk ends*. New York: HarperCollins.

Silverstein, S. (1981). *The light in the attic*. New York: HarperCollins.

Stafford, W. (1992). *The animal who drank up sound*. Ill. by D. Frasier. San Diego, CA: Harcourt Brace.

Starbird, K. (1963). December leaves. In *Don't ever cross a crocodile*. Ill. by K. Dalton. New York: Lippincott.

Swenson, M. (1993). *Complete poems to solve*. Ill. by C. Hale. New York: Macmillan.

Teasdale, S. (1954). Falling stars. In *Stars tonight*. Ill. by D. Lathrop. New York: Macmillan.

Thurman, J. (1985). Flashlight. In *Flashlight and other poems*. Ill. by R. Rubel. New York: Atheneum.

Thurman, J. (1985). The night wind. In *Flashlight and other poems*. Ill. by R. Rubel. New York: Atheneum.

Tippett, J.S. (1981). Sunning. In *Good dog poems*. Comp. by W. Cole. New York: Scribner.

Viorst, J. (1972). *Alexander and the horrible, terrible, no good, very bad day*. Ill. by R. Cruz. New York: Atheneum.

Viorst, J. (1981). Just before springtime. In *If I were in charge of the world and other worries*. Ill. by L. Cherry. New York: Atheneum.

Westcott, N. (1988). *The lady with the alligator purse*. Boston, MA: Jay Street.

Whitman, W. (1975). Night on the prairies. In *Room for me and a mountain lion: Poetry of open spaces*. New York: M. Evans.

Worth, V. (1978). Acorn. In *Still more small poems*. New York: Farrar, Straus & Giroux.

Worth, V. (1984). Seashell. In *All the small poems*. New York: Farrar, Straus & Giroux.

Worth, V. (1987). Dog. In *All the small poems*. Ill. by N. Babbitt. New York: Farrar, Straus & Giroux.

Worth, V. (1987). Magnifying glass. In *All the small poems*. Ill. by N. Babbitt. New York: Farrar, Straus & Giroux.

Worth, V. (1987). Safety pin. In *All the small poems*. Ill. by N. Babbitt. New York: Farrar, Straus & Giroux.

CHAPTER 12

Leading Grand Conversations

Deborah Wells

ON A RECENT visit to Sue Burtch's second grade classroom, I noticed Shane, the smallest of eight children sitting in a literature circle comparing Rapunzel with *The Paper Bag Princess*, a modern fairy tale by Robert Munsch. Shane listened intently to the discussion while trying to get a turn to speculate why Munsch might have decided to write this book. After John and Charles shared their ideas, Shane spoke. Because his ideas were very similar to others', I wanted to see how his teacher would react: Sue listened carefully and gave undivided attention; her body turned toward Shane, her eyes met his, she matched his smile, and nodded her encouragement. Judging from the teacher's reaction, Shane knew that his ideas about books were important.

Shane's comments, like those of all his classmates, are received by a warm and accepting audience, who take their lead from a caring teacher. Even though Shane's reading ability is less well developed than others in his class, and his comments are not always directly related to the conversation, he joins discussion groups eagerly and confidently.

How do teachers like Sue help all children

believe their ideas are valued? How do teachers help their students develop the confidence to use language as a tool for exploration? Most important, how can teachers encourage students to view a literature discussion as a "grand conversation," rather than a "gentle inquisition"?

Readers can be trusted to find meaning in a text. When teachers value their students' responses, literature discussion groups provide a safe place for children to use language to explore important ideas and issues. From these discussions, grand conversations can emerge—instances of genuine dialogue that reveal the power of literature to move and inspire.

Classroom Conversations: Who Talks? Why? How?

Insightful teachers invite all children to join in the conversation by creating a community of learners—a community in which members find meaningful ways to use language to learn about themselves and the world of literature. Their book discussions resemble natural conversations, with the ebb and flow of shifting

Illustration from The Paper Bag Princess *by Robert Munsch, illustrated by Michael Kusugak. Published by Annick Press Ltd. in 1980. Reprinted by permission of the publisher.*

topics punctuated by students' thoughts and questions. However, book discussions in some classrooms still sound like interrogations: the teacher fires off questions to direct the topic and assess students' comprehension. Such a teacher-controlled discussion is illustrated in this discussion of *Harriet the Spy* by Louise Fitzhugh. The teacher tries to get a group of fifth grade students to examine one of the themes in the book—what makes people rich.

Luann: (retelling an incident from *Harriet the Spy*) She said that Sport's house smelled like old laundry and everything was kind of old looking and her house didn't smell...and she asked herself, does that mean we are rich and everything? What makes people rich?

Teacher: What do you think about that? That was good that you noticed that, Luann. What do you think?

Mark: I know what makes people poor and rich.

Teacher: What does, Mark?

Mark: Money.

Teacher: Okay, Does that make...

Lee: A poor person can get rich and lose all his money and live in a rich house. They only have to pay a down payment and get in.

Teacher: Do you think that money is the only thing that makes people rich?

Mark: No.

Lee: Yeah. No.

Luann: Personality.

Matt: Some people could invent something.... They might get money that way.

Teacher: Okay, it's true that money does make you rich. But I think that there are other things that make you feel rich, too.

Amanda: Yeah. Like your clothes.

Teacher: How about your friends?

Mark: Yeah.

Lee: You wish.

Teacher: Okay, you're getting a little silly. Let's stick to what we are talking about. So Harriet is trying to figure out whether she is rich and what makes people rich. She's trying to understand that. Luann?

Luann: She wants to find out if Harrison Withers and his cats all eat the same food....

In this exchange, Mark, Lee, Matt, and Amanda continue the view that being rich means wealth and material goods. Their teacher is able to get Luann to suggest that wealth could mean other things, such as a good personality, but the other students keep their positions despite the teacher's attempts to change their perspectives. Rather than promote a collabo-

Leading Grand Conversations

rative, mutual construction of meaning, the teacher tries unsuccessfully to get her students to accept a value she has and her interpretation of the passage Lee introduced.

The teacher is in control of the exchange. She gives several students a chance to answer, but she controls who speaks and what counts as an acceptable interpretation. When the students' answers are different from the expected response, the teacher does not tell them the answer. Instead, she asks another question that seems to suggest a different response. The exchange ends when Luann introduces a new topic— Harrison Wither and his cats.

Labeled I-R-E (initiation-reply-evaluation), this type of interaction pattern is common in many classrooms (Mehan, 1979), as mentioned in Chapter 10. But while it may be useful for reciting certain kinds of information, reviewing facts for a test, or checking comprehension, this interaction pattern is not the same as that found in natural conversation. Bloome (1987) labels this kind of discussion a "procedural display," because the content, interpretations, and larger meanings are lost as students (and teachers) go through the motions of getting through a lesson. Instead of scaffolding—building on and expanding students' thinking—procedural display is characterized by teachers shaping students' responses so that the "right," or expected, answers surface. These book discussions are gentle inquisitions led by a teacher who controls the content and interactions. In this setting, students may read the assigned text and wait for the teacher to initiate the "discussion." To check students' comprehension, teachers ask a series of questions, nominate speakers to reply, and evaluate the accuracy of the responses. This interaction pattern conditions students to view literature discussions as a time to prove what they have learned from a text. Many children learn this pattern early in their school experiences, and it takes time and trust to elevate their idea of a discussion to the idea of a real dialogue.

Genuine dialogues are collaborative and sound more like natural conversations. The following example from a discussion of Betsy Byars's *After the Goat Man* demonstrates what can happen when teachers give up some of their control and encourage students to guide the discussion. The novel is about a boy named Figgy and his friends, Ada and Harold. Figgy lives with his grandfather, the Goat Man, an elderly man who is about to lose his farm.

Tim: I want to talk now.

Teacher: Okay.

Tim: I thought the Goat Man would be more sensitive near the end because, well, he helped Figgy out.

Carrie: It was different. That grandfather just walked with Harold to where Figgy was, and he was real quiet and he just, he really cared. I think he really cared.

Teacher: That part of the story was real, real touching for me, too, because Betsy Byars [told us] he was real grouchy and hated children, and then you're seeing a different side of him.

Joy: I thought the grandfather was getting close to Figgy and I thought, well, it was kind of sad. What happened to his grandfather?

Teacher: If you look at page 112....

Tim: Another thing. His rabbit's foot. I thought his rabbit's foot like had a name. I thought it would be like a main character.

Teacher: The rabbit's foot?

Tim: Yeah.

In this group, students nominate themselves when they have something to say. As they discuss the change in the grandfather's character, they also describe the feelings the text evokes. As in natural conversation, speakers choose when to speak, they tell about themselves, and they build on previous comments. In this discussion, the teacher is a participant, sharing her reaction to Byars's story. As in the first example, the teacher asks questions, but these questions are genuine requests for information or clarification. When a new topic is introduced, the teacher responds to it, but later returns to Joy's question.

How Do Teachers Help Students Gain Confidence in Expressing Their Ideas?

Lunchrooms, playgrounds, and classrooms with a substitute teacher—all these are noisy places, filled with children actively engaged in conversation. In these naturally occurring conversations, topics emerge from a common need or interest. Turns to talk are negotiated or taken when (and if) someone has something to say. Responses are modified and shaped by the listener's reactions and replies. The amount of time a person speaks is usually determined by the speaker or listeners, who interrupt to take their turn. In natural conversations, children argue, speculate, question, and share. When the topic moves to important issues—allowances, school, books they have read—the conversation can become a meaningful dialogue.

In genuine dialogue, meanings are jointly constructed. Participants create new meanings through language that emerges through collaboration. Dialogue occurs when participants gain a deeper insight into the issues being discussed (not just when they voice opinions). Participation is enhanced when there is a concern that all group members have oppor-

tunity to speak and previous speakers' responses are acknowledged. Participants show interest nonverbally as well as by asking questions or seeking clarification. Finally, there is a flexible, rotating leadership; the dialogue is not dominated by a single individual. These characteristics are also traits of successful literature discussion groups—groups that engage in genuine dialogue.

Integrating this type of language into the classroom requires teachers to consider the book discussions they wish to have and to address their role in a discussion group. Some teachers see themselves as the leader whose role is to guide the discussion by checking readers' comprehension and "covering" the story. In this case, a question-answer pattern is an efficient way to proceed. Some teachers, though, view their role as a participant in book discussions—as a fellow reader. The dialogue in those groups is collaborative: all participants share interpretations, make connections between literature and their own lives, and gain new insights. Genuine dialogue in a literature discussion group requires time and patience. By the time children have been in school for a few years, most have acquired the traditional ways of interacting. They are accustomed to being asked questions and giving the safe and correct answers—or the wrong ones. Changing this habit requires trust and risk taking.

In discussion groups that Maryann Eeds and I (1989) worked with, we found that teachers initially had a difficult time turning the conversation over to students. The teachers acted as discussion directors: they asked questions and shaped students' responses toward specific ends. Nevertheless, all the groups had moments of insight and collaboration. For example, the readers who discussed Natalie Babbitt's *Tuck Everlasting* shared in a grand conversation. When *Tuck* was discussed, teachers really listened, encouraged students to think deeply about what was said, and supported inquiry as students discussed life and death issues. With time and understanding, grand conversations can be a part of all literature discussion groups.

How Can Teachers Help Children Participate in Grand Conversations?

If you listened in on book discussions across grade levels and paid close attention to the kinds of comments being made, you might reach one overwhelming conclusion about teachers' talk: it is not necessarily the *amount* of teacher talk that makes a difference; rather, it is the *quality* of the teachers' responses—the genuine questions, the acknowledgments, and the replies (Eeds & Wells, 1989).

In a successful literature discussion group, the teacher is not the central focus—the book and the readers' responses are. The teacher is a collaborator, a reader who contributes but does not dominate the discussion. This does not mean that teachers sit back biting their tongues, wishing they could just "teach." Teachers *are* responsible for finding that teachable moment, that invitation to share knowledge about authors and their craft. Teachers are also responsible for creating an atmosphere that allows students to show their involvement with the text and consider the importance of the ideas the author presents. Successful literature discussion groups enable participants to gain new insights about the text and about themselves. For this to happen, teachers have to help children develop the habit of mind, the way of thinking about a text, that will enable them to share their responses with others and profit from the ensuing dis-

Jacket design from Natalie Babbitt's Tuck Everlasting. ©1975 by Natalie Babbitt. Reprinted by permission of Farrar, Straus & Giroux, Inc.

cussion. There are several types of comments that encourage students to closely examine the text and create meanings that might not emerge without such supports. Three specific kinds of teacher comments are common to natural conversations and literature discussion groups: encouragement, synthesis, and inquiry.

Encouragement

Encouragement comments serve to keep the conversation going by demonstrating the listener's interest and involvement. In discussion groups, teachers show they are listening by nodding, agreeing, or making statements that encourage speakers to elaborate on their responses. In the following discussion of *Tuck Everlasting*, the students develop theories about why the Tuck family waits so long to see their children, and the teacher encourages their ideas.

> Debora: What Mandy was saying, she was talking about the boys when she first started off where in the book it says somethin' about the boys and it's in Chapter 2, and I think she made a good, uh, response about meeting them every 10 years.... Yeah, I don't think that's very good to meet your sons every 10 years. They wouldn't get to know you or anything like that.
>
> Mandy: Yeah, but like I was saying, if they were angels, they could, uh, maybe God wouldn't let them see them except for that...they could only turn human every 10 years.
>
> Teacher: Hum.
>
> Mandy: And besides that, it said, "going down" to see them.
>
> Teacher: Good point. That's what made you think that they might be in heaven, hm?
>
> Mandy: (to Debora) Didn't you think so?

The teacher in this excerpt (from Eeds & Wells, 1989, p. 21) does not judge the students' responses, she listens. A simple "Hum" encourages Mandy to continue speaking, to extend her turn to talk. "Good point" praises Mandy's strategy of using the text to support her answer. The teacher's use of encouragement allows students to see that she is genuinely interested in what they have to say. As students share their hypotheses, Debora adds to Mandy's comments as new ideas emerge, and Mandy refers back to the text to support her theory.

The teacher is the leader in this conversation, but her comments do not control the direction of the discussion. Instead, she helps the group establish an interaction pattern that allows students to do most of the talking, to engage in an active construction of the text.

Synthesis

Synthesis comments also serve to maintain conversation. They are usually nondirective and give students the confidence to use language in an exploratory way. One type of synthesis comment is an empathetic response to label a feeling (for example, "Oh, you felt anxious when Winnie was in jail"). Other synthesis comments occur when the teacher repeats or restates speakers' ideas, which explicitly acknowledges their responses. Inclusive and personal pronouns may be used to encourage involvement and create a dialogue that includes everyone (for instance, "Yesterday we wondered if the Tucks might be angels, but today some people have a different idea"). Synthesis comments may be accompanied by a request for agreement that the paraphrase was correct ("Is that what you meant, Mandy?"). By encouraging students to speak and by synthesizing their responses, Shannon, the teacher leading the following grand conversation (from Eeds & Wells, 1989, p. 20–21), is able to move discussion from a question-and-answer model toward genuine dialogue in which readers frequently discuss the central truths the text holds for them:

> Jonathan: Yeah, what I thought was, it upset me and I couldn't figure out what it was.... It starts on page 8. It says, "It's no use having *that* dream," and over here it ends and says, "I was having *that* dream again," and it's talking about a dream and it says "we're all in heaven and none of this had ever happened." What happened?

Mandy: I want to know why they were in heaven, I mean, I want to know if it's a down-to-earth story or it it's happening in....

Teacher: Oh. She wants to know if the story's taking place....

Mandy: (interrupts) I think I've got it now. It could be that they're, them two are angels going down to see their children, or something like that.

Teacher: She's wondering if, in the story, that the people are angels and they are going down to see their sons and they only get to see them...

Mandy: Every 10 years.

Teacher: Every 10 years. Aha.

Inquiry

Inquiry comments allow teachers to model their thought processes, think aloud, and demonstrate how *they* construct meaning from text. Teachers can share their own predictions, inferences, and verifications with students. Inquiry comments can also help the group become involved with the text, engaging them in a literary experience that allows them to enter the story world. In the following example, in which the dialogue about *Tuck Everlasting* continues, the teacher acknowledges the previous speaker and mentions the gaps left by Babbitt when she describes the "stranger." The teacher asks questions that reveal her reading processes:

Teacher: Debora mentioned the stranger...and I wondered...did you notice that the author didn't tell you everything about the man? I wondered what would be the reason why she wouldn't tell you?

Jonathan: Well, I was thinkin', when I get to the man, I was starting to think about the title, *Tuck Everlasting*, and the prologue and it started to piece together, like they're gonna live forever or somethin' like that. And I started to

fade away with that angel theory thing and I figured like if that spring was everlasting, maybe that guy has tasted it before; he also lives forever and he's trying to find out if there's more people.

Teacher: Maybe the stranger drank some of that water and he thinks, "If I'm gonna live forever, maybe there are other people who are also going to live forever." Hum. That's an interesting theory. We'll have to find out if that's the case.

Jonathan shows evidence of his own inquiry as he eagerly voices his changing interpretation, his theory about the connection between the title and the mysterious stranger. The teacher synthesizes Jonathan's comments and provides encouraging comments. She points out they will have to read to find out in order to generate hypotheses about what may happen. None of the participants claim to have the answer; they are satisfied with the inquiry process as they construct meaning together.

Some Thoughts

Teachers should reflect on their roles in a literature discussion group. Through encouragement, synthesis, and inquiry, they can invite students to engage in a critical discussion of a text. By using an interaction pattern that is like natural conversation, students become comfortable talking with one another and reflecting on the responses that are given. In contrast, the nature of talk in many classrooms is oppressive for its participants. When teachers are always in control—introducing topics, nominating speakers, and evaluating their replies—students may become passive and uninvolved. In those instances, literature discussion groups may be no more than a procedural display, going through the motions of "discussing" a text. Changing the interaction patterns in discussion groups can empower students to engage in a dialogue about a text in which participants talk and listen, speculate and argue, and explore the text's potential meanings. Through encouragement and synthesis, teachers can establish literature groups that allow students to become personally involved with the text, to engage in inquiry, and to critique in a natural and satisfying way.

References

Bloome, D. (1987). Reading as a social process in a middle school classroom. In D. Bloome (Ed.), *Literacy and schooling* (pp. 124–149). Norwood, NJ: Ablex.

Eeds, M., & Wells, D. (1989). Grand conversations: An exploration of meaning construction in literature study groups. *Research in the Teaching of English*, 23, 4–29.

Mehan, H. (1979). *Learning lessons*. Cambridge, MA: Harvard University Press.

Children's Literature

Babbitt, N. (1975). *Tuck everlasting*. New York: Farrar, Straus & Giroux.

Byars, B. (1974). *After the Goat Man*. New York: Viking.

Fitzhugh, L. (1964). *Harriet the spy*. New York: HarperCollins.

Munsch, R. (1980). *The paper bag princess*. Buffalo, NY: Firefly.

CHAPTER 13

"So What Do I Do?" The Role of the Teacher in Literature Circles

Kathy G. Short and Gloria Kauffman

AS EDUCATORS MOVE toward collaborative approaches to teaching and learning with students, one of the most frequently asked questions is: "But what about the role of the teacher?" Because teachers have become dissatisfied with traditional roles in which they impose curriculum on their students, some have assumed a laissez-faire stance. From this hands-off position, they create classroom environments for learning and stand back to let the curriculum emerge from the students. Dewey (1938) argues that educators constantly engage in this kind of "either-or" thinking, rather than considering other options. In this case, the option is a collaborative effort in which teachers and students construct curriculum together.

We believe that the same kind of "either-or" thinking has pervaded considerations of the teacher's role in literature discussions. Some educators argue that the teacher must be present as a guide to support students in taking discussions to a greater depth. Others insist that teachers should not be present be-cause their greater power and social prestige have an inhibiting influence on students' constructions of their own meanings and development of independent strategies. Instead of trying to argue for or against teacher presence in literature circles, we are interested in understanding the different potentials that exist in small group discussions when teachers are and are not present. We also believe that much of the support and demonstrations that teachers provide for discussion occur *outside* of the actual literature circle experiences.

In this chapter, we consider the teacher's role in establishing a classroom environment that supports literature circles and encourages dialogue among students. The issues that we raise are pulled from many years of experience with literature circles. We illustrate the role of the teacher by drawing on examples from Gloria's (one of the author's) fifth grade students who discuss two picture books with and without her presence in their literature circles. The first book, *Baseball Saved Us* by Ken Mochizuki, focuses on a young Japanese

American boy in an internment camp during World War II who deals with prejudice through playing baseball. Gwen Everett's *John Brown: One Man Against Slavery* is the powerful story of John Brown's belief in the equality of all people, and his 1859 raid on a U.S federal arsenal in Harper's Ferry, Virginia, which led to his execution.

Establishing a Supportive Environment for Literature Circles

When we first worked with children in literature circles (Short, 1986), we spent a lot of

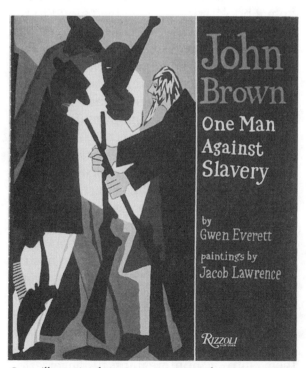

Cover illustration from Gwen Everett's John Brown: One Man Against Slavery. *©1993 by Gwen Everett. Paintings by Jacob Lawrence. Art ©1993 by Founders Society, The Detroit Institute of Arts. Reprinted by permission of Rizzoli, New York.*

time thinking about our role within these groups. Initially, our students had difficulty figuring out how to talk about books, so we considered the kinds of demonstrations we could offer of ways to talk about literature. Gradually, we realized that we were influencing the groups more through what we did outside the literature circles than within the discussions. In particular, key aspects of our roles became to create a sense of community, plan extensive experiences with books, establish a broad thematic context, provide multiple demonstrations of effective book talk, and organize the logistics of the groups.

A necessary condition for powerful discussions about literature is a strong sense of community in the classroom (Short, 1990). We quickly realized that children are not going to talk about connections and issues that really matter in their lives if they do not trust and know well the people with whom they are sharing. In the discussion of *Baseball Saved Us*, Ruben talked about how he felt about being the last one picked for teams. John raised the issue with Arthur that Arthur "hardly ever uses the team, but is one team by himself." The honesty of these fifth grade boys, all of whom were popular children in the school, is a reflection of their willingness to be vulnerable—an attitude they did not take early in the year. We have found that our major focus at the beginning of the year has to be on building this sense of community, for without community, we have no chance of collaboratively constructing meaning with students.

We also recognized that if students have no interest in books or have not had previous experiences with literature, they will not respond positively to literature circles and will not be able to draw from a wide range of literature connections when they talk. With students who lack these literature experiences, we immerse them in books by providing more class time for independent reading, reading aloud, Readers Theatre, and talking with partners, small groups, and the whole class. Sharing is particularly important in allowing students to become more comfortable talking about their enjoyment of a book with another person.

Another feature of the supportive environment is the relationship of literature circles to the broader issues and themes being explored in the classroom. When we first began literature circles, we simply chose individual books that we saw as great pieces of literature and offered them for student selection. We soon realized that experiences with even a great book are enhanced if that book relates to other literature and to personal or class inquiries. Now our literature circle books connect with a broader classroom theme or focus. *Baseball Saved Us* and *John Brown* were related to the broad concept of "discovery," which the class had been exploring from various perspectives throughout the year. This broad concept led to a classroom focus on "rights" and to small inquiry groups about slavery, children's rights, animal abuse, and women's rights. By placing the literature circles within these broader thematic contexts of children's inquiries, the students brought many more connections and ideas to their discussions. Both groups that discussed *Baseball Saved Us* made connections with racism, slavery, the Holocaust, and illegal Central American immigrants because of earlier class discussions and questions.

When our literature circles relate to a broader classroom focus, we find that the most powerful demonstrations about talk occur during whole class read-aloud discussions rather than in the literature circles. When Kathy (one of the authors of this chapter) was working with second grade students who primarily saw their literature circles as time to "tattle" on the behavior of others, she began reading aloud picture books on ecology and having short whole-class discussions before arranging students into small groups to discuss text sets about ecosystems (Short & Armstrong, 1993). Instead of mandating a specific procedure for how students should conduct their literature circles, these class discussions provided demonstrations of how they could talk about their books with one another.

Books read aloud provide shared experiences from which students draw ideas and connections for their discussions. Both literature groups on *Baseball Saved Us* (with and without the teacher present) made many connections between internment camps and concentration camps. These connections came from a book that had been read aloud to the class, *Devil's Arithmetic* by Jane Yolen. In addition, as the students discussed *John Brown* they brought up an issue from a previous class discussion of Frances Temple's *Grab Hands and Run* about illegal immigrants and whether it is "good or bad to risk your own life for other people."

We often use the whole-class discussion as a place to introduce particular reading strategies such as webbing, "Sketch to Stretch," and "Save the Last Word for Me" (Harste, Short, & Burke, 1988). These strategies become part of a repertoire that students are encouraged to use in their literature circles when they need to get more deeply into a book. Often, we have students first try these strategies with a partner because these partner activities help students become more comfortable in working and talking with another person. Pairing students puts them into a nonthreatening conversation where their participation is essential. "Say Something" and "Written Conversation" are two partner strategies that have been particularly effective for us in introducing students to ways of talking with and listening to others (Harste, Short, & Burke, 1988).

Instead of solving problems for students, we work constantly at reflecting and brainstorming with them as to how they might define and solve problems themselves. At the beginning of the year, Gloria often had students meet for five to ten minutes at the end of their literature circles for a whole-class reflection. She first asked, "What did you discuss in your groups today?" because she wanted to put primary emphasis on their discussion of meaning, rather than on their behaviors. She then asked, "How did your groups go today?" and students described what was working well and where there were still problems. When teachers always take the responsibility for solving students' problems, students can become unable to function in groups without teacher presence. Instead of trying to set up the groups ahead of time so carefully that students know exactly what to do, Gloria initiates literature circles knowing that some will be chaotic. Students then come together to reflect on what *they* can do to make the experience more productive.

Kathy often introduces literature circles to students by asking them to think about how they talk with friends about a movie or television show. Children realize they do not ask the same kinds of questions or talk in the same ways about movies that they do in traditional reading instruction groups. Instead, movie talk centers on such topics as their favorite parts, events that confused them, the endings, and connections they made with their own lives. By encouraging them to make a list of what they discuss with their friends when they really talk, teachers can help students begin to build their own framework for book discussions. When teachers list topics for discussion on the chalkboard, students often adopt that list as a template for their groups. If, however, students create their own list of topics, they see it as "possibilities" they can ignore or adopt—depending on the direction of the discussion.

We also recognize that an important part of our role as teachers is working with students in setting up the groups (Short & Klassen, 1993). Because we believe that student choice is essential to literature circles, we introduce the books to the class, give students

Sketch to Stretch

After reading a book, each student makes a sketch (a quick drawing) of what the story meant to him or her. The focus is not on an illustration of the story but on their own personal connections and meanings. In a group, each person shows his or her sketch, lets others comment on the meanings they see in the sketch, then shares his or her own meaning. The group talks about the different ideas students have raised in their sketches.

from Harste, Short, & Burke, 1988

Save the Last Word for Me

During reading, each student selects 3 to 5 quotes from the text that are interesting, powerful, confusing, or contradictory. Then students write each of their quotes on the front of a 3" x 5" card, and, on the back they write why they selected each quote. In a group, one person begins by sharing one of his or her quotes without commenting on why the quote was chosen. The group then briefly discusses their responses to that quote—why they see it as important. When the discussion subsides, the person who selected the quote gets the "last word" and tells why he or she chose it. The group then moves on to another student. Younger children can show a page from a picture book, and the others in the group can share their responses, letting the child who chose that page have the last word.

from Harste, Short, & Burke, 1988

Say Something

Two students share the reading of a short story together. The first student begins by reading aloud several paragraphs or a page of text to the other student. When the reader stops, both "say something" about the story by making a prediction, sharing personal connections, asking questions, or commenting on the story. The second reader then reads aloud a chunk of text and again stops so that both can "say something." The two readers continue alternating the reading of the story, commenting after each reading, until the story is completed.

from Harste, Short, & Burke, 1988

Written Conversation

Two students have a silent conversation by talking on paper. They share one piece of paper and a pencil and talk about a book by writing back and forth to each other. Because writing slows down the conversational process, they are encouraged to really "listen" to each other as they write. No talking is allowed except with young children who often need to read what they have written to each other.

from Harste, Short, & Burke, 1988

time to browse, and then invite them to make their book choices through a sign-up sheet or ballot. Because they choose their own group, some students in a particular group need support in reading the book and may need to read with a partner, listen to a tape, or have the book read aloud to them. When students are reading longer chapter books, they often need to meet for short (10 minute) literature circle discussions each day so they can share favorite parts, clear up confusion, and establish

reading goals for the next day. After children finish their books they can then engage in more focused and intensive discussions.

We now understand that literature circles depend on a new set of social relationships and beliefs about learning and teaching. Until we examined the broader context within which literature circles were functioning, we found that we were constantly frustrated with the lack of depth in students' talk. Literature circles are not an activity to "add" to traditional classroom structures or simply a better way to teach reading. They depend on collaborative relationships between and among teachers and students and a curriculum based in inquiry.

Supporting Talk Within Literature Circles

While we believe that the major role of the teacher is to establish the environment in which literature circles function, teachers also have a role within the circles. We do not think that teachers should or need to be part of every literature circle. When teachers carefully set up a context that supports literature discussion, students are able to thoughtfully explore alternative interpretations and connections with their peers. In our close examination of the talk among Gloria's fifth graders, we noted that all the children (teacher present or not) moved into dialogue on significant issues related to the book and their lives. The *Baseball Saved Us* group that met without Gloria raised issues about racism, the author's writing style, connections with their own lives, and distinctions between concentration and internment camps. They spent time talking about Renee's argument that the boy "was trying to show people that even though he's different than them, he's still a person" when he hit the home run. Sean offered another perspective when he pointed out, "I felt that this kid's kind of lonely and that he takes all his anger out on the ball."

The Values of Talk Among Students

In circles in which the teacher is not present, students are freer to explore their own agenda and issues from "kid culture" (Newkirk, 1992). In the *John Brown* literature circle that met without Gloria, students engaged in a long debate about whether they would risk their lives for another person and whether it was better to fight for the slaves' freedom or quietly buy them and set them free. Their central issue was whether freedom itself or the way in which one becomes free was more important. This debate led to confusing connections with amnesty issues and each participant trying to prove his or her point. As we read through the transcript of the group's discussion, we realized that, had we been present, we would have stepped in to resolve the debate early in the process because students appeared to be arguing the same issues repeatedly without moving forward. Had we entered the circle, however, perhaps students would not have been able to deal with their own agenda in the time they needed to talk themselves out of the deadlock.

Students can also learn how to sustain their discussion without constantly relying on the teacher to move their talk to deeper issues or to solve their problems. We heard many examples of children bringing the discussion back to the book when they felt they had digressed. We also found instances of the discussants referencing one another, asking clarifying questions, making connections with their own experiences and other literature, reminding one another that all had the right to their opinions, and asking permission to

change the topic. They were able to operate effectively because they were becoming experienced with literature circles and had previously struggled through unproductive discussions. We believe that if we had consistently facilitated their discussions, they would not have developed the abilities to sustain productive conversations on their own.

An additional advantage of "independent" literature circles is that the groups are able to meet more frequently because students need not wait for the teacher's presence. Scheduling demands are greatly eased when teachers do not have to rotate among literature circle meetings so they can always be present. Instead, groups can meet concurrently, with the teacher periodically joining in.

Teachers' Contributions to Literature Discussions

On the other hand, we do not believe that teachers should *never* be present in literature circles. As underscored by others in this volume, the teacher has a valuable contribution to make as a member of the group by sharing connections and interpretations. When we initially started literature circles, we saw our role as providing open-ended interpretive questions at critical points to keep the discussion going or as encouraging students to think more deeply about a book. Gradually we realized that our questions still kept the focus of the group on us and that students were not necessarily developing their own strategies for thinking critically about their reading. We wanted to move from leading the discussion to becoming a member of the group, and so we reduced questions and started contributing our connections and opinions. If we wanted to know whether students understood a particular part of a book, we talked about our connection rather than asking a series of questions. In the *Baseball Saved Us* discussion, students were not making any comments at all about the boy's interaction with the guard, but instead of asking pointed questions, Gloria simply commented, "The guard intrigued me. This kid was out to show this guard he could do it." The students picked up on this comment and made some insightful comparisons between their fathers and the guard.

We still do ask questions in the groups, but they tend to be of two types. One type is "real" questions about issues or events for which we do not have answers and truly want to know what students think. Another type of question asks students to expand on a particular opinion or interpretation. Students often give brief pronouncements in the group such as "It's a boring book" or "I liked the dog" that tend to discourage, rather than invite, responses from others. These comments are reminiscent of whole class discussions in which teachers move quickly from student to student to gather viewpoints, working to ensure participation and attention. In these staccato exchanges, students are not often asked to explore their responses; they have learned if they say *something*, the teacher will move on to the next person. When students make these brief, unexamined comments in our literature circles, we accept the comments, but then ask them to explain. For example, when Tara wondered aloud what black people might think of whites, Gloria commented, "That's interesting. What were you thinking when you said that?" Our questions are genuine: we want to understand why a student is thinking in a particular way.

> *"Older children have become so conditioned to teachers providing answers that they often assume that any time the teacher talks, the interpretive work is finished."*

We also know that if we can encourage students to share more of their thinking instead of making telegraphic pronouncements, they will have a stronger base for group dialogue.

At the beginning of the year, we find that, as teachers, we need to share our ideas using very tentative language (such as "maybe," "not sure," "could be," and "wonder if"), so that students do not think the ideas put forth by teachers are the "right" ones. In particular, older students have become so conditioned to teachers providing answers that they often assume that any time the teacher talks, the interpretive work is finished.

In the literature discussions with Gloria's students, we noted that Gloria made statements that built on ideas children introduced but pushed their thinking to consider other connections or perspectives. For example, when David commented that John Brown thought there would not be freedom without bloodshed, Gloria explained that it bothered her that the "way to overcome something was to kill to make things better." Later in the discussion, when the students were talking about slavery and racial hatred, Gloria raised the issue that "a lot of the white people were fighting to end slavery, but they didn't want to live with blacks or have anything to do with them, which is what I see today." Her comment challenged the children to consider slavery and hatred as they exist in our world today, rather than in a distant past. Throughout the discussions, we found many examples in which Gloria's comments connected the children's topics to deeper societal problems, to relationships in the classroom or community, and to the issues and literature shared in earlier classroom conversations and inquiry. She accepted their topics but also encouraged them to extend and to think through their positions on particular issues.

By studying group discussion with a teacher present, we realized that although we had made progress in moving away from asking questions to participating as members of the group, there were still teacher behaviors that cued students to attend to the teacher rather than the group. We saw many examples of "active listening" in which Gloria continuously acknowledged students' comments with background sounds such as "Hmmm" and "Yeah." We realized that this active listening actually cues students to the teacher and that no one needs to play this role when students meet without the teacher. In fact, we saw more students interrupting one another when the teacher was present, almost as if students competed for attention. They also seemed to talk at the same time more often in the presence of the teacher, possibly because Gloria could sort out their comments and help the group continue. In her absence, students had to listen more carefully to one another.

Moving Between Conversation and Dialogue

Rather than focus in depth on a particular issue when they initiate a book discussion, students tend to talk about their favorite parts and their related experiences, examine the illustrations, retell parts they found confusing, and engage in social chatter. Their talk is often tentative as they toss out many different ideas and connections with the book that gain little or no response from others. This is the kind of talk that teachers rarely value but which we believe plays an essential role in discussants' growth. Through these conversations, stu-

dents have a chance just to enjoy the book, share their initial responses with one another, build a sense of community, and begin to consider a wider range of possible interpretations and issues (Short, 1993). Gloria rarely joins groups during their initial sharing and exploration. While she values this talk, she finds herself getting impatient with their meanderings, their "kid" connections, and stories. Instead, she provides the time they need to share these initial connections and then joins the groups as they are ready to move into more focused discussions of particular issues and need her support.

At times the conversation in a group moves naturally into a dialogue in which students intensively critique and inquire together (Peterson, 1992). At other times, students need support to create a dialogue. When students in a particular literature circle announce after a day or two that they are finished with their discussion, that is when we know they are ready to move into focused inquiry. At this point, our role as teachers involves joining the group to serve as scribes while they brainstorm and web possible issues and connections that bear further discussion (Kauffman & Yoder, 1990; see also Bromley's Chapter 9 in this volume). During this brainstorming or webbing, we can add our own ideas to the web so those ideas are considered but not imposed. If the web is drawn on a large sheet of paper in the center of a table, everyone has access to it, and the group can decide what they want to discuss at the next meeting.

We always ask literature circles to end their meetings by making a plan for what they will talk about next. By reaching an agreement on an issue for discussion, students have a beginning point for the next meeting and do not need to depend on the teacher to start the group. They also have time to think and prepare for that discussion. Their preparation may involve selective rereading toward certain ends, adding ideas to their logs, or doing related research.

As students continue their literature circles, they add to the web new issues that come up in their discussions. They rarely discuss everything on their web but use it as a set of possibilities for focusing their talk. If a group is struggling, we might suggest they try a particular strategy such as "Sketch to Stretch" or "Save the Last Word for Me," but they decide whether they want to use the strategy. Because of their many experiences with literature discussion, Gloria's fifth grade students were able to move into dialogue on their own and did not use any of these strategies as a group. Instead, they opted to use these strategies for responding in their literature logs.

Because we have found that literature logs support students in thinking more deeply about their responses to a book, we ask students to write in their logs two or three times a week (see also Chapters 20 and 21). We want them to view their logs as a place to think about a book and preserve their thinking for possible sharing in the literature circle. Students decide which days they will write and what forms their entries will take—free writes, webs, charts, or sketches. Each day, immediately before their groups meet, they reread their logs as part of their preparation for the group discussion.

Another role that we play in the circles is to take notes on the group discussion. These notes are essential to our evaluation of the kinds of talk and thinking occurring in the groups. We also use our notes to think about the kinds of demonstrations or experiences we might introduce into the classroom and to evaluate the growth of particular students. While in the groups, our note taking keeps us so busy that students cannot continuously look to us for guidance, and we are not tempt-

ed to dominate the talking. Students view the notes as beneficial when we use them to provide a summary of that day's discussion or to refer to a particular comment made earlier in the discussion. Besides notes, an occasional audio- or videotape of ourselves interacting in literature circles makes us more aware of our own group behaviors and contributions.

Rethinking Our Role as Teachers

As we work with our own students and other teachers in exploring literature circles, we see two extremes in how educators view their role in these discussions. One extreme is to simply put students into groups without supportive structures or demonstrations. These groups rarely evolve beyond sharing and social conversation, and can, in fact, become destructive in terms of student relationships—when students tease one another, for example. At the other extreme, some educators have used direct instruction and careful modeling of "how to do" literature groups. As group leaders, these teachers take on the role of asking questions to push student thinking, or they carefully structure the groups by assigning particular roles to students. Literature circles are *not* cooperative groups where students work together in different roles to accomplish a task: they are collaborative groups where students think together to create new understandings.

Instead of modeling what students *should* do, we believe teachers need to provide demonstrations within meaningful contexts of what students *might* do in literature circles (Smith, 1981). We also need to plan for and provide opportunities for students to reflect on the content and processes of their group discussions. We want to collaborate with our students in ways that support them in their current thinking and challenge them to consider new possibilities. But just as we ask children to examine and push their thinking, so must we as teachers more closely examine our own beliefs, practices, and interactions in the classroom.

References

Dewey, J. (1938). *Experience and education*. New York: Collier.

Harste, J., Short, K., & Burke, C. (1988). *Creating classrooms for authors*. Portsmouth, NH: Heinemann.

Kauffman, G., & Yoder, K. (1990). Celebrating authorship in literature circles. In K. Short & K. Pierce (Eds.), *Talking about books: Creating literate communities* (pp. 135–154). Portsmouth, NH: Heinemann.

Newkirk, T. (1992). *Listening in*. Portsmouth, NH: Heinemann.

Peterson, R. (1992). *Life in a crowded place*. Portsmouth, NH: Heinemann.

Short, K. (1986). *Literacy as a collaborative experience*. Unpublished doctoral dissertation, Indiana University, Bloomington, IN.

Short, K. (1990). Creating a community of learners. In K. Short & K. Pierce (Eds.), *Talking about books: Creating literate communities* (pp. 33–52). Portsmouth, NH: Heinemann.

Short, K. (1993). Making connections across literature and life. In K.E. Holland, R.A. Hungerford, & S.B. Ernst (Eds.), *Journeying: Children responding to literature* (pp. 284–301). Portsmouth, NH: Heinemann.

Short, K., & Armstrong, J. (1993). Moving toward inquiry: Integrating literature into the science curriculum. *The New Advocate*, 6, 183–199.

Short, K., & Klassen, C. (1993). Literature circles: Hearing children's voices. In B. Cullinan (Ed.), *Children's voices: Talk in the classroom* (pp. 66–85). Newark, DE: International Reading Association.

Smith, F. (1981). Demonstrations, engagement, and sensitivity. *Language Arts*, 58, 103–112.

Children's Literature

Everett, G. (1993). *John Brown: One man against slavery*. New York: Rizzoli.

Mochizuki, K. (1993). *Baseball saved us*. New York: Lee & Low.

Temple, F. (1993). *Grab hands and run*. New York: Orchard.

Yolen, J. (1988). *Devil's arithmetic*. New York: Viking.

CHAPTER 14

Following Children's Leads Through Talk Story: Teachers and Children Work to Construct Themes

Kathryn H. Au

STUDENTS HAVE MUCH to say about books—and possibly even more to say when discussion leaders allow them to offer their own interpretations and construct their own themes, as Short and Kauffman argued in the previous chapter. And when students are invited to carry out discussion in culturally familiar ways, they produce the most insightful talk of all. In this chapter I take you into a third grade classroom in Honolulu, Hawaii, to show how the teacher uses a culturally familiar way of organizing discussion. In contrast with traditional questioning strategies, this form of discussion gives children more opportunity for personal interpretation and exploration of a theme.

Constructing the Theme of a Story

Constructing a theme can be a challenging task for children because they must reach for ideas that encompass the text as a whole. Lukens (1990) calls a theme the idea that holds a story together:

> In storytelling "What happened next?" is a question about chronology and narrative order. "Why did it happen?" is a question about conflict and plot. But when we ask, "What does it all mean?" we begin to discover theme (p. 87).

Teachers consider theme an important aspect of literary understanding. Even preschool and kindergarten children appear to gain some sense of theme when they are exposed to literature and given opportunities for discussion (Lehr, 1991). But exactly how do discussions contribute to students' ability to grapple with story themes?

To learn more, I observed in the classroom of an expert teacher who allowed her native Hawaiian students opportunities to construct their own themes for stories (Au, 1992). The children were reading "Magic in a Glass

Jar" by Rhoda Bacmeister, a story about a brother and sister, Uki and Shuzuko, who find a caterpillar and watch it turn into a beautiful moth. Uki and Shuzuko are able to appreciate this experience because their grandmother, as a girl growing up in Japan, had learned to raise silkworms. At the start of the lessons, the teacher had planned to use the theme of learning from grandparents to tie discussion of the story together. However, in the course of their discussions, the students developed a theme of their own—that of the importance of freedom, of letting the moth go free. Their talk showed that the students understood the teacher-proposed theme of learning from grandparents, but they simply found their own theme more compelling. I looked closely at how the teacher used a culturally responsive way of organizing discussion that allowed students to develop their own themes instead of being limited to the theme she had proposed.

Talk Story

People of different cultural backgrounds have learned to organize their conversations in different ways. Different cultures have different rules governing speaking, listening, and turn taking, and it is by observing these mutually recognized rules that participants collaborate to converse (Erickson & Shultz, 1982). When with peers, Hawaiian children frequently engage in a speech event known as "talk story." Watson (1975) defines talk story as "a rambling personal experience narrative mixed with folk materials" (p. 54). In talk story, collaboration with others is more highly valued than individual performance. Children often narrate stories together, each supplying separate pieces of information, corroborating claims, or building on one another's words in rhythmic turn taking. Children speak in their home language, Hawaii Creole English, a non-mainstream variety of English. Here is a brief example of talk story in which the primary speakers are two six-year-old Hawaiian children, Keahi and Kona (brackets indicate overlapping speech):

Keahi: You know—you know, if he kidnap das mean he wants you for good, too.

Kona: —he can fly—and den—

Keahi: [Yeah.]

Kona: [Afta he] can pick you up he can take you away (Watson, 1975, p. 56).

Keahi begins with a point, which Kona elaborates. There is overlapping speech as Keahi agrees with Kona, and Kona then continues.

The literature discussions I have observed resemble talk story in that two or more students collaborate to produce a response to the teacher's question. Often, the teacher calls on a child to respond but still allows others to comment on the chosen child's answer or to add answers of their own. At times the teacher does not call on a particular child, and then any child may contribute to the discussion. This kind of joint performance or collaborative talk contrasts with what might be called conventional classroom recitation, described in earlier chapters as when the teacher asks a question or otherwise initiates a topic, chooses a student to answer, then evaluates the response.

When teachers who are inexperienced in working with Hawaiian children attempt to conduct discussions following the rules for conventional classroom recitation, they run into trouble. Often the student chosen to answer will suddenly grow shy and refuse to respond, while others will call out the answer (Boggs, 1972). Inexperienced teachers frequently try to silence the other children to give the chosen student a chance to answer. Usually, however, the other children refuse to be quiet. From the teacher's viewpoint, it seems as if the children are deliberately breaking the rules for speaking and turn taking; the children see no reason not to speak up and help the discussion along, especially when they have ideas to contribute.

Why do young Hawaiian students behave this way during conventional classroom recitation? One reason is that they may be uncomfortable in activities that single them out in front of their peers and that stress individual achievement rather than group cooperation (Au, 1980; Gallimore, Boggs, & Jordan, 1974). Because the responsibility for answering falls on only one person in conventional classrooms, the recitation reflects the value of *individual* achievement. Talk story reflects a different value—group cooperation—as the children work together to answer the teacher's questions and interpret the story.

In mainstream settings, the use of conventional recitation gives the teacher the ability to control the course of discussion. Just the opposite is often the case when teachers attempt to use recitation with young Hawaiian students. Teachers who insist that only the chosen child answer spend most of the time reprimanding children who appear to be speaking out of turn, which consumes much of the time scheduled for discussion and academic learning. When recitation is used in reading lessons, Hawaiian children discuss fewer story ideas and make fewer logical inferences about the story than when discussions are conducted in the culturally familiar talk-story form (Au & Mason, 1981).

Teachers who conduct lessons in the talk-story form seem to maintain a balance between their own rights in the discussions and those of the children. They accomplish this by observing the principles of *breathing room* and *equal time*. Teachers give children breathing room by al-lowing them to produce responses cooperatively. Except when students stray from the topic of discussion, teachers always seem to accept answers given in Hawaii Creole English, although they paraphrase these answers in standard English. Teachers observe the principle of equal time by trying to give all the children in the group a turn to speak. Teachers may call on children to ensure that those less successful in obtaining turns to speak have a chance. Teachers apply the principle of equal time to themselves by trying to draw answers from the children rather than lecturing them. A student, not the teacher, may have the longest uninterrupted turn of speaking during a discussion (Au, 1980).

The Talk-Story Discussion

To understand how themes developed through discussions in the talk-story form, I studied videotapes made in the third grade classroom of Joyce Ahuna-Ka'ai'ai (Center for the Study of Reading, 1990). Joyce taught a series of four lessons based on "Magic in a Glass Jar" to a group of seven native Hawaiian students. The lesson to be analyzed here, the last in the series, was about 25 minutes long, the typical length of small group reading lessons in Joyce's classroom. I focus on four segments of discussion that show how Joyce and her students collaborated to construct a theme for the story.

"Born to Be Free"

About halfway through the story reading, Keala, one of the girls in the group, begins bidding for a turn and then seizes the floor (brackets mark overlapping speech):

> Teacher: Okay, let's think about the story
> |a little bit.|

Keala: [Mrs. Ahuna—]

Chad: I picked it up.

Keala: It's like on "Born to Be Free" 'cause there's this tiger. It was first a little one. And then this lady picked him up.
[And finally it was—]

Teacher: [Oh, I saw that one.] They had to do what
[at the end?]

Keala: [It's sad.]

The teacher allows Keala to speak not by calling on her but by commenting that she too knows about the movie Keala calls "Born to Be Free." (Keala seems to be thinking of the movie "Born Free," which is actually about a lion not a tiger.) The topic introduced by Keala becomes the focus of discussion.

Next, the teacher tries to get Keala to explain the connection between the movie and the story "Magic in a Glass Jar."

Teacher: They had to do what?

Keala: It fighted. It was the one that was so rough.

Teacher: And what did they have to do at [the end of the story?]

Alex: [It's a wild thing.]

Keala: It wasn't wild. When they—when they started
[feeding(?) it]

Teacher: [But Keala,] what did they have to do at the end of the story?

Keala: They had to let it go.

The teacher raises the question of what happened at the end of the story three times before Keala answers it directly. Alex's comment seems to bolster Keala's point, but she responds by contradicting him ("It wasn't wild").

These two segments show several characteristics of the talk-story form of discussion. There is a lot of overlapping speech—two peo-

ple talking at the same time. The teacher allows the students to introduce their own topics, as long as these do not move the group away from discussion of the story. In contrast, during conventional classroom recitation it is usually the teacher's questions, not the students' ideas, that determine the topics to be discussed. Through her comments and questions, the teacher validates Keala's topic. However, she does not allow Keala to dwell on details of the movie's plot but immediately takes the initiative to link the movie with the story. Because Keala introduced the topic, she becomes the main speaker among the students. Other students have the right to support or dispute the claims of the main speaker, as Alex did with Keala.

"You Can't Keep Things Forever"

The teacher does not state the connection between the movie and story implied by Keala; instead, she moves the discussion back to the theme of the story. Although she does not mention the theme of freedom, the students pick up on it immediately.

Teacher: Why do you think the author wrote this story? What did he want—What did he want you to learn from it?

Chad: about moths

Teacher: About moths. What—what else?

Natasha: [caterpillars]

Kamalu: [You can't keep things in—] you can't keep things
[forever]

Chad: [in jars]

Kamalu: They have to come—[like moths]

Darralyn: [how to take care of it]

Kamalu: [You can't keep them in a glass jar forever.]

Natasha: [You can keep a dog or cat forever,] but like insects you cannot keep 'em
[forever]

Teacher: [Okay]

Natasha: they have to be
[free]

Chad: [hey, once] I kept one lizard forever

Keala: [born to be free]

Teacher: [Excuse me,] is there anything else
that they were telling us—[she was
trying to tell us]

Keala: [Yeah]

Teacher: about?

When the teacher asks why the author wrote this story, the children quickly move into a discussion of the theme—in this case, freedom. Chad and Natasha mention moths and caterpillars, and Kamalu makes the point that you can't keep moths in a glass jar forever. Natasha comments that there is a difference between insects and animals such as dogs and cats, which you can keep "forever." Chad mentions lizards as another example of an animal that can be kept forever. The teacher repeats her question twice, perhaps in an effort to get the discussion back to the theme she has planned to develop—that of learning from grandparents. Both times the students continue to focus on insects, or, in Keala's words, "how you keep them alive and [how] you got to let them go." Only later, when the teacher asks directly how Uki and Shuzuko learned about caterpillars, is she able to reintroduce the theme of learning from grandparents.

This segment of discussion shows other characteristics of lessons conducted in a talk-story form. The teacher initiates the discussion with an open-ended question; she does not call on any student to be the main speaker, and several students share the floor. Much overlapping speech occurs as several new but interrelated ideas are presented in rapid succession by Chad, Natasha, and Kamalu. Keala chimes in at the end to link their ideas to the point she made

earlier. The students' comments do not trigger any teacher questions, as they did in the previous segment of discussion with Keala. Instead, the teacher seems to let the discussion continue until she is certain of the direction the students are taking. At that point the teacher asks about another possible theme, again in an open-ended way.

"There's Almost a Lesson Here"

A few moments later, the teacher asks a more focused question about the theme: "So what do you think, besides learning about the butterfly, what else did we learn from this story?" She calls on Chad, who does not answer at first. Then Darralyn, Alex, Kamalu, and Chad make remarks about silkworms, cocoons, and life cycles, and Kamalu states, "If they didn't have her [the grandmother], then Uki and Shuzuko wouldn't know about caterpillars." The teacher moves quickly to build on Kamalu's point:

Teacher: What does that say about the grandmother and the information the
grandmother had?

Keala: That she's smart and that sometimes
no one can disagree.

Alex: Every—

Keala: And some and um da kine.

Teacher: Darralyn, what were you gonna say?

Darralyn: That, um—forgot.

Teacher: [There's almost a lesson here.]

Keala: [Okay, so they're also—]

Teacher: Besides about the caterpillars, there's
almost a lesson here that has to do—

Keala: [That if they didn't—]

Darralyn: [That Shuzuko and Uki—]

Keala: [If Obasan wouldn't—]

Darralyn: [thought]

Keala: [caterpillars]

Teacher: [Keala, you] know that Darralyn's talking, so just give her a chance.

Darralyn: Uki and Shuzuko learned caterpillars from Obasan.

Teacher: They learned about caterpillars from Obasan.

As the teacher asks a question to develop the theme of learning from grandparents, Keala and then Alex start to speak. However, the teacher calls on Darralyn, perhaps because she has not recently been active in the discussion. Darralyn says she has forgotten what she was going to say (recall how children sometimes respond poorly when singled out), and the teacher again asks about the theme ("There's almost a lesson here, besides about the caterpillars"). Keala begins to answer, but the teacher waits for Darralyn, who gives the answer the teacher seems to be looking for.

Joyce later explained to me that because the discussion was being videotaped, she felt the need to make it go according to plan by firmly establishing the theme of learning from grandparents. Under the pressure of being videotaped, she departed from the talk-story form and reinforced the speaking rights of just one student, Darralyn, to make her point. There was overlapping speech, but only because Keala made several false starts and never finished stating her idea. Joyce succeeded in getting her theme stated, as the comments by Darralyn and Keala show, but the talk involved fewer students and was not as rich in ideas as earlier discussions around the theme of freedom for the moth.

> **"Talk story and other culturally familiar forms of discussion can support a genuine exchange of ideas about literature among teacher and students."**

Conclusions

I have found that lessons conducted in the culturally familiar talk-story form seem to contribute in several ways toward helping Hawaiian children construct their own themes for stories. First, students initiate their own topics of discussion. If what a student says is related to the story, the teacher will help to establish the student's topic as the focus of discussion. For example, Keala saw a connection between a movie and the story, which the teacher helped her to explore.

Second, the talk-story form of discussion permits several students to present their ideas, one right after the other, without teacher intervention. Especially in situations in which the teacher has not called on any particular student to speak, each is free to build on another classmate's ideas. Students, not the teacher, decide when they have something to contribute, and they can speak directly to one another and not just through the teacher.

Third, the talk-story form of discussion maintains a balance between the speaking rights of the teacher and students. While the talk-story form permits students to construct their own themes, it does not prevent the teacher from guiding the discussion and presenting her own thoughts. At times the teacher may choose to help students explore their chosen themes, while at other times she may choose to advance her own insights. In this lesson, the talk-story form allowed both the students' and teacher's themes to be explored. As a result, both students and teacher achieved their purposes during the discussion.

All students come to literature discussions with a rich store of knowledge and experiences, many of them gained at home. I have seen that when teachers draw on students' existing knowledge and conduct discussions in culturally familiar forms, students have the opportunity to explore literature in a deep and meaningful way. I believe that talk story and other culturally familiar forms of discussion can support collaboration and a genuine exchange of ideas about literature among teacher and students.

References

Au, K.H. (1980). Participation structures in a reading lesson with Hawaiian children: Analysis of a culturally appropriate instructional event. *Anthropology and Education Quarterly*, 11, 91–115.

Au, K.H. (1992). Constructing the theme of a story. *Language Arts*, 69, 106–111.

Au, K.H., & Mason, J.M. (1981). Social organizational factors in learning to read: The balance of rights hypothesis. *Reading Research Quarterly*, 17, 115–152.

Boggs, S.T. (1972). The meaning of questions and narratives to Hawaiian children. In C. Cazden, V. John, & D. Hymes (Eds.), *Functions of language in the classroom* (pp. 299–327). New York: Teachers College Press.

Center for the Study of Reading (1990). *Teaching reading: Strategies from successful classrooms*. Six-part videotape series. Urbana-Champaign, IL: University of Illinois.

Erickson, F., & Shultz, J. (1982). *The counselor as gatekeeper: Social interaction in interviews*. New York: Academic.

Gallimore, R., Boggs, J.W., & Jordan, C. (1974). *Culture, behavior and education: A study of Hawaiian-Americans*. Newbury Park, CA: Sage.

Lehr, S.S. (1991). *The child's developing sense of theme: Responses to literature*. New York: Teachers College Press.

Lukens, R.J. (1990). *A critical handbook of children's literature* (4th ed.). Glenview, IL: Scott, Foresman.

Watson, K.A. (1975). Transferable communication routines: Strategies and group identity in two speech events. *Language in Society*, 4, 53–72.

Children's Literature

Bacmeister, R. (1964). Magic in a glass jar. In W.K. Durr, J.M. LePere, & R.H. Brown (Eds.), *Windchimes* (pp. 68–77). Boston, MA: Houghton Mifflin.

CHAPTER 15

Collaborative Story Talk in a Bilingual Kindergarten

Jennifer Battle

The old nun would read from her favorite books, usually biographies of early American presidents. Playfully she ran through complex sentences calling the words alive with her voice, making it seem that the author somehow was speaking directly to me. I smiled just to listen to her. I sat there and sensed for the very first time some possibility of fellowship between a reader and a writer, a communication, never intimate like that I heard spoken words at home convey, but one nonetheless personal.

—Richard Rodríguez, Hunger of Memory (1982, p. 60)

"Read me," she would insist, following me around with the book [The Funny Little Woman, Mosel, 1972] in her hands. Each time I read the story, Akemi repeated more of the dialogue. "My dumpling, my dumpling! Has anyone seen my dumpling?" became Akemi's leitmotif. She had accomplished her first complete English sentence.

—Vivian Paley, Wally's Stories (1981, p. 123)

THE LURE OF literature—its narratives, its sounds, its images—engages second-language learners as it does native English speakers and becomes a pathway to acquiring a new language. Researchers report substantial benefits, including improved scores on sections of standardized tests, for second-language learners from frequent exposure to children's literature (Elley & Mangubhai, 1983; Feitelson et al., 1993; Roser, Hoffman, & Farest, 1990), successful early forays into reading and writing (Farest, 1991; Larrick, 1987), and demonstrations of language growth through, for example, literacy events such as dramatized story retellings (Seawell, 1985). Building evidence attests that, with some adaptations, what is good for native English speakers for learning language and becoming literate is also good for second-language learners. A restricted curriculum, characterized by less than the richest exposure to language, may actually raise obstacles for language acquisition and cognitive development.

What happens when stories are read aloud in English to children who are most comfortable speaking another language? A class of bilingual kindergarten children in Texas taught by Cris Contreras has become deeply involved in the stories she reads to them each day in English. Much like Richard Rodríguez and Vivian Paley's Akemi, the native Spanish speakers in this classroom connect with the stories. They respond, ask questions about illustrations and characters, and share personal experiences. Ms. Contreras is a teacher who demonstrates that good stories invite good talk, that good talk represents clear thought, and that language learning is tied to both.

Creating a Context for Language Learning with Story Time

Ms. Contreras makes her classroom a friendly place to investigate topics through literature. Children nap with books, listen to books, reenact books, and take books home to read. They explore a great variety of literature in many ways. A library center prominently located near the area rug where the children gather for story reading provides easy access to bookshelves and cozy places with pillows to sit on while browsing. To supplement the permanent classroom collection, Ms. Contreras brings in books (both in English and Spanish) from the public library. These books reflect the theme or topic of units currently under

study—whether science, social studies, or literature. The stories Ms. Contreras reads aloud also relate to the hands-on experiences and fieldtrips that support a deeper understanding of a particular topic (for example, bones or seeds). She gives special attention to selecting the books read aloud—books that will engage her students and that are appropriate for their interests. Ms. Contreras wants her second-language learners to have excellent language models, so she is careful to select books with high-quality text. She also wants to stimulate lively conversations, so she chooses books with positive representations of ethnic groups, strong thematic content, and stimulating illustrations.

In this classroom filled with books and stories, Ms. Contreras reserves a special time after lunch to read aloud to her students. Her first purpose is always for children to enjoy these stories: "My main objective is to nurture a love of reading," she says emphatically. She reads from books that tie into a literary unit—groups of related books organized into sets by author, genre, theme, or topic. The children talk before, during, and after the read-aloud, but they also respond in other ways. For example, the day she read *Angelina Ballerina* by Katharine Holabird, Ms. Contreras added a pink ballet tutu to the housekeeping center for children to slip on to become a dancer. Children used green construction paper to fashion Peter Pan hats for themselves the day they read Mary Hoffman's *Amazing Grace*. And the day they listened to *The Girl Who Loved Wild Horses* by Paul Goble, they took their stick horses with stuffed paper heads to the park for a good run.

Most of all, though, Ms. Contreras creates a classroom environment where it is safe to talk. She seems to accomplish this in three overlapping ways. First, she carefully avoids correcting children's language. To ensure that they feel comfortable voicing their ideas, Ms.

Cover illustration from Paul Goble's The Girl Who Loved Wild Horses. *Illustration ©1978 by Paul Goble. Reprinted by permission of Macmillan Books for Young Readers, an imprint of Simon & Schuster Children's Publishing Division.*

Contreras makes no overt demands on the children's language production. Instead, she encourages them to share their thoughts and commends them for their efforts. She responds to children's messages in ways that demonstrate her interest in what they have to say, rather than in which language forms they use.

Second, Ms. Contreras encourages children to ask questions, make observations, and give their opinions throughout story reading events. She values their responses, and they are eager participants. Perhaps one of the most pronounced characteristics of Ms. Contreras's story sharing style is her way of accepting children's responses. After inviting responses, she fixes her attention on the speaker. Even when

a child's story talk falters or when responses are cryptic, her attention demonstrates her interest in ideas and seems to help children gain confidence with their new language, however hesitantly, in the group setting. She provides support for children to communicate their ideas in other ways as well: at times she accepts children's responses by repeating or paraphrasing their language; at other times, following the children's lead, she adds interesting bits of related information or pulls their ideas together.

Third, Ms. Contreras does not *require* the children to talk during story time; participation in story time is strictly optional. However, most of the children are eager participants—perhaps because of the frequent opportunities to speak and the comfortable atmosphere. Throughout story reading events, children make comments and ask questions. When Ms. Contreras finishes reading, she invites still more ideas. Open-ended questions such as, "How did this story make you feel?" or "Tell me what you thought about this story" prove irresistible for children's participation. Although they take advantage of opportunities to discuss, several children confide they still have more to talk about.

All this support, encouragement, listening, and patience pay off. The following conversation illustrates how Ms. Contreras supports responses by collaborating with the children as they discuss the emergence of the first mammals on earth after reading Jan Brett's *The First Dog*.

> Joseph: A long, long time ago there used to be [dinosaurs] and they died.
>
> Ms. C: A long, long time ago there were dinosaurs. Then all the dinosaurs...
>
> Pedro: Died.
>
> Sky: Caput.
>
> Ms. C: Died. They passed away. Yes. Then there were...were there people when there were dinosaurs?

Yvonne: No. Yes!

Ms. C: No.

Pedro: Cave people.

Ms. C: No. No, there weren't.

Pedro: When they died, then they will...

Yvonne: Then the cave people came.

Ms. C: Then after all the dinosaurs died, then there were cave people. There were people that lived in caves. Después que murieron todos los dinosaurios... [After all the dinosaurs died...]

Victor: Salieron los hombres—las personas. [Men appeared—the people.]

Ms. C: Habían personas que vivían en cuevas. Por eso les nombraban así "Cave man, cave woman, cave boy." "Cave" es una cueva. [There were people that lived in caves. That's why they called them "Cave man, cave woman, cave boy." "Cave" is a cave.]

Adam: A cave...cave...cave.

Ms. C: Está gente vivía durante el tiempo que habían los primeros animales. [These people lived during the time when there were the first animals.]

Pedro: Cave teachers.

Ms. Contreras also asks children to elaborate on their responses, guiding children to support their ideas, as in this conversation she had with Yvonne about *Amazing Grace*:

Ms. C: She's [Grace's] practicing. Está practicando.

Yvonne: She don't know what to be.

Ms. C: She likes being everything. If this is what you want to do, all you have to do is...

Yvonne: Practice.

Ms. C: Practice and work hard.

Yvonne: And "put your mind to it."

Ms. C: Have you heard that line before?

Yvonne: It was in the book.

Ms. C: It was in the book? Was it in the book?

Yvonne: Yes.

Ms. C: I don't remember those words in the book.

Yvonne: Read it.

Ms. C: Maybe you heard it from "The Little Mermaid?"

Yvonne: No. It's in the book.

It was not long before Yvonne (with the help of the book) convinced Ms. Contreras, and her pleased teacher encouraged her to talk further about what made this story idea important.

So Much to Notice and So Much to Say

Ms. Contreras and her bilingual kindergarten children discuss a wide range of topics that seem important, interesting, or new to them. They talk about book features, such as the Caldecott Medal and even the books' publication dates; they talk about book language—its rhyme, lilt, and meaning; they talk about illustrations; and they talk about literary elements—characters, setting, and plot. Two things happen in these conversations that seem especially central to the language learning that occurs. The first is the willingness of the children to "connect" with the story and to express those personal associations. The second is the collaborative effort that story "talkers" engage in to make meaning—to interpret the text together.

Personal Associations

Ms. Contreras models personal associations with literature by telling life stories, demonstrating how the read-aloud stories are intimately connected to her life as teacher and mother. Her responses show the children that

Illustration from Abiyoyo *by Pete Seeger. Illustration* ©1986 *by Michael Hays. Reprinted by permission of Macmillan Books for Young Readers, an imprint of Simon & Schuster Children's Publishing Division.*

she values reading children's literature as a time to think about her world and what is important to her. To introduce *The Art Lesson* by Tomie dePaola, Ms. Contreras brought in her collection of books by dePaola and his poster of familiar nursery rhymes that she intended to hang in her son's room:

> All of these books are mine, because you know what? I love the way he draws. This is what I'm going to hang in Elias's room. But before I hang it up, I wanted to show it to you.

Even more important, Ms. Contreras helps children bring *their* story associations to the surface. She helps them recall classroom or life experiences that connect with the theme

of a story or a character's feelings. She prods gently for instances in which the children have had occasion to feel the same way. The conversation presented here is part of a discussion about *Abiyoyo* by Pete Seeger. Rogelio explains that when the townspeople ostracize the boy and his father, he feels sad for them:

Ms. C: Why does it make you feel sad?

Rogelio: Because they [the townspeople] made them live on the edge of town.

Ms. C: That's right. They told them, "You have to go to the edge of town. You can't live with us anymore." It's kind of like when I tell you you have to go stand at the fence. How does that make you feel?

Rogelio: Sad.

Ms. C: Sad. That means I remove you. I make you go away (many children groan loudly).

Ms. C: Because...was the father following the rules?

Rogelio: No!

Ms. C: No. He was tricking people, and they didn't like it.

Pedro: And the boy was making too much noise.

Through opportunities to identify with and share personal experiences, the children come to realize how they are similar to the characters in their stories. They had nearly all experienced being scared when spending the night at a friend's house—just like Ira in Bernard Waber's *Ira Sleeps Over*:

Adam: My mom, she didn't like me...um... going my friend, but...but she now learned that I'm big. I can go.

Ms. C: When you're older, you're gonna spend the night with your friend.

Katherine: Una vez me dió miedo a la casa de Fernanda, una amiga. [One time I got scared at Fernanda's house. She's a friend.]

Ms. C: Fernanda? María Fernanda? Yo la conozco. Fuiste a la casa de ella? [I know her. Did you go to her house?]

Family Pictures by Carmen Lomas Garza stimulated personal associations for the teacher as well as the children. In the following conversation, however, these urban children seem somewhat removed from the chicken killing scene in Lomas Garza's book. Nevertheless, they still love to eat "caldo":

JoJo: I ate one chicken. My grandma made it.

Ms. C: Now when your mother makes some chicken, where does she get that chicken? Does she go out to the backyard and kill a chicken?

Juan: You buy it from HEB [a local food market].

Joseph: We go to Popeye's.

Sky: Because there wasn't no store there.

Ms. C: Aquí estan matando la gallina. Mira. [Here they're killing the chicken. Look.] I saw this happen once. I didn't want to look anymore. My mama did this. We had chickens and my mama got one and she picked it up by the head and she swung it like this....

Pedro: Ugh. And it died.

Ms. C: Yeah. Yeah. It died. And then she dipped it in water, and guess what fell off?

Child: What?

Pedro: The head?

Ms. C: The feathers. Then they cut the head off, and then they cleaned it. They took off all the feathers.

Sky: Teacher, don't say that gross stuff. I hate it.

Ms. C: Del pollo van a hacer caldo de pollo. [With the chicken they are going to make chicken soup.]

Children: Mmmmm.

Ibeth: I love caldo.

Joseph: When they get the chicken neck and they swing it around, that breaks the neck.

Children's talk about personal and classroom experiences they share provides them with a rich way to connect with stories. Their conversations illuminate the children's deep involvement in the stories through their identification with, and empathy for, the characters and their problems. Talking about stories gives these bilingual Mexican American children a chance to reflect on their own lives and to express those reflections. Both children and teacher learn more about the stories and one another—each individual's tastes, dreams, problems, and talents.

Interpretive Conversations

Just as native language speakers respond to stories on many levels (Martinez et al., 1992; McGee, 1992), so do these bilingual children demonstrate insights that represent inference and interpretation. Besides engaging in lively conversations that follow the plot action, these children speculate beyond the story events. For example, in the following excerpt Pedro is particularly concerned for the safety of the young cave boy in *The First Dog* because the boy had to spend the night in a tree to avoid a threatening saber-toothed tiger:

Ms. C: Why do you think he [Kip] spent the night in the tree?

JoJo: 'Cause they were friends.

Sky: 'Cause there was trouble all around him.

Ms. C: Right. He didn't know if he [the saber-toothed tiger] was gone or not. Se quedó en el árbol. Tenía miedo. Toda la noche se quedó en el árbol. En la madrugada es cuando habló con el perro. [He stayed in the tree. He was afraid. All night he stayed in the tree. At dawn is when he talked to the dog.]

Pedro: What about...uh...why did the mom didn't call him?

Yvonne: Where's the mom?

Ms. C: There's another good question. Where *is* his mom?

Juan: At home.

Ms. C: Maybe she's at home cooking.

Roberto: I know where she is...

Alondra: There's no telephone.

Roberto: She's at the end of the page. [The last illustration in the story shows a pic-ture of the people Kip lived with near a cave.]

Ms. C: She's at the end of the page?

Alondra: There's no telephones.

Ms. Contreras recapitulates in Spanish this distressing story event sparked by Pedro's concern for the whereabouts of Kip's mom when Kip is in such danger. She turns the question back to the group for pondering. Several children offer to explain why Kip's mom did not call her son back to the cave. The children's involvement in the story seems to spur their collaborative grappling with and negotiation of ideas.

These kindergartners are learning to listen to one another's notions about a situation and to pose alternatives in a conversational style. Sometimes they explore a possible solution to a character's problem or hypothesize explanations for a character's actions. They build on classmates' responses and seem to come to a deeper understanding of the story. These interpretive conversations occur at critical moments in the story conflict or when strong personal associations are evoked. For example, in the following conversation about the story *Angelina Ballerina*, the children work together to explain the motivation behind Angelina's remarkable change in behavior (Angelina's parents have signed her up for ballet lessons and bought her a tutu. Suddenly Angelina is keeping her room clean, and she is no longer late for dinner or for school.):

Ms. C: Ahora sí está escuchando lo que dice su mamá. Le está haciendo caso y cuando su mamá le dice, rápido lo hace. [Now she is really listening to what her mother says. She is minding her, and when her mother tells her, she does it quickly.]

Pedro: You know why she does it?

Ms. C: Why?

Pedro: If she don't do it, they might take her out.

Yvonne: No...

Joseph: The mother or the father might take her out.

Ms. C: You think they might take her out of the class?

Sky: She did it because she is happy now because she is in the dance class.

Yvonne: She wants to do it because she is too happy that she is going to school, and she's doing everything what her Mom says.

Ms. C: Katherine?

Katherine: Cuando no lo hace ella, le van a llevar back el vestido. [When she doesn't do it, they're going to take the tutu back.]

Ms. C: ¡Que suerte! Joseph? [What luck!]

Joseph: She wants to do that.

Ibeth: When they bought that ballet dress that's what they did for her. If she didn't want to help or go to school, and then they would take it back.

Response in Two Languages

These children are grouped according to language dominance for language arts, science, social studies, and math instruction. However, during story time Ms. Contreras gathers all the children around her rocker and uses both English and Spanish to share stories and guide story talk. The children express their thoughts in the language they choose spontaneously. Their language proficiencies in English and Spanish, as revealed by testing conducted at the school, range broadly between non-Spanish, limited-English speaker to non-English, fluent Spanish speaker. The demands of communication in two languages during story time affect both the teacher and the children. When there are speakers of two languages in a classroom, neither of which speak the others' language, adaptations can be made to traditional story time routines to accommodate these language differences. For Ms. Contreras, it makes sense to summarize each story in Spanish before reading each aloud in English. This modification of a typical story time routine seems to provide support for the children who have not yet developed a sufficient level of proficiency in English. Ms. Contreras explains:

I'm asking my English speakers to do what my Spanish speakers do all the time. I have found there is definitely an advantage to telling the story first in Spanish and then reading it in English. I don't have to stop and translate. I mean, it made the children think in both languages, which I thought was great. I feel like being in this classroom they know that their language is valued. I feel like they don't stop learning Spanish. It's there. They appreciate it. They want to speak it, and they come with more of a background than a child who doesn't speak Spanish at home.

Although both languages are used to communicate feelings, opinions, and ideas, it is interesting that most of the teacher's and the children's talk during story time is in English, regardless of language dominance. Alejandro and Arturo speak Spanish exclusively during story time. Victor, on the other hand, speaks Spanish most of the time—except when he chants story refrains. Hector and Katherine respond in speech characterized by code-switching within utterances—using both languages in the same sentence. The remainder of the children speak predominantly in English. The teacher, however, takes responsibility to support bilingual understanding of the story by moving freely and regularly between the two languages as she feels it necessary.

Language Awareness

Involvement in story talk also stimulates conversations that focus more directly on puzzlement *about* language, such as the print children notice in the books. In Ms. Contreras's class the children began to notice rhyming sounds and interesting language: when she displayed the illustration of Tommy's twin aunts in Tomie dePaola's *The Art Lesson*, they talked about similar-sounding Spanish words:

Ms. C: Oh! Look at these.

Yvonne: They're both the same.

Ms. C: What are they?

Sky: They're twins!

Pedro: They're Chinese.

Ms. C: They're twins. Éstas son primas que son "cuatas."

Juan: Son "cuates."

Ms. C: Son "cuatas." When they're girls, they're called "cuatas."

Ibeth: One day we went to a flea market. There was a man who have "cuetes."

Ms. C: Oh, "cuetes." Cuetes and cuates sound alike. That's firecrackers.

These conversations about language also demonstrated the children's awareness and sensitivity to language form. In the following conversation, for example, Victor recites in Spanish the refrain contained in the story of *The Little Red Hen* by Paul Galdone. Ibeth, who is also a fluent Spanish speaker, picks up on a language form that does not sound quite right to her:

Victor: Yo no, dijo el gato. Yo no, dijo el perro. Yo no dijo *la* ratón.

Ibeth: La rata!

Translations

In this class the members collaborate in supporting meaning making across two lan-

Illustration from Tomie dePaola's The Art Lesson. ©1989 *by Tomie dePaola. Reprinted by permission of The Putnam Publishing Group.*

guages. Translation is one major way in which understanding among classmates is fostered. Although the teacher takes primary responsibility in this area, the children contribute either by requesting or providing translations when they identify a need. Informal translation takes place within conversations that focus on a specific topic relating to a story, such as seeking clarification about an illustration, as in this example from the discussion of *Abiyoyo*:

Juan: What's that red stuff?

Yvonne: That red stuff is blood.

Katherine: Es sangre. [It's blood.]

Pedro: Look at the sangre! It looks like sangre, that red...

Ms. C: It does look like sangre.

Enactments

In addition, Ms. Contreras and the children use nonverbal demonstrations (enactments) within their conversations, which provide another vehicle for supporting communication across two languages. Physical movements or actions represent concrete examples of the significance of story concepts, words, or ideas. The teacher often uses this type of demonstration to illustrate such character actions as "to sigh" or "to sniff." These demonstrations give the children a chance to engage by imitating the movement. Not only is dramatic enactment consistent with the observations of young children's responses made by Hickman (1981) in her benchmark study, it may also help seal meanings for children acquiring their second language.

Some Suggestions

Cris Contreras and her bilingual kindergartners show that when children's ideas are invited, accepted, and valued, there is opportunity for children to become collaborative language learners and meaning makers in a classroom community. A second language seems best acquired in learning environments that acknowledge communication and meaning as central to the learning experience. Students' motivation to communicate in Cris's class is enhanced by quality stories carefully chosen to provide excellent language models, story problems or thematic substance worth discussing together, and a teacher eager to share and receive. Allowing children to freely use their two languages to respond to stories validates their native language, enhances the cognitive development so crucial to academic success, and gives greater opportunity to demonstrate language competence. Because Cris's classroom provides an environment in which students' anxiety is low, her students are eager participants in story discussions. When teachers like Cris open discussion to

children's original expressed thoughts and feelings, the children are more likely to become bilingual learners.

References

Elley, W.B., & Mangubhai, F. (1983). The impact of reading on second language learning. *Reading Research Quarterly, 19*, 53–67.

Farest, C. (1991). *Talking and writing authors: Hispanic kindergarten children write in a literature-rich classroom.* Unpublished doctoral dissertation, University of Texas, Austin.

Feitelson, D., Goldstein, Z., Iraqi, J., & Share, D. (1993). Effects of listening to story reading on aspects of literacy acquisition in a diglossic situation. *Reading Research Quarterly, 28*, 70–79.

Hickman, J. (1981). A new perspective on response to literature: Research in an elementary school setting. *Research in the Teaching of English, 15*, 343–354.

Larrick, N. (1987). Illiteracy starts too soon. *Phi Delta Kappan, 69*, 184–189.

Martinez, M., Roser, N.L., Hoffman, J.V., & Battle, J. (1992). Fostering book discussion in elementary classrooms through response logs and a response framework. In C.K. Kinzer & D.J. Leu (Eds.), *Literacy research, theory, and practice: Views from many perspectives* (pp. 303–312). Chicago, IL: National Reading Conference.

McGee, L.M. (1992). An exploration of meaning construction in first graders' grand conversations. In C.K. Kinzer & D.J. Leu (Eds.), *Literacy research, theory and practice: Views from many perspectives* (pp. 177–186). Chicago, IL: National Reading Conference.

Paley, V.G. (1981). *Wally's stories.* Cambridge, MA: Harvard University Press.

Rodríguez, R. (1982). *Hunger of memory: The education of Richard Rodríguez.* New York: Bantam.

Roser, N.L., Hoffman, J.V., & Farest, C. (1990). Language, literature, and at-risk children. *The Reading Teacher, 43*, 554–559.

Seawell, R.P. (1985). *A micro-ethnographic study of a Spanish/ English bilingual kindergarten in which literature and puppet play were used as a method of enhancing language growth.* Unpublished doctoral dissertation, University of Texas, Austin.

Children's Literature

Brett, J. (1988). *The first dog.* San Diego, CA: Harcourt Brace.

dePaola, T. (1989). *The art lesson.* New York: Putnam.

Galdone, P. (1973). *The little red hen.* New York: Clarion.

Goble, P. (1978). *The girl who loved wild horses*. New York: Macmillan.

Garza, C.L. (1990). *Family pictures: Cuadros de Familia*. San Francisco, CA: Children's Press.

Hoffman, M. (1991). *Amazing Grace*. New York: Dial.

Holabird, K. (1983). *Angelina ballerina*. New York: Potter.

Mosel, A. (1972). *The funny little woman*. New York: Dutton.

Seeger, P. (1963). *Abiyoyo*. New York: Macmillan.

Waber, B. (1972). *Ira sleeps over*. Boston, MA: Houghton Mifflin.

CHAPTER 16

Our Journey Toward Better Conversations About Books

Veronica González, Linda D. Fry, Sylvia Lopez, Julie V. Jordan, Cynthia L. Sloan, and Diane McAdams

"Literature offers us images to think with."

—Chambers, 1985, p. 3

WE HAVE ALWAYS believed in the power of teachers and students learning together. This belief affects how we teach across all subject areas, especially language arts. Most recently, we have become more involved with our students in literature study—exploring our varied interpretations of stories and books through discussion and writing—and it has been an exciting time. For the past few years, we have systematically planned our daily read-aloud time to maximize its effect. Whether we call it story time or read-aloud, it has evolved in each of our classrooms from a teacher-directed activity to a child-centered experience, from too little time to ponder a good story to a blocked time for thinking, writing, and talking about literature. We feel we are moving together toward richer conversations

in our classrooms—now places where ideas are welcomed, explored, and supported—from the kindergarten classes all the way down the hall to the upper elementary classes.

Because we teach at different grade levels (kindergarten, first, second, and fourth), we believe that much of what we have learned applies broadly. We hope that this "story" of our experiences will be useful to others who quest for better ways to share literature and to initiate and conduct better book talk with children.

Where We Started

Children's literature has always been a part of all our classrooms, but we now realize that it was not a constant and strong part of our lives. On the surface we were doing the right things to promote book talk: for example, we had classroom libraries, and we read aloud to our students. In kindergarten, we chose books to support children's learning in math, science, and social studies and planned extension activities based on stories read aloud. At the primary level, story time was also a daily event in which the children talked about the stories as they answered our (often knowledge-based) questions. By fourth grade, read-aloud time was, at best, a few minutes after lunch when there was time. After reading a chapter (or sometimes only part of a chapter because of time constraints), the children would sigh, the teacher would apologize, and the class would move on to the "real" curriculum. Occasionally, good readers were assigned a novel to read on their own, and corresponding worksheets promised to help with the tasks of introducing vocabulary and monitoring comprehension chapter by chapter. At none of the grade levels did we make time to *really* talk about books, as the children and the stories deserved. We were frustrated because some of the children who should have been avid readers were not; many of the children were finding too little time to read; many of the children did not have good reasons to think and express that thinking precisely; and lots of the children needed more support for their reading and writing than they were getting—especially the social and collaborative support that comes from interacting with peers. We wanted children to share our passion for good stories, but we were not quite convincing them we meant it.

Language to Literacy: The Beginning

In 1989 our district began offering extensive inservice training in a literature project called Language to Literacy (see Roser, Hoffman, & Farest, 1990, for a description), and we knew immediately that we had found something we could work with to address our concerns. Language to Literacy, as also described in Chapter 8, is a read-aloud program in which stories are organized into units centering around a theme, genre, topic, or an author's or illustrator's works. Each unit for primary-age children came to us in a tidy book bag, containing a minimum of ten quality children's picture books designed for a "one-a-day" read during a two-week period. A guide for each of the units suggested open-ended discussion prompts, language-centered extension activities, and a bibliography of related books. For middle graders, the units focused on the thematic connections among selected novels or chapter books as well as related reading materials. The focusing book was to be read aloud by the teacher, with the children either reading along in their own copies (from the book bag) or forming book clubs to read from thematically related books.

We looked forward to the part of the unit guide that suggested the format for a huge Language Chart to accompany the unit, which we used in the same way as Roser and Hoffman discuss in Chapter 8. For example, if we read books about mischievous heroes and heroines who use their wits to avoid trouble, three headings on the chart for this "Mischief Maker" unit may be "What was the big trouble?" "How did our hero save the day?" and "What do you think?" Daily, we could enter the books we were reading on the language chart and begin to discover patterns as to how these stories worked and depended on one another.

From the beginning, we displayed the unit books in our classroom library centers, where children were (and still are) encouraged to preview and read even before the books are read aloud to the whole class. In the Language to Literacy read-aloud plan, a new story (or chapter) is introduced; then we reflect and predict together, read aloud to the class, and stay open to discussion before, during, and after. When we first began to use these LtL units, we did just these things and then recorded the children's language on the Language Charts, where our accruing written evidence prompted more comparisons across books. We offered literature extension activities as we found time.

As we began to think of story time as a more cohesive undertaking, our enthusiasm kept pace. Literature was beginning to assume a far more important place in our classrooms, a prominence we had intuitively known it deserved but simply had not quite known how to bestow (while meeting our other obligations). There was no doubt that children were reading and talking and choosing to do both. But we soon found that literature units, comparative book talk, and extensions required more time than we had previously devoted to literature. Because we believed that read-aloud time was important, as did the administration at the district and school levels, we decided to devote some of our reading "instruction" time to reading aloud good books and talking about them in more meaningful ways. Until then, we had kept literature study separate from formal reading instruction time. We went even further: our literature unit studies began to bridge to other subjects, such as science and social studies, and made our language arts program more complete by connecting reading and writing.

There were many other changes that occurred in our classrooms that first year as we began to use the LtL units. Perhaps the most important change was that we felt it "legitimate" to share good literature in the classroom. With this validation, we discovered the value of sharing books in related units. The world of children's literature expanded for our students. They seemed to explore themes more deeply and to develop a much stronger sense of authors—as evidenced by their specific, knowledgeable book requests, their library book choices, their paperback book club orders, and the books they were bringing from home. Many of our students were more motivated to read on their own.

From the beginning, our experiences supported the wisdom of Routman's (1991) observation: "Reading aloud [to children] is...the single most influential factor in young children's success in learning to read" (p. 32). To our delight, the children's interest in reading that was sparked at school was extended to the home. Parents soon began to notice a difference in their children and offered positive comments such as, "I can't believe they're reading so much" or "I can't get his nose out of a book!"

The immediate positive payoffs of using Language Charts were evident from the beginning. The charts were providing support for our book talk as well as major visible advertisement for the value we placed on it in our classrooms. And, as Chapter 8 also verifies, the children *were* talking. In addition, some of the suggested Language Chart structures introduced the children to story elements—setting, character, problem, and so on—so even the youngest students were acquiring the "language of literature." Children's understanding of story structure and literature's universal themes became apparent not only as they talked but also as they wrote their own increasingly well-developed stories.

Despite these pluses, the best use of the Language Charts remained to be discovered. Because they were structured by their headings, the charts were teacher controlled and not very personal. At their worst, they could function like big "worksheets on the wall" filled out by us with suggestions from the children.

Perhaps these predetermined "categories" of comparison too rigidly affected the direction in which talk moved or even cut off more variant responses. So, although the class discussions had moved steps beyond where we had started, we believed that our story and chapter discussions were still less than they *might* be. We reasoned that we could look for part of the solution by altering the prescribed nature of the Language Charts. Still, we had come a long way in just one year; literature was a central feature in our classrooms, and we were talking about that literature, but we were not yet certain we were truly *discussing* it.

Learning to Discuss Stories

During our second and third years implementing thematic literature units, we were invited to join a Language to Literacy collaborative research project and found ourselves in the midst of a terrific support group of teachers and professors who were struggling with the same issues: How can we make story discussions richer and more meaningful? How can we invite the quiet or apprehensive children to participate in discussions? How can we enter the study of literature without leaving its joy?

Introducing Literature Response Journals

Together we began to look for ways to encourage children to enter literature more fully and to participate more actively in literature discussion. We knew we wanted more of them to share, support, and negotiate their genuine responses. We knew we wanted to preserve the personal meanings and connections that children made, and we knew that we wanted them to talk together without so much teacher-child-teacher interaction. We decided to add response journals to our literature study. Our

research team talked about advantages and misuses of journals. We wondered if giving all children some quiet minutes after reading a story or chapter to write their own ideas might give those ideas time to form and be a way to preserve them until they could be shared.

To introduce the literature response journals into the literature units, we bound sturdy colored paper with plastic ring bindings into journals that almost immediately seemed to serve as a catalyst for writing. After reading a story (or chapter) from a particular unit, we directed the children to "take just a few minutes to write what you are thinking or feeling about the book." We modeled for the students by busily writing in our own journals as they wrote in theirs and by sharing our journals as a member of the group. After writing for only a few minutes in these personal response journals, we gathered on the rug or in the classroom library center to talk. The children proudly read verbatim from their journals—something we had not anticipated. Kindergartners, at the beginning of the year, scribbled and drew their thoughts but nevertheless "read" solemnly from their entries during discussion. They also were eager to share and discuss their entries.

The introduction of response journals seemed an important change in our story time procedures. The journals connected reading to writing, extended the meaning of the text, and seemed to give the children more ownership of their literary experience. With the use of response journals, children had the opportunity for the first time to hear some of their peers' original thoughts about stories. Still, we suspected that the children's thinking about literature was richer and more varied than their written responses revealed. Many of those initial responses were statements such as, "I like the part...," "This is a good story," or "I like the illustrations." Then we introduced a second variation in our literature unit studies: we stopped interrogating children and simply issued invitations to talk. Over time, though, we noticed a change. The second grader whose journal is reproduced in the figure on the next page wrote in response to Tomie dePaola's *The Kids' Cat Book* in October (on the left of the figure) and in March. Not all these changes, we felt, could be explained by development alone. This student's response demonstrates a sophisticated literary critique initiated by an invitation to reflect on the literature.

Reconsidering Our Invitations to Talk

Influenced by Chambers (1985) who writes about giving children open-ended invitations to express their views about stories,

we began to initiate book talk by encouraging children to share what they noticed about a story—what they most wanted to say. With them gathered around us, journals in hand, we at first stayed active to keep the talk more collaborative than just a variety of responses by the students without a continuous thread of dialogue and interpretation. "Who else *noticed* something like Robert did?" we would ask. Now, as we look back, we think we were teaching conversational skills more intently than we were launching "literary arrows" (see also Chapter 2). Even so, our children's observational powers seemed to take some leaps:

"Did you notice, Teacher, that the colors of the edges are the same as in the picture?" asked a kindergartner examining *I Am Eyes Ni Macho*, a panoply of African scenes by Leila Ward.

Illustration from I Am Eyes Ni Macho *by Leila Ward, illustrated by Nonny Hogrogrian. Illustrations ©1978 by Nonny H. Kherdian. Reprinted by permission of Greenwillow Books, a division of William Morrow & Company, Inc.*

González et al.

The Kids Cat Book

I liked the .Crulie hair cats. Theiry whiskers are even Crulcd. And when the cats and mice were raped up. The book was fun to read,

The Kid's Cat Book

3-2-92

This story is very interesting. My favorite parts are when he goes home with all the cats and cats. I also like when all the mice and cats were waped up. This book teaches you alot about cats. In the back of the book it tells you 8 interesting things about cats. I also like some of the illustrations a lot. This book has lots of links to literature they are

The Paion Books, The Cloud Art Lesson, The Cloud Book and lots more. They are all by Tomie de Paola and a lot of imformation. because of them give you information.

"Yes," the teacher answered her, "I think we might try to do some art with border patterns."

"I love Africa," one student sighed with satisfaction.

"Do you?" asked the teacher. "Tell us why."

"Because," came the confident reply, "Africa copied the zoo!" [A child-initiated discussion ensued as to just how Africa and the zoo are alike.]

Again influenced by Chambers and our research team discussions, we also talked to our classes about aspects of the story that still puzzled *us*, that seemed unresolved or open to interpretation: for example, we might say, "I'm still wondering why Maniac (from Jerry Spinelli's *Maniac Magee*) was willing to go home with Amanda at the end of the book. I can't help thinking things in the neighborhood hadn't been totally resolved." Children, too, began to talk about what they wondered about or puzzled over. From illustration to plot to theme, we considered unresolvable issues together and tried to untangle things to understand.

As a third part of our "framework" of invitations to talk, we recalled our own personal satisfactions and connections with the books' incidents and images or thought aloud about other books that the story reminded us of. We prompted children's personal connections with the story's meaning or their ideas about related pieces of literature, again modeling aloud: for instance, we might say, "Dicey (from *Dicey's Song* by Cynthia Voigt) and Maniac seem alike in a lot of ways."

The children's observations, wonderings, and links to life and literature shaped the discussion in new ways, probably because they had new ways to think about literature, which we saw evidence of in their journals. In response to E. B. White's *Charlotte's Web*, Paul wrote:

I thought this book was sad at the end. because he said no one would every take his Charlotte's

place and when Charlotte died. I'm wondering how come spiders don't get to see their kids.

In response to Arthur Ransome's *The Fool of the World and the Flying Ship*, Danielle connected with a life experience and wrote in her journal:

This book remins me about when I was 3 I tought you coughd fly without any thing I trad the first time I scrched my nee seond time I fell on my nose and fanilly I said. I CWIT.

Lin's journal showed connection with *Leo the Late Bloomer* by Robert Kraus:

Leo was a late bloomer he got his grort sput at his right time. Right now I have need of a growt spurt.

Travis used his journal to think about how he might respond if he were Toad of *Frog and Toad* by Arnold Lobel:

I like this book I have read it a lot of times but I still like it I like the part when toad was yelling at his seeds I wd never do that I don't think my seeds at home are growing but I'm not going to yell at them to grow.

We noticed, too, that when we began to write and talk about *our* own personal connections with the literature, our willingness to share seemed to influence the children's talk and writing. During the first quiet minutes when the story was finished, Alison wrote in response to Deborah Nourse Lattimore's Aztec myth, *The Flame of Peace*:

The book has to many lord. The picture are weared. The numbers are weared. The book is similer to *Legened of the Blue Bonet*. I like this book very much. I think the boy is brave and clever.

During story talk, Ronnie González (Alison's teacher and one of the authors of this chapter) talked about her own reactions to the story, which she wrote in her own journal:

This story made me think of my Mexican heritage and the thought that I am part Aztec, also. It made me feel very proud to know that Two Flint had brought peace to the Aztec people....

Later, Alison opened her journal page to add to her entry, writing excitedly, "My Great great Grama is Azteck indian!"

The changes we made in discussion procedures seemed to encourage children to share their responses more freely. We were beginning to see more talk at all levels. We experimented with different seating arrangements so that the students could sit face to face. Linda, who teaches fourth grade, arranged her desks in a U-shape. Children in primary grades scooted to sit in a wider circle on the story rug. We teachers realized that we needed to be just another member of these conversational groups rather than their autocratic leaders. It worked: discussions were becoming conversations, with children speaking about what was important to them, talking with one another, and building on previous remarks.

The changes we made by introducing journals and the adapted conversational "framework" soon began to affect the way we used the Language Charts as well. Some of us took broad invitations ("What did you notice or observe?" "What are you wondering about?" and "What are you reminded of?") and adapted them to general headings for our charts—"Observations," "Wonderings," and "Connections." In some of our classrooms, we labeled "Connections" as "Links to Literature and Life." At times, we removed headings and simply captured what children had to say.

Some of us divided our classes into small discussion groups to follow up on the larger class discussions. Certain children became scribes for the groups to capture the most salient ideas from the large group discussion as well as the intimate reflections of the small

Cover illustration from William Armstrong's Sounder. ©1969 by William Armstrong. Illustrations ©1969 by James Barkley. Reprinted by permission of HarperCollins Publishers.

group. The Language Charts now held what children had decided to record—still in their language but now in their written conventions as well. In second grade and higher, the children took over the production of the entire chart—words and illustrations. As an example, compare the Language Charts (on the next page) of fourth graders' responses to *Sounder* by William Armstrong from two different years—the first chart using the more focused format and the second, an open-ended alternative.

Sounder by William H. Armstrong	
How does the boy feel about his dog?	What do you think the boy wants?
He feels Sound is a good dog.	He wants to learn to read.
He is worried about Sounder starving.	He wants the dog to live.
The boy feels sad.	
He's sad because can't find Sounder's body.	He wanted his dad to have a perfect cake.
He's still missing him and he wants him home.	He wants his father out of jail.
He feels sorry for Sounder because of the way he looks.	He wants the jailer dead.
He felt bad when Sounder died.	He wants his mom to be happy. He wants to go to school. He wants to learn to read the book he found.

Sounder by William H. Armstrong

I wonder how the white men had found out how the boy's father stole the ham at first. I wonder why whites used to be so mean to blacks.

Why was the man with the red face so careless with a Christmas cake, breaking it up and dropping it on the floor instead of cutting it in half and putting it neatly back into the box?

The boy's father gets sent to the chain gang and the boy goes to look for his dad. How does he feel having all these people being mean to him? It would be scary wandering around for years. The boy's mother must be worried. I would be worried if my kid was gone for years and I didn't know where he was.

This book made me wonder what it would be like to be poor and to have to steal to keep my family alive.

The author makes it sound so real. It's sad. It really makes you wonder what's going to happen. It keeps you on your toes.

This chapter made me think of what it was like back then and how it would be like to be poor. Also, how the food tasted. If it was real and there was barely any food at all, stealing might cross my mind. The punishment would probably be hanging, but I would do it for my wife and children.

I still wonder if the mom will ever turn to her own self again. What I mean is like when she used to read stories to them and talk to them—not like she is doing now because all she is doing now is humming, ignoring them.

I wonder what if would be like if my companion (dog) died. I think it would be even worse if I didn't know if we was dead or alive and I didn't know where he was because he might be suffering.

Some Postscripts

At first we attempted to set a time limit (just five minutes) on getting the children's reactions to a story on paper; however, we found that we ourselves were writing more and more. We were telling children, "Finish writing your thoughts; we have just about a minute left," as we furiously scribbled our own thoughts, reluctant to stop. Because we had wanted to make journal writing enticing and enduring, we deliberately planned to "limit" it through time constraints—stopping before children were ready. We secretly enjoyed their groans when we asked them to stop—it meant we had not overdone a good thing. Although our time limits have become much more flexible, we still see children find moments throughout the day to return to their journals to include additional thoughts (and we smile with satisfaction).

We think the journals are especially helpful to those children who were apprehensive about verbalizing their ideas. Some children just seem to feel more comfortable writing their ideas first—in a personal journal that need not ever be read by another. Those early "discussions," which consisted of reading journal entries aloud, have succumbed to natural conversational flow. Through the years and over time, there is more and better discussion. When disagreements erupt among classmates, they turn to their books and their classmates to garner support. Discussions seem to last longer and are not always resolved to each person's satisfaction—as good discussion may never be. By adapting our strategies, we think we have provided a more challenging (but supportive) environment in which to talk about books.

We believe the whole idea of discussing literature with one another and recalling special memories and thoughts drew our classes closer together. Other changes seemed to occur very naturally in our classrooms, too. Literature study has become the focus of the reading curriculum; classroom libraries are more important than ever. Our children are becoming readers who appreciate the excitement an author can generate. They devour sequels of the read-aloud selections, books by the same author, and books with themes similar to the unit books.

Previously, even the good readers would complete a book and say little more than "That was a good book" before picking up another. With all the changes in the read-aloud program, children read a book and want to find someone with whom they can talk. The use of Language Charts and especially the response journals has greatly changed the way we deal with literature in our classrooms. Story time has evolved from simply a time to read a story and talk briefly about it to an in-depth discussion of literature. Through Language to Literacy, our children have become critical thinkers beyond their years.

We devise our own units now, and each year a new group comes to us and we begin the process anew. Typically, there are a few students who have worked with Language to Literacy teachers in previous years who assume the lead. But around the first of November, it is as though a light turns on in our classrooms. Students begin to really talk with one another. They start asking what we are going to read next. They are no longer looking for "the right answers"; instead, we come together on equal footing to *really* talk about what we are listening to and reading. These children share our passion for good books and good talk.

Notes

The authors wish to express appreciation to Kay Montgomery, principal of Braun Station Elementary, better known as the most requested read-aloud guest in each of our classrooms; to Nora Forester and Kathy Jongsma, who have supported us in many ways; to our faculty who continue to learn with us; and to the rest of our research team—Jim Hoffman, Nancy Roser, and Miriam Martinez.

References

Chambers, A. (1985). *Booktalk: Occasional writing on literature and children*. New York: HarperCollins.

Roser, N.L., Hoffman, J.V., & Farest, C. (1990). Language, literature, and at-risk children. *The Reading Teacher*, 43, 554–559.

Routman, R. (1991). *Invitations: Changing as teachers and learners* K–12. Portsmouth, NH: Heinemann.

Children's Literature

Armstrong, W.H. (1969). *Sounder*. New York: Harper-Collins.

dePaola, T. (1979). *The kids' cat book*. New York: Holiday House.

Kraus, R. (1971). *Leo the late bloomer*. Ill. by J. Aruego. New York: Simon & Schuster.

Lattimore, D. (1987). *The flame of peace; A tale of the Aztecs*. New York: HarperCollins.

Lobel, A. (1979). *Days with Frog and Toad*. New York: HarperCollins.

Ransome, A. (reteller). (1968). *The fool of the world and the flying ship: A Russian tale*. Ill. by U. Shulevitz. New York: Farrar, Straus & Giroux.

Spinelli, J. (1990). *Maniac Magee*. Boston, MA: Little, Brown.

Voigt, C. (1982). *Dicey's song*. New York: Atheneum.

Ward, L. (1978). *I am eyes ni macho*. New York: Morrow.

White, E.B. (1952). *Charlotte's web*. Ill. by G. Williams. New York: HarperCollins.

Other Responses to Literature

CHAPTER 17

Exploring Literature Through Drama

Lee Galda and Jane West

WHEN DOROTHY READ *Mr. Popper's Penguins* by Richard and Florence Atwater to her third grade class, the children spontaneously waddled about the school for several days imitating penguins walking together. When a biography of Helen Keller was hot property among these same students, they pretended to be blind, and some created a sign language by tracing out letters in one another's palms. Children, even those beyond kindergarten, have a natural inclination toward the dramatic. Acting occurs freely in their play. Perceptive teachers can capitalize on children's natural inclination to dramatize and enhance the delight-filled learning it brings about while increasing the joy of experiencing books.

Why Drama?

The spontaneous, unstructured, dramatic play that young children do in a home living room and the games they play in the backyard are similar to the kind of dramatics teachers can sponsor to enhance children's experience of story and let them live a little longer in the spell of a good book (Cullinan & Galda, 1994). Collaborative experiences involving drama as a way of responding to literature promote dialogue among students and between students and teachers that helps students explore and expand their responses to literature (Edmiston, Enciso, & King, 1987; O'Neill, 1989; Verriour, 1985).

Jess and Leslie, the boy and girl best friends in Katherine Paterson's *Bridge to Terabithia*, were masters of dramatic play. Paterson described Jess's psychological transformation as he approached the kingdom of Terabithia, the pair's imaginary world across the creek:

> The closer he came to the dry creek bed and the crab apple tree rope the more he could feel the beating of his heart. He grabbed the end of the rope and swung out toward the other bank with a kind of wild exhilaration and landed gently on his feet, *taller and stronger and wiser in that mysterious land* [italics added] (p. 46).

What happened to Jess as he became a part of the dramatic play with Leslie exemplifies Vygotsky's (1978) notion of play as the creation of an imaginary situation, the game of let's pretend: "In play a child always behaves beyond his average age, above his daily behavior; in play it is as though he were a head taller than himself" (p. 102).

Drama as a form of play in response to story helps children become "taller and stronger and wiser" in a number of ways. Children involved in drama as a response activity learn about literature and language as they explore texts, re-create scenes, become characters, and reflect on their experiences with books. Dramatic response activities lead toward the development of narrative competence, increased literary understanding, increased comprehension, oral language development, and the opportunity for empathetic emotional insight. Through participating in story drama, children experience appreciation of literature through telling, responding to, and analyzing stories. Beginning with social dramatic play in the preschool years, children learn the significant aspects of narrative and narrative structures including beginnings, middles, and endings in terms of both sequence and linguistic markers such as "once upon a time." Other markers, such as the use of the past tense, also appear in children's play and indicate children's understanding of a narrative convention. They learn to distinguish between a story world and the real world; they learn about voice and audience as they read different characters' voices, narrators' voices, and voices that comment on the drama from the audience's point of view (Wolf & Pusch, 1985).

Children who play in response to literature learn a great deal about literature in general as they explore characters and events and consider motivation, point of view, character development, and sequence. Thinking and talking about a book in preparation for dramatic response often brings about deeper understandings of what has been read. Playing about stories also seems to increase children's comprehension of what they read. The opportunity to discuss and reenact stories they have listened to helps children comprehend better than do activities that involve drawing or discussion only (Galda, 1982; Pellegrini & Galda, 1982).

Drama can also serve as an immensely rewarding oral language experience as children plan, recall, argue, and create voices other than their own (Galda, 1984). Playing about stories provides ideas and models for language use, "makes verbalization easy and natural, increases presence of mind, and develops inventiveness" (Moffett, 1968, p. 91). Drama generally improves communicative abilities as children must listen attentively and react, use language to achieve desired effects with their audience, use varied linguistic styles, and shift roles and points of view (Moffett, 1968). The complex language that children use for planning and the decontextualized language that they use for playing are similar to the language they need to use for writing. In these ways, dramatic play may contribute to general language competence (Pellegrini, 1984).

Play also allows children to experience and express feelings in a safe situation as they pretend to be other people in other times and places. This can widen their range of experience and deepen their insights and empathy, which enriches their responses to the books

> "*Children involved in drama as a response activity learn about literature and language as they explore texts, re-create scenes, become characters, and reflect on their experiences with books.*"

they read. While play about fiction enhances emotional understanding, play about nonfiction can do so as well. When children enact events and processes, such as the Cherokee Nation leaving their homes and beginning their journey on the Trail of Tears in the United States, they not only understand more about the complexities of the events, but they also forge stronger emotional connections.

In addition, engaging in story drama enriches children's understanding of physical and emotional aspects of life. When a child pretends to be Rumpelstiltskin and flies into a rage, the emotional content of a rage is experienced by player and audience alike; thus, the concept is better understood than if "rage" is merely read or defined by a teacher (P. S. Koskinen, 1993, personal communication).

Story drama involves all our modes of human communication—reading, writing, speaking, listening, and gesturing. It encourages creativity and facility with the modes of discourse. Story dramatization also involves logical thinking, planning, and effective evaluation of self and others. Drama in response to literature can bring opportunities for expressing, organizing, and clarifying human experiences through the other performing arts—music, dance, and song.

Kinds of Story Drama

There are many forms that dramatic activity can take—pantomime, spontaneous reenactment, interpretation, improvisation, role playing, and Readers Theatre, among others. Whatever form drama takes, it can serve as a compelling invitation to respond to literature.

Pantomime

Pantomime involves conveying meaning or story through facial expressions and body language such as shrugs and gestures. Children should be familiar with what is being pantomimed so that they recognize characteristics that mark the story or character. Whether watching or doing, children involved in pantomime are focused on defining characteristics of a character, story, or scene. To present a pantomime, they must think and talk about how characters look, feel, and act, which involves in-depth thinking about the story.

Reenactment

Reenactment also entails looking back closely at a book after it has been read. Children can talk about the story's significant events as they briefly plan their presentation. This talk provides opportunities for their exploration of sequence, structure, cause and effect, and other issues. Spontaneous reenactment requires no props, costumes, or script. What it does require is thorough familiarity with the story to be reenacted. Children who present the drama must attend to sequence and character language. Children who watch the performance must do so as well and often coach from the audience if a classmate overlooks an important part. Attentive listening is crucial when listening and watching a story's reenactment. Stories from folklore lend themselves to this kind of dramatic response because of their simple, straightforward plots and often melodious, repetitive language. Nonfiction that describes events or processes also can be explored through spontaneous reenactment.

Interpretation

Oral interpretation provides students opportunities for rereading favorite scenes or stories. In these rereadings, the pitch, tone, tempo, and volume of voices alter to suit the characterizations and events. Students discuss the personalities of characters and how those personalities might be reflected in their voices. Effective oral reading as well as literary understanding are encouraged in this response activity.

Improvisation

Improvisation requires students to extrapolate from the story to enact an original scene. It is a way to answer the question that many children ask at the end of a particularly enjoyable story: What happened next? That is, what happened when Goldilocks got home? What happens to Jess and May Belle? Stories with straightforward characterization, such as the stereotypes found in folklore, offer younger students opportunity for successful improvisational experiences. Older children who enjoy stories with more fully developed characters can explore these characters through improvisation as well. In both cases, readers talk about characters—what they are like, how they act, how they feel—as they plan their improvisation and often return to the text to support their ideas or look for additional details.

Role Playing

Role playing also encourages students to probe deeply into characters and explore motivation and point of view as it relates to characters' actions and reactions. Best done with meaningful episodes from memorable stories (both fiction and nonfiction), role playing offers students the opportunity to try on someone else's life, personality, perspective, and voice. Opportunities for interpreting characters' actions, perspectives, and use of language in different ways are present when children respond through role playing.

Readers Theatre

Readers Theatre involves the same kind of close scrutiny of texts, characters, and events and the use of oral language to plan and discuss, but it adds the dimension of writing. In preparing for Readers Theatre children craft a written script that reflects the events and characters they have read about. This activity also requires them to encode *everything* that they want their audience to know because they are not allowed to use movement or gestures to convey meaning. When writing their script children attend closely to the language, deleting unnecessary phrases such as "he said." Through the role of a narrator, they convey necessary information about time, place, and movement.

As we have said, the range of literature-related dramatic response is wide. Simple rhythm and movement experiences can be based on poetry and song. Improvisation or reenactments of stories make more purposeful use of story structure, sequence, and language, while remaining spontaneous and unrehearsed. Role or scene playing is bit more complex, involving more discussion and planning. Readers Theatre makes use of text as script and dramatic interpretation. The most complicated way to use dramatic response is scripted drama in which players memorize lines for their respective parts and perform for an audience. We focus our attention here on a less complicated response mode—improvised and unrehearsed story dramatization in which children take on characters' roles.

Responding Through Story Drama

A secure classroom atmosphere is crucial for ensuring that children feel comfortable when you introduce story drama. They need a relaxed, safe environment in which mistakes are acceptable, people and conventions are flexible, and there is a familiar structure with reasonable limits. It is best if the first story drama you try is short and simple: Cinderella's flight from the ball or Rumpelstiltskin's name being guessed, for examples. Initially, choose children you know will participate fully and well. (These are not necessarily the best readers or writers, the math stars, or those with unblemished behavior.) Get involved yourself if you feel comfortable doing so.

Begin by telling or reading a story. As you talk with the children, note the most important parts of the story. Decide together on an episode to reenact, such as the following passage from *Charlotte's Web* by E. B. White in which Wilbur meets Charlotte face to face for the first time:

> "Salutations!" said the voice.
> Wilbur jumped to his feet. "Salu-what?" he cried.
> "Salutations!" repeated the voice.
> "What are they, and where are you?" screamed Wilbur. "Please, please, tell me where you are. And what are salutations?"
> "Salutations are greetings," said the voice. "When I say 'salutations,' it's just my fancy way of saying hello or good morning. Actually, it's a silly expression, and I am surprised that I used it at all. As for my whereabouts, that's easy. Look up here in the corner of the doorway! Here I am. Look, I'm waving!"
> At last Wilbur saw the creature that had spoken to him in such a kindly way. Stretched across the upper part of the doorway was a big spiderweb, and hanging from the top of the web, head down, was a large grey spider. She was about the size of a gumdrop. She had eight legs, and she was waving one of them at Wilbur in friendly greeting. "See me now?" she asked.
> "Oh, yes indeed," said Wilbur. "Yes indeed! How are you? Good morning! Salutations! Very

pleased to meet you. What is your name, please? May I have your name?"
> "My name," said the spider, "is Charlotte."
> "Charlotte what?" asked Wilbur, eagerly.
> "Charlotte A. Cavatica. But just call me Charlotte."
> "I think you're beautiful," said Wilbur (pp. 35–37).

After deciding on the episode for reenactment, break it into segments: unseen, Charlotte greets Wilbur; Wilbur sees Charlotte waving; Charlotte reveals her name. Next, analyze the characters' emotions, motivations, and physical appearances: Why did Charlotte decide to befriend Wilbur? Why was Wilbur so excited to meet her? How did Wilbur feel when he finally saw Charlotte? What made Charlotte so beautiful to Wilbur? How did Charlotte look waving from the web? How did Wilbur react physically when he saw her? Then, determine the setting: Where are Charlotte and Wilbur in this scene? How does the barn play a part in what happens? Talking about books in this way leads children back into the book and allows them to delve more deeply into the stories they have created as they read.

After this initial discussion and planning, allow students to choose actors and plan for five or ten minutes before going "on stage." Do the scene several times, letting different children take turns at the parts.

As you plan and do story drama, begin in individual response and move into collaborative literary analysis. Kindergarten children who consider how the three billy goats Gruff and the troll sound and move are going through the same process as are older students who consider what they have read to plan improvisations or Readers Theatre based on a scene from *Bridge to Terabithia*. Like any worthwhile response activity, story drama takes readers deeper into the book they have read.

Illustration from Jeanette Winter's Follow the Drinking Gourd. ©1988 *by Jeanette Winter. Reprinted by permission of Alfred A. Knopf, Inc.*

Story Drama Across the Curriculum

Folktales and other stories are great material for dramatic playing, but, as mentioned earlier, drama need not be restricted to fiction. Drama is also an excellent way to experience content area "stories" such as those of the invention of the telephone, the discovery of penicillin, or the experiences of immigrants as they have moved from one country to another. In the latter case, taking others' viewpoints in such multicultural drama can evoke discussion that increases understanding (Gimmestad & DeChiara, 1982).

When planning nonfiction drama, choose a short episode, just as you would with fiction. Putnam (1991) offers the following recommen-

dations for dramatizing nonfiction. Determine what the children already know and what they would like to learn about the designated topic. Read or tell the section to be dramatized, being sure to clarify word meanings and causal relationships and to make connections with the children's own experience. As you read, stop and let the children briefly dramatize important information or events. Then, after one overview of the entire passage, act it out again, following the guidelines for story drama earlier. After the reenactment, ask what the children have learned and provide an opportunity for them to respond independently, such as writing in a learning log, illustrating the information, or writing a narrative.

Literary genres can also be combined for integrating drama into the curriculum. For example, a social studies unit on the U.S. Civil War that discusses the underground railroad might include readings of historical fiction such as *Follow the Drinking Gourd* by Jeanette Winter, nonfiction such as Ellen Levine's *...If You Traveled on the Underground Railroad*, and poetry such as "Harriet Tubman" by Eloise Greenfield. After reading or hearing the selections, the teacher might lead children in dramatizing some of the more interesting parts or even the parts that are more difficult for the children to understand. Based on information in these three selections, the children might become hungry runaway slaves with the task of getting food—beginning with hunting or stealing a chicken, building a small fire, and then hiding until the smoke dissipates and there is less danger of attracting attention, coming out of hiding when it is safe, cooking the meat quickly, and then covering the evidence before running again. Other brief events for dramatizing include inventing and using signals to communicate with other travelers (such as knocks on windows, passwords, or tapping stones together), getting into hiding places (trapdoors, tunnels, fake floors), or arriving at a station and being able to eat, bathe, change clothes, and receive medical attention for the first time. Older students might reenact several major aspects of a journey, with a focus on the roles of various people involved: the station master, the conductor (Harriet Tubman and Peg Leg Joe, two real-life conductors, are mentioned in these books), friendly strangers, slave hunters, and fugitive slaves. The children might even follow the clues in the song from *Follow the Drinking Gourd*.

Evaluating Story Drama

After each performance, the performers and audience can evaluate what they have done and seen, first noting things they liked—what they enjoyed watching—and then things that might be done differently, always thinking about improving their own performances. When teachers evaluate children's participation in story drama, they look for focus on the task: did they stay within the confines of the drama? The children should also respond to one another's characters meaningfully within the frame of the drama: did they react appropriately to their coactors? Involvement in drama should be more than another exercise to get through: did the children move beyond playing parts to "becoming" the characters? Anecdotal notes about children's participation in dramatic activities are an important part of ongoing assessment in language arts.

Conclusions

When children experience literature through drama, they understand literature and literary elements more deeply. Drama involves children in talking and thinking about what they have read, helps them closely connect with books, and allows them to explore their emotional responses to what they have read or listened to. When children have played about a story they have become part of that story, and the story has become part of them. They are truly "taller and stronger and wiser" because of it.

References

Cullinan, B.E., & Galda, L. (1994). *Literature and the child* (3rd ed.). Ft. Worth, TX: Harcourt Brace.

Edmiston, B., Enciso, P., & King, M.L. (1987). Empowering readers and writers through drama: Narrative theater. *Language Arts, 64,* 219–229.

Galda, L. (1982). Playing about a story: Its impact upon comprehension. *The Reading Teacher, 36,* 52–55.

Galda, L. (1984). Narrative competence: Play, storytelling, and story comprehension. In A. Pellegrini & T. Yawkey (Eds.), *The development of oral and written lan-*

guage in social contexts (pp. 105–117). Norwood, NJ: Ablex.

Gimmestad, B., & DeChiara, E. (1982). Dramatic plays: A vehicle for prejudice reduction in the elementary school. *Journal of Educational Research*, 76, 45–49.

Moffett, J. (1968). *Teaching the universe of discourse*. Boston, MA: Houghton Mifflin.

O'Neill, C. (1989). Dialogue and drama: The transformation of events, ideas, and teachers. *Language Arts*, 66, 147–159.

Pellegrini, A.D. (1984). Symbolic functioning and children's early writing: The relations between kindergartners' play and isolated word-writing fluency. In R. Beach & L.S. Bridwell (Eds.), *New directions in composition research* (pp. 274–283). New York: Guilford.

Pellegrini, A.D., & Galda, L. (1982). The effects of thematic fantasy play training on the development of children's story comprehension. *American Educational Research Journal*, 19, 443–452.

Putnam, L. (1991). Dramatizing nonfiction with emerging readers. *Language Arts*, 68, 463–469.

Verriour, P. (1985). Face to face: Negotiating meaning through drama. *Theory into Practice*, 24, 181–186.

Vygotsky, L. (1978). *Mind in society*. Cambridge, MA: Harvard University Press.

Wolf, D., & Pusch, J. (1985). The origins of autonomous texts in play boundaries. In L. Galda & A.D. Pellegrini (Eds.), *Play, language, and stories: The development of children's literate behavior* (pp. 63–77). Norwood, NJ: Ablex.

Children's Literature

Atwater, R., & Atwater, F. (1938). *Mr. Popper's penguins*. Boston, MA: Little, Brown.

Greenfield, E. (1978). Harriet Tubman. In *Honey, I love: And other love poems*. New York: HarperCollins.

Levine, E. (1988). *...If you traveled on the underground railroad*. New York: Scholastic.

Paterson, K. (1977). *Bridge to Terabithia*. New York: Crowell.

White, E.B. (1952). *Charlotte's web*. New York: HarperCollins.

Winter, J. (1988). *Follow the drinking gourd*. New York: Knopf.

CHAPTER 18

Responding to Literature as Art in Picture Books

Barbara Z. Kiefer

IN AN ESSAY on response to literature, Britton (1977) writes that the goal of the reading program should be to produce children who "read more books with satisfaction" and who "read books with more satisfaction" (p. 110). That statement encompasses all that we might hope for when we think about supporting children's responses to literature. We want them to broaden the type and number of books they read, but most of all we want to help them deepen their response to a single book—to read it with *more satisfaction*.

Certainly, in all the writing and research that have accompanied our thinking about response to literature, Rosenblatt's (1978) theory of aesthetic response, as mentioned in earlier chapters, plays a pivotal role in helping us plan to reach this goal. Yet seldom have we stopped to consider the meaning of aesthetic response beyond its application to literature. Aesthetics is a philosophical discipline having to do with the theory of fine arts. Kaelin (1989) suggests that aesthetics "may be

thought of as the discipline concerning itself with artistic communication—with the description of creativity of works of art, of artistic appreciation" (p. 71). As Elliott Eisner explains, aesthetics raises the question, "What do I know about art and what is my response to it?" (Brandt, 1988, p. 7).

Such questions are central to the study of literature. They may help teachers take children beyond the usual queries so typical of many reading lessons—"Who was the main character?" or "What was the theme of the story?"—toward gathering children's responses to "How did that story make you feel?" or "How has that work changed the way you experience the world?" Although a theory of aesthetic response applies to a literary work of art, it can also extend beyond literature to other art forms. Even while much writing and research that address children's response to literature include discussion of picture books, seldom is the picture book considered as a separate and unique art form that may evoke very different aesthetic responses. In fact, in the past, some researchers even suggested that illustrations in picture books were detrimental or even harmful to children (Bettelheim, 1976; Samuels, 1970). Groff (1973), for example, went so far as to argue,

> To the degree that it dilutes the opportunities for the child to respond to a word story, the modern picture book becomes a nonliterary commodity. It can limit the child's interest in real books and even impart a neutral or negative attitude towards words (p. 28).

More recently, however, we have recognized the importance of picture books to children's language and literacy development. We need to extend these perceptions to recognize the potential of the picture book for developing children's aesthetic awareness as well. To do that, we need to understand that a picture book is a combination of image and idea that is different from a work of literature. Bader (1976) has declared that as an art form the picture book "hinges on the interdependence of pictures and words, on the simultaneous display of two facing pages, and on the drama of the turning page" (p. 1). Marantz (1983) argues that picture books "are not literature (in other words, word-dominated things)," but rather a form of visual art. The picture book, he tells us, "must be experienced as a *visual-verbal* entity if its potential values are to be realized" (emphasis added, p. 154).

Teachers can show children how to discover these potential values and deepen their aesthetic responses by helping them understand how illustrators communicate artistically and how illustrations contribute to the meaning of a picture book. To do this, we need to understand that visual art and verbal art forms are not identical; while both language and visual art have a meaning expressing potential, the two cannot be matched at a "word" or "sentence" level as some have tried to do. Gombrich (1982) argues that although both language and visual images have the capacity to express, arouse, and describe, the visual image is most effective in arousing emotions, while it is unable to match "the statement function of language" (p. 138).

Even so, when we consider how meaning is expressed, verbal and visual art have much in common. Both authors and artists have certain elements available for conveying meaning, creating character and setting, propelling the plot, and developing mood and theme. The author chooses sounds and words—the phonetic and morphemic systems of language. The artist uses line, shape, color, value, and texture—the elements of art. Both language and art have syntactic and semantic properties. We recognize the syntactic or structural properties of art in its organization of lines and color, its semantic properties in the ways in which lines and colors evoke metaphors such as quiet, warm, or angry. In addition, both authors and artists can choose to organize these elements through certain principles of composition, and both use terms like balance, rhythm, and pattern to describe these principles. Finally, the word "style" can be used to encompass the conscious and unconscious *choices* of these elements and principles by authors or artists to convey meaning within their particular aesthetic form (Kiefer, 1993; 1994).

For the picture book illustrator these stylistic choices include the traditional visual elements and principles of composition mentioned earlier. However, unlike an artist who deals with only a single two-dimensional surface, the illustrator must extend these choices to the design of the entire book. In addition, the illustrator must consider factors unique to book production and make choices about what will appear on the endpapers or what typeface will be used for the words. Also important to a picture book's overall manifestation are the illustrator's choices of viewpoint from which each scene will be observed and the pictorial content and details that will support and extend the text.

Thus, in first understanding and evaluating our own responses to picture books and then in helping children broaden and deepen their aesthetic awareness and response, we should consider the literary choices made by the author and how those choices affect us. In addition, we must also consider how the illustrator has chosen to convey meaning through certain elements of art, principles of composition, and other factors relating to picture book design.

Examining an Illustrator's Stylistic Choices

A picture book that provides examples of how the illustrator's choices can contribute to our aesthetic experience is John Steptoe's *Mufaro's Beautiful Daughters*. The book is Steptoe's tribute to the ruins of a great civilization found in Zimbabwe (which European scientists had ignored for years) and to the contrasts and similarities between the lives lived in the past and those in the present. These contrasts and similarities are realized through the characters of two sisters—Nyasha, who is as kind and loving as her sister, Manyara, is bad tempered and selfish (Steptoe, 1987).

Steptoe's artistic choices brilliantly represent this underlying tension. For example, beginning with the cover painting and the soft green endpapers, the book's dominating color scheme is of cool greens and blues that evoke the lush flora of the African setting. Into each double-page spread, however, Steptoe adds a touch of contrast by using accents of

Illustration from John Steptoe's Mufaro's Beautiful Daughters. ©1987 *by John Steptoe. Reprinted by permission of Lothrop, Lee & Shepard Books, a division of William Morrow & Company, Inc., with the approval of the Estate of John Steptoe.*

reds and oranges, the color complements (or opposites) of green and blue. In addition, Steptoe used a fine pen to create his forms through crosshatching (the criss-crossing of tiny lines), sometimes overlaying these lines with washes of color. The textures created by the crosshatching and the smooth white areas on each page further extend his theme and add to the tension of the story. This is also true of Steptoe's use of value—the varying degree of light and dark within the composition. By developing strong contrasts between light and dark, he again reinforces the theme, lending three-dimensional form to each figure and high drama to each double-page spread.

Steptoe's characters come fully alive, and they move with great dignity within the pages of the book because of these stylistic choices. In addition, the composition of each double-page spread has been carefully considered so that flowing forms lead the eye across the page and onto the next. Alternating perspectives also lend variety to the total book design and reinforce the contrasting viewpoints: sometimes we look down on the scene, sometimes we look straight ahead, and other times we look up from below. Finally, Steptoe's meticulous research adds authenticity to such details as the embroidered garments of the characters in the final wedding scene and to the flora and fauna in the lush setting.

Mufaro's Beautiful Daughters won the Boston Globe-Hornbook Award for Illustration in 1987 and the 1988 Caldecott Honor Medal, the only book named that year as an honor book. There is no doubt the book has become a modern classic for all ages; it is a work of art that touches us all deeply. This is due in large part to Steptoe's carefully chosen elements of art and book design that convey the depth of this story. Choices such as these are at the heart of the deepest aesthetic responses that result from experiences with an artistic expression—a fine picture book.

Engaging Children with the Art of the Picture Book

It is not necessary for teachers to be experts in art history or art appreciation to engender the deepest aesthetic responses in children. Just by thinking about the meaning-making potential of the pictures as they interact with the words or ideas in a book, and by recognizing the emotional effect of the illustrator's artistic choices, teachers can help children respond more fully to the art of picture books through talk and other classroom activities.

As I have researched children's responses to picture books across grade levels and settings, I have had many opportunities to observe how children's talk about picture books helps deepen their aesthetic understanding. I observed and recorded (Kiefer, 1994) potent examples of children's meaning making with Maurice Sendak's *Outside over There*. This book has received both praise and criticism from adult readers; many adults have argued, in fact, that it is not a book for children at all. Kimmel (1982) argues that *Outside over There*, along with Molly Bang's *The Grey Lady and the Strawberry Snatcher* and Chris Van Allsburg's *The Garden of Abdul Gasazi*, is "far too unusual or sophisticated to attract many children" (p. 37). However, the book is both visually and verbally compelling, in spite of the fairly brief printed text. It is rich in verbal and visual meaning, and it represents a range of Sendak's artistic choices that allows children to wonder and question as well as to admire. I listened as the book was read aloud to a class of first and second graders and watched as their teacher, Mrs. Hall, helped deepen the children's responses during repeated visits both to this book and others by Sendak.

The children seemed to be intrigued by this book from the outset, possibly due to Mrs. Hall's enticing summons, "I have a special new storybook to share with you. Come up close.... It's one of *those* books." If she had hoped to invite them to look closely and think deeply about the book, she certainly succeeded. Mrs. Hall's introduction to *Outside over There* recreated the intimacy of a parent-child read aloud, and she skillfully drew their attention to the book with her opening comments and questions in the conversation reproduced following. Her introduction also invited children to look carefully at all parts of the book, make connections, and predict what they might find inside:

Mrs. Hall: I have a special new storybook to share with you. Please come up close, very, very close. It's one of *those* books. What did you say about this book, Hildy?

Hildy: Is that from the Bible?

Mrs. Hall: (pauses) The author—

Child 1: Maurice Sendak.

Child 2: I know! Ohh! She also wrote *Where the Wild Things Are*.

Mrs. Hall: Maurice Sendak. Look what I just did. I flipped to the back pages. Why?

Child 3: They tell something.

Mrs. Hall: I thought there might be a picture of Maurice Sendak and wanted to see. (The end flap was blank.) Maurice

Illustration from Maurice Sendak's Outside over There. ©1981 *by Maurice Sendak. Reprinted by permission of* HarperCollins.

Responding to Literature as Art

Sendak is a man, and I thought we might have some information on the back pages.

After the children made further comments about the book, Mrs. Hall leafed through the title and dedication pages and asked, "What would you expect to find in this story just from looking?" Children offered many predictions: "flowers," "little people," "boats," "a whole bunch of babies." Holding the book open to face the children, Mrs. Hall began to read, and they began their initial talk about the book, particularly its pictures. As the children worked toward their own meanings, Mrs. Hall's comments ceased almost entirely. She was willing to follow the children's leads and support their attempts to interpret. She also welcomed the children's silence; sometimes she let as much as a minute go by before she turned a page or before someone spoke.

As Mrs. Hall read, the children predicted, wondered, inferred, and made connections as Sendak's unique vision opened up their own imaginations. Within the first pages of the book, the children pointed out details in the illustrations and told what they thought was happening:

Child 1: Look, there's those people (the goblins).

Child 2: They're taking stuff from her.

Child 3: They're on every page, and there's a boat in the water.

Child 2: And they're taking stuff.

Child 4: And there's a dog and children.

As the story's excitement builds and the goblins climb through the window to kidnap Ida's baby sister, the children used the illustrations to make inferences and predictions about what might happen:

Child 1: I think they're trying to scare her because they got up on the ladder—the ladder to move something. They can go around and get up to take the ladder.

Child 2: And they're trying to scare her.

When Ida discovers that the goblins have taken her sister and left another baby made of ice, the children made still more comments about the details conveyed by the pictures. They were fascinated with the visual subplots in the illustrations, particularly with a ship that appears outside the window, first caught in a storm, then sinking, and then reappearing later with the goblins who have stolen Ida's sister.

Child 1: Look at the baby's eyes

Mrs. Hall: Look at the eyes. Tommy?

Tommy: Um, they're getting more flowers like in the picture. See there and there? (He turns the page.) More flowers are coming.

Child 2: There's still more flowers. See there's...(excited).

Child 3: There's the sea and there's the boat and it's wrecked.

Child 4: Yeah.

Child 5: It could have been his Papa's.

Child 6: And right there.... There's lightning in there.

Child 1: Ooooh! See? And there's that boat.

Child 2: We just said that.

Child 1: It's like that goblin poem.

Child 3: "An' the Gobble-uns 'll git you ef you don't watch out!"

As Ida sets off to rescue the baby, the children wondered about her magic "raincoat" and speculated about where her absent sea captain father and her mother might be. They were particularly taken with a picture depicting Ida floating in the sky on her yellow cloak. A ship sails in harbor, and stairs lead over a rocky land bridge, its shape partially obscured by billowing storm clouds that barely allow the moon to peek through. The goblins cross beneath the bridge, carrying the baby.

Child 1: Look at that shadow.

Child 2: Like they're going to *take her*.

Child 3: Ummm—Is that a crack there? Is that a crack?

Child 4: It looks like there's a special light there and it's there. Maybe down there it gets to the ship, the light in the picture...

Child 5: And it has a moon coming up and everything.

Child 6: It could be a path.

Several: Yeah!

Mrs. Hall: A path to where?

Child 6: I don't know—goblin kingdom.

Child 7: It...oh...

Child 8: Outside over there!

Child 7: Yeah! Into outside over there!

Mrs. Hall: I like that, don't you?

Child 9: I was gonna say that.

When the story was finished, Mrs. Hall brought the children's attention back to the total book experience by asking, "What does this book make you think about?" and she listened intently to their responses and drew out support for the children's ideas with thoughtful probes.

Mrs. Hall: What does this book make you think about, Jennie?

Jennie: It made me feel sad.

Mrs. Hall: Why would you say that?

Jennie: Because they took the baby away. They did a couple things that were real sad, but the ending made me feel better.

Hildy: It's sort of like in the old times because of the pictures and stuff.

Mrs. Hall: What did the pictures make you think about?

Hildy: Well, they're sort of lushy and stuff.

Mrs. Hall: Mmmm, that's lovely. Tommy?

Tommy: Okay, ummm...it...there's time in it because it starts from the day, it goes all through night, and back to day again.

Child 2: And the moon—it changes.

Mrs. Hall ended the discussion by making certain that the book was placed into the hands of a child. In the coming days, it became a central part of this classroom community of readers (Hepler & Hickman, 1982). Moreover, during this first reading and book conversation, Mrs. Hall helped spotlight the book's potential. Her remark that *Outside over There* was "one of those books" was a reference to what she called books with "secrets"—details that promise to bring children back to the pages to make new discoveries. Mrs. Hall also invited children to make connections with other books through such observations as noting the author, and then she allowed children time to gather their thoughts about Sendak and his other books. Later, one child made an intertextual connection on her own as she quoted from James Whitcomb Riley's *Little Orphant Annie*. And, when one child mistook Sendak for a woman, Mrs. Hall did not correct but rather demonstrated how readers inspect the end flap to find material that "tells something."

This picture book reading experience represented collaboration rather than competition among these participants in classroom discourse, and the children's talk set the stage for further understanding. Instead of a list of comprehension questions found in many reading textbooks or literature "response guides," Mrs. Hall's questions were on target for an aesthetic experience. Questions such as, "What does this book make you think about?" or "How does this book make you feel?" reflect a genuine desire to hear what children have to say and a willingness to listen, which are both crucial to children's deep understandings and important responses to the artistry of author and illustrator. Thus, Mrs. Hall initiated an exploration of Sendak's book that would take some of these children into better understandings not only of the art of the picture book but also, perhaps, of themselves.

In the days and weeks that followed, she brought in more books by Sendak and invited children to talk and compare and create artistic and written products. She also read the book again several times. Some of the children suggested that time was of great importance in the book because they had noted movement through day and night and in the positions of the moon (a recurring symbol in Sendak's books). Children who noticed five tiny butterflies on the page that shows Ida rescuing her sister were sure that the five goblins had turned into butterflies. Two second grade boys who had pored over the pictures decided at this juncture that Ida's experience was really a dream. They felt they knew this because they had seen the shepherd asleep on one of the double-page spreads. It was a dream, they said, because you "count sheep when you dream."

When I returned to Mrs. Hall's room a year and a half after completing my first visit, she had just read *Outside over There* for the fifth time, following an illustrator study of Maurice Sendak. She was now teaching a combination third and fourth grade, but many of the children whom I had observed in her first and second grade were now in this older group.

Two girls, eight and nine years old, sat down with me and the book, eager to talk about what they thought it was really about. As they looked at the pictures in which Ida has discovered that her sister is missing and a ship caught in a storm is visible, they explained:

Terri: She's (Ida's) so happy, and then she notices the baby's gone. Then she gets kinda mad.

Tina: There's the father's ship.

B.K.: How can you tell?

Terri: We can't, but that's what we're thinking.

Tina: She's getting mad, and the flowers keep growing, and then there's the shipwreck out there.

Terri: It's kinda like if she's mad, outside here it's mad.

Tina: She has to take care of the baby, and that's her responsibility.

Terri: She feels bad, and she's all mad and that's why the storm is there.

The girls' recognition of the possibilities of meaning in this book are every bit as profound as any of the adult critiques that I have read, and I would guess that Sendak would be very satisfied with their interpretations and appreciation. Indeed, Sendak (1993) tells of receiving a 14-page letter from a 12-year-old girl telling him how much she hated *Outside over There*. As he read her detailed account of what she disliked on each page, it became clear to him by the end of her letter that she had clearly received a meaning he had been trying to convey through the art and words. He reports that she still disliked the book, but for him, the important thing was that she had taken so much time, considered it so carefully, and had such strong feelings about it.

Children Become Aesthetic Readers

As mentioned before, teachers do not need extensive training in art to develop aesthetic responses in children. Mrs. Hall valued the art in picture books and was genuinely curious about children's responses. She asked questions to help children think about their emotional and intellectual responses to stories. She gave children time to look at books and time to talk about books—trusting them to become astute observers and meaning makers through the art of picture books. She helped children make connections with other books and other art forms. She helped deepen initial reactions by giving children opportunities to write and create art in response to picture books. Finally, she revisited picture books with children many times, encouraging them to bring new experiences and understandings to each encounter.

Over time, children in Mrs. Hall's class (and up and down the halls of schools everywhere) become sensitized to the magic and artistry of picture books that demand close scrutiny. With only a budding knowledge of the language of art principles and design, children apply these principles readily as they compare different illustrated versions of the same folktale for their effects on response. They pour over delightful endpapers in Lois Ehlert's *Red Leaf, Yellow Leaf* or those in Paul Zelinsky's interpretation of the Grimm Brothers' *Rumpelstiltskin*. They speculate about the choice of typefaces, comparing the calligraphy used in *Outside over There* with the chiseled typeface in Gerald McDermott's *The Stonecutter*. And they enlist the aid of art specialists to gain insights into how illustrators often borrow cultural or historical conventions to support and enhance story interpretations. For example, children can compare photographs of hide paintings done by Native Americans of the Northern Plains with Paul Goble's illustrations for his retellings of Native American folktales. They can delight in finding tributes to great artists within the pages of modern pic-

ture books. Sendak, for example, refers to Pieter Bruegel's "The Fall of Icarus" in *Outside over There*, while Tord Nygren includes works by DaVinci and Picasso in *The Red Thread*.

Langer (1953) has argued that an artwork is an expression of an artist's ideas, something that takes shape as the artist attempts to communicate a vision that discursive language cannot properly express. The resulting piece of art gives us "forms of imagination and forms of feeling inseparably" (p. 397). Certainly, this is the kind of experience that Mrs. Hall provides children and that all teachers can effect through looking carefully, listening intently, and sharing their own ideas in response to picture books.

References

Bader, B. (1976). *American picture books: From Noah's ark to the beast within*. New York: Macmillan.

Bettelheim, B. (1976). *The uses of enchantment: The meaning and importance of fairy tales*. New York: Knopf.

Brandt, R. (1988). On discipline-based art education: A conversation with Elliott Eisner. *Educational Leadership*, 45, 6–9.

Britton, J. (1977). Responding to literature. In Meek, M., Warlow, A., & Barton, G. (Eds.), *The cool web: Patterns in response to literature* (pp. 106–111). New York: Atheneum.

Gombrich, E.H. (1982). *The image and the eye: Further studies in the psychology of pictorial representation*. Ithaca, NY: Cornell University Press.

Groff, P. (1973). The picture book paradox. PTA *Magazine*, 67, 26–29.

Hepler, S., & Hickman, J. (1982). "The book was okay. I love you": Social aspects of response to literature. *Theory into Practice*, 21, 278–283.

Kaelin, E.F. (1989). *An aesthetics for art educators*. New York: Teachers College Press.

Kiefer, B.Z. (1994). *The potential of picturebooks: From visual literacy to aesthetic understanding*. New York: Merrill/Macmillan.

Kiefer, B.Z. (1993). Visual criticism and children's literature. In B. Hearne & R. Sutton, (Eds.), *Evaluating children's books: a critical look. Aesthetic, social and political aspects of analyzing and using children's books* (pp. 73–91). Urbana, IL: Graduate School of Library and Information Services.

Kimmel, E. (1982). Children's literature without the children. *Children's Literature in Education*, 13, 38–43.

Langer, S.K. (1953). *Feeling and form.* New York: Scribner.

Marantz, K. (1983). The picture book as art object: A call for balanced reviewing. In R. Bator, (Ed.), *Signposts to criticism of children's literature* (pp. 152–155). Chicago, IL: American Library Association.

Rosenblatt, L. (1978). *The reader, the text and the poem: The transactional theory of the literary work.* Carbondale, IL: Southern Illinois University Press.

Samuels, S.J. (1970). Effects of pictures on learning to read: Comprehension and attitudes. *Review of Educational Research*, 40, 397–408.

Sendak, M. (1993, July). Panel discussion of *Down in the dumps with Jack and Guy.* New York: HarperCollins.

Steptoe, J. (1987). Mufaro's beautiful daughters. *The Horn Book Magazine*, 64, 25–28.

Children's Literature

Ehlert, L. (1992). *Red leaf, yellow leaf.* San Diego, CA: Harcourt Brace.

Grimm, J., & Grimm, W. (1986). *Rumpelstiltskin.* Retold & Ill. by P.O. Zelinsky. New York: Dutton.

McDermott, G. (1975). *The stonecutter: A Japanese tale.* New York: Penguin.

Nygren, T. (1988). *The red thread.* New York: Farrar, Straus & Giroux.

Riley, J.W. (1983). *Little Orphant Annie.* Ill. by D. Stanley. New York: Putnam.

Sendak, M. (1981) *Outside over there.* New York: HarperCollins.

Steptoe, J. (1987). *Mufaro's beautiful daughters.* New York: Lothrop.

Additional Resources for Teachers Interested in the Art of Picture Books

Bang, M. (1991). *Picture this: Perception and composition.* Boston, MA: Bullfinch.

Cummings, P. (1992). *Talking with artists.* New York: Bradbury.

Marantz, S. (1992). *Picture books for looking and learning: Awakening visual perceptions through the art of children's books.* Phoenix, AZ: Oryx.

Martin, D. (1989). *The telling line.* New York: Delacorte.

Shulevitz, U. (1985). *Writing with pictures: How to write and illustrate children's books.* New York: Watson Guptill.

CHAPTER 19

Writing as a Way of "Getting To" What You Think and Feel About a Story

Elaine Handloff and Joanne M. Golden

Laura Ingalls Wilder is a good author because she captures your imagination. She does that by making things seem like your really there.

As fifth grader Lindsey's journal entry shows, a reader responds to literature by making personal connections and links with text. Lindsey has played an active role in making meaning during and following her reading of the *Little House* books. She has engaged in a literary transaction—anticipating, inferring, and integrating her ideas with those of the author. In these and other ways, readers and authors together create story worlds. Journal entries, such as Lindsey's, illustrate what we can learn about the active role of the reader.

Why Response Journals?

Although reader response journals are being used in many classrooms, not many teachers and teacher-researchers have closely inspected the positive influences of journals on literacy processes. In one study of three fourth graders' responses to a novel, Wollman-Bonilla (1989) found that journal writing contributed to the development of reading strategies, knowledge of literature, ability to communicate ideas, self-confidence, and motivation to read. In another study in a junior high, students themselves reported the positive effects of journals on their understanding of literature (Tashlik, 1987). In a study of middle school learning disabled students, writing in journals resulted in favorable attitudes toward reading and an increase in involvement with books (Oberlin & Shugarman, 1989). In fact, during the course of 18 weeks, students who had previously read an average of 1 book per year read 20 books each.

Several investigators have explored different ways of structuring journal writing in the classroom. In her reading workshop, Atwell (1987) used student-to-student as well as student-to-teacher writing. She found marked differences in the kinds of writing students engaged in, depending on the audience for whom it was intended. When writing to peers, students wrote more affective descriptions than when they wrote to their teacher, and they tended to ask peers for book recommendations. Audience was also an influence on journal responses in a study by Heiden and Schmitt (1991). They developed a procedure in which sixth grade students conversed through their journals with university students who had read the same books. By the end of the experience, the sixth graders employed new types of responses and were more willing to relate personal experiences to story events. Dekker (1991) also observed a range of responses when she encouraged her second and third graders to talk about books before writing in their journals.

These studies illustrate the potential of response journals to develop literacy abilities and provide insights into how readers respond to literature. Further inquiries into the journal as a means of observing students' responses to literature might focus on topics such as how students develop responses to literature through journal writing, what patterns of response are evident at different grade levels, how book choices influence responses, and what role the teacher plays in the process.

A Close Look at Response Journals

In the fall of 1990, Elaine Handloff initiated a program in her fifth grade reading class that involved students in responding in a journal to books they were reading independently. This was one part of the classroom reading program, which also included whole and small class discussions of literature, extension activities, as well as the required basal. The rationale for the journal writing program was based on a desire to incorporate more writing into the reading program, to provide students opportunities to become more consciously aware of their reactions to the books they read, and to establish more personal interaction between students and teacher. Elaine's observations from this program were the basis for a paper written for Joanne Golden's graduate course in literature for the middle school. From this point, we formed a collaborative research team and designed a study of journal responses for the following school year. In our study, we explored the responses to literature written by a small group of students who used journals as part of their reading program during their fifth and sixth grade years in Elaine's classroom.

Getting Started

During the second week of the next school year, Elaine told her students they would read independently and regularly as part of their ongoing reading program, and they could choose any book that interested them. She also asked them to write freely in response to their reading twice a week for 15 to 20 minutes in designated journals. The journals were to reflect students' thoughts and feelings about the books rather than their retellings. In addition, Elaine asked the students to support their statements and opinions with evidence from the book. She shared samples of written responses from previous students on an overhead for discussion. Periodically, she wrote comments in the journals to support students' responses (for example, "interesting thought" or "good support") as well as questions to encourage more fully developed responses ("How does she make you feel as though you're right in the story?" or "Why do you think that will happen next?").

What We Learned After One Year

At the end of the school year, we inspected closely the students' first and last 10 entries. We marked and categorized the smallest meaningful units of response according to Squire's (1964) system, but modified the categories to reflect more closely the nature and variety of what we actually found in the journals (see the table on the next page). Throughout this chapter, as we cite examples of journal entries, we provide the coded label based on the categories represented in the table (for example, an "I" after an entry means it is interpretive).

Our comparison of journal entries of fifth graders from the beginning to the end of the school year showed some interesting patterns. First, as expected, students increased the length of their entries. Second, they wrote more statements to support their responses. Third, and perhaps most interesting, their journal entries reflected a noteworthy shift from "narrative"(N) to "interpretive"(I) statements. Linda's journal entries illustrate this shift over time:

> *Fall entry*
> Ramona gets the part in the church nativity scene (N). She wants her mother to make her a sheep suit but her mother doesn't have enough time (N).

> *Spring entry*
> Harriet is the nosiest child I've ever met (I). She is just so much fun (I). I think it's because she has a boring 'Ole Golly'. (Yes, that's her name) and has to entertain herself (I).

Rather than indicating a hierarchical order of responses, we viewed interpretive responses as reflecting a more complex reaction to the literature than narrative responses. While this analysis informed us about group patterns, we also wanted to learn how individual students responded to literature, so we decided to continue the inspection through the following year.

A Closer Look at Lindsey

The next fall Elaine was assigned to the sixth grade, and nine of her previous year's students stayed with her, which provided us with the opportunity to study those nine students' journal responses during a longer period of time. To illustrate how literature responses served to inform us about individual readers, we focus our discussion on the journal entries of just one student during her fifth and sixth grade years—Lindsey, whose journal entry is in this chapter's opening.

We considered Lindsey to be an above-average reader whose patterns of response reflected those of her eight other second-year classmates, but with a few differences. Like her classmates, Lindsey's responses included literary judgments during the study, but her entries contained more judgments than the other students'. In the fall of her fifth grade year, however, 50 percent of Lindsey's responses were literary judgments, but by the spring of sixth grade, only 22 percent of her responses were literary judgments. Unlike the group's pattern, Lindsey showed a sizable increase in her use of personal statements. Only 9 percent of her entries were personal statements in the fall of fifth grade, but they had increased to 25 percent in the spring of sixth grade. Other differences between Lindsey's responses and the group's were her extensive use of interpretive statements and entries that continued to increase in length across both years.

In examining Lindsey's journal entries, one question we considered is what this

Categories of Responses to Literature

Category Name	Definition	Examples
Interpretive (I)	making inferences or predictions; explaining the work or relating it to something else; expressing the theme of the work; discussing characters, setting, or other literary elements	"I think the rats will escape in time." "Marcy probably won't win the election because she is a snob." "Jim knows now that friends are important." "I think the main character is funny." "What will Steve do?"
Literary Judgment (LJ)	assessing or rating the author's or illustrator's style; classifying genre; pointing out use of language or literary devices; evaluating the literary work	"This book is scary and exciting." "The author is very creative." "The illustrations are beautiful and really go with the text." "This is a great book." "This is a humorous mystery." "It made me feel like I was in the story."
Narrative (N)	literal retelling of the story; listing of literal aspects of the work, such as names of characters	"This story is about a 10-year-old boy named Steve who has to move to a new neighborhood." "The book I'm reading is *The Secret Garden*."
Personal (P)	statements about how the student felt while reading and what book the student wishes to read next; statements expressing personal interest.	"I'm glad the kids were able to get out of the house in time." "I like this book." "I wonder what will happen next." "I am going to look for the sequel to this book to read next."
Personal Associational (PA)	references to ties to the student's own life; references to how the student would feel or react if he or she were in the character's place	"I'm a lot like Jason because I hate math and I have a bratty brother." "If I were Jane, I would be really scared."
Prescriptive (Pr)	statements regarding what the character "should" do or have done	"His parents should let him choose his own friends."
Miscellaneous (M)	unrelated matters, such as number of pages read	"I am on page 61." "I saw the movie."

The code (S) indicates the response is supported.

length (or written fluency) means, particularly in light of her dramatic drop in offering literary judgments (LJ). Had Lindsey really demonstrated growth as a reader and responder during this time period? A close examination of her entries presents an interesting picture. Consider Lindsey's entry in September of her fifth grade year:

> This book is good (LJ). It expresses my feelings in some places (PA). It shows feeling (LJ). I recemend this book to anyone who has a situation like Mitch and Amy have (LJ). I also recemend this book to anyone who loves to read (LJ).

Although four of the five statements in this entry reflect literary judgments, they are entirely unsupported, and it seems that Lindsey may be unclear about (or reluctant to express) why she likes this book. The fifth statement in the entry represents the first that is expressed in a different way. This kind of repetition of an unfocused literary judgment was typical of many of the students' responses in the earliest entries. By February of fifth grade, however, Lindsey expressed more specific literary judgments—although they were still largely unsupported:

> I think this book is good (LJ) because it has detail (LJ). The author knows how to capture your imagination (LJ). She also has adventure around every corner (LJ). She also keeps you hanging in suspense (LJ). I think Bianca and Patience are determined (I).

By September of her sixth grade year, Lindsey demonstrated more conscious awareness of why she considered a book to be "good" through her personal (P) responses:

> I'm glad that Jack came back even if he did scare them (P). When he got lost I was sad (P), and when they were in the middle of the river my knees were shaking (P). That's how good Laura Ingalls Wilder writes (LJ).

An entry from the end of her sixth grade year shows that Lindsey had taken a big leap from simply declaring a book is "good" and recommending it to anyone who likes to read. She began, instead, to identify specific characteristics of an author's style of writing:

> I think Julie Campbell writes well (LJ). She makes it seem as if you're really there (LJ) because she describes things so well (LJ). For example, when she described the "ghost" boat, I gasped just like Trixie and Honey did (P)! I felt as if I were really there (LJ).

The reason for the large decrease in literary judgments becomes more clear. The repetition of the "this book is good" type of statement was replaced by fewer, but more clearly articulated and better supported, literary judgments. Lindsey seemed not to become less judgmental about the books she read, but rather more sophisticated in her expression of her judgments. This particular pattern was typical of other students during the two-year period as well, which suggests the possibility that a prolonged opportunity to experience journal writing may help some students to develop in expressing their responses to literature.

Lindsey's second divergence from the group pattern was her sizable increase in personal statements. Again, a careful examination of the actual entries offers a perspective on what this change reveals about Lindsey's growth as a reader. Lindsey included some personal statements in her earliest entries, but they did little to indicate how she was responding, as is evident in the following entry from the beginning of her fifth grade year:

> I think I will like it (P). He's going to make a journal about the trip he's taking (N). I think its going to be a good book (P). I get to see what the author has to say about the different places (P).

By the end of sixth grade, Lindsey's personal statements showed closer engagement with the literature:

> I'm glad that Honey is okay (P). If I was Trixie I would be whiter than the whitest thing on the Earth (PA)! I'm not sure whether or not to believe that Gordie McDuff really isn't a Scottish man (P). I wonder if Kathryn Kenny is Julie Campbell's daughter (P) because they certainly write alike (LJ-S). I wonder who Gray Cap (a pickpocket) really is (P) *and* how he knows that Honey has a valuable necklace (P). I wonder if Honey's necklace is a copy or the real thing (P). Mystery books are my favorite (P).

Lindsey appears to have developed a sense of the genre of mysteries that she enjoys to the extent that she asks questions as she reads to help direct her. This level of interaction suggests the likelihood that Lindsey is successfully comprehending what she is reading. It is evident that she is an active participant in making sense of literature, a trend that continued to develop throughout the second year.

Lindsey's decided preference for interpretive statements was unusual in comparison with her classmates. What exactly do her frequent interpretive statements tell us about the processes Lindsey undergoes while reading, which she incorporates into her writing? From her very first entries, Lindsey's interpretive statements show that she is really thinking about what she is reading. The following entry is from October of fifth grade:

> Henry is in a real bad situation (I), but I think he can help (I). Whenever he gets into bad situations he can always get out of it (I). He can handle things well (I). Henry knows how to take care of hiself (I).

Lindsey's faith in Henry is further illustrated by the well-supported interpretive comments in the following entry:

> Henry can handle things well (I), because he always has something planned (I). Like when they couldn't get the pool in, he remembered the secret Indian secret (N). I think it worked well (I).

By the spring of her fifth grade year, Lindsey's use of interpretive statements had increased dramatically (to 54 percent of her entries). Her February entry was exclusively interpretive, which was remarkably different from the group pattern. In addition, many of the statements were used as support for other interpretive responses:

> Henry is the kind of boy you would call creative (I). The reason he's creative is because he can make good artwork, like posters (I-S), can think of good ideas (I-S), and can think of good names for things (I-S). Midge is not the typical kind of girl (I). She does not giggle all the time (I-S), scream at things like snakes and spiders (I-S), and can be a boy's best friend because of that (I-S). Uncle Al is the kind of Uncle that isn't mean (I) and doesn't spoil you (I).

Although Lindsey's use of interpretive statements decreased during the second year, she continued to support her responses:

> I think I know he's homesick (I) because he's always wishing his mom and dad are there (N-S).... I think Jens is a good sailor (I) because he's good at climbing the ropes (N-S) and making knots on them (N-S).

One final sample of Lindsey's entries shows her continuing use of interpretive statements, but with an added twist of real-life knowledge providing the support:

> I think Trixie was smart (I) and dumb to go into the dumbwaiter (I) because it could've been the secret (I-S) and she could've run out of air and not have gotten out of there at all (I-S).

Although Lindsey's use of interpretive statements throughout the study did not increase in a steady progression, her ability to use interpretive statements in different ways is apparent. She articulated her interpretive statements in greater depth by supporting them more fully both with different types of statements and with knowledge drawn from life experience. It seemed likely that the second year of journal writing had offered Lindsey the opportunity to build on her skills.

The final aspect to consider regarding Lindsey's growth during the two-year period was her steady increase in the length of her entries (fluency). This discovery seemed particularly interesting because it was also typical of the group. Certainly, part of Lindsey's increased fluency can be attributed to her additional use of support for her ideas and her more elaborated responses. Equally important is that Lindsey, like other writers in Elaine's class, became more experienced at writing in her journal and spent more time actually writing. In the initial stages of the program, students often spent as much as 10 minutes thinking about what to write before ever putting pen to paper. As the program continued, they gradually needed less of their writing time to organize their thoughts. We believe the students became more aware of their reading responses and approached the journal writing prepared to express their responses.

> *"Using student journals, teachers have a unique 'window' available to them to observe literacy processes in each of their students."*

sight into how their students are reacting to what they read both during the reading process and after reading is completed. For the classroom teacher, this is a real benefit of response journals; teachers have a unique "window" available to them to observe literacy processes in each of their students.

A close look at Lindsey's journal entries over time suggests the possibility that long-term journal writing may well extend and sensitize students' responses to literature. In an era of increasing class size, journal writing offers a viable option for individualizing instruction in literacy and getting to know one's students far better as participants in literacy processes than is possible in other classroom activities. Like Lindsey, some students may feel more comfortable expressing thoughts in a journal—using writing as a way of "getting to" what they think and feel about literature.

Writing as a Way of "Getting to" Reading

Analysis of individual students' journal entries can offer teachers a great deal of in-

References

Atwell, N. (1987). *In the middle: Writing, reading, and learning with adolescents.* Portsmouth, NH: Heinemann.

Dekker, M. (1991). Books, reading, and responses: A teacher-researcher tells a story. *The New Advocate, 4,* 37–46.

Heiden, D., & Schmitt, P. (1991). An authentic literary experience: Sixth-graders and preservice teachers in shared response. *Reading Horizons, 32,* 128–138.

Oberlin, K., & Shugarman, S. (1989). Implementing the reading workshop with middle school LD readers. *Journal of Reading, 32,* 682–687.

Squire, J. (1964). *The responses of adolescents while reading four short stories.* Urbana, IL: National Council of Teachers of English.

Tashlik, P. (1987). I hear voices: The text, the journal and me. In T. Fulwiler (Ed.), *The journal book* (pp. 171–178). Portsmouth, NH: Heinemann.

Wollman-Bonilla, J. (1989). Reading journals: Invitations to participate in literature. *The Reading Teacher, 43,* 112–120.

CHAPTER 20

"Playing the Part My Ownself": Connecting Life with Literature Through Dialogue Journals

Judith Wells Lindfors

IN HIS RESPONSE journal, Kenny, a university football player, commented on his reading of *The Color Purple* by Alice Walker:

> The author wrote this book as if there were a bunch of small letters put together. Each one of these letters began with the salutation Dear God. The words were wrote down in the book as someone would say it, not actually the correct spelling. I thought this was very good, it helps me speak as if I was playing the part my ownself...

This chapter is about Kenny and three of his peers who, like Kenny, brought their "own-selves" into the texts they read and the texts they wrote while they were enrolled in what we (Connie Juel and I who were team teaching) came to call "the athlete course." It was a one-semester university course in which 25 student athletes tutored at-risk African American and Mexican American first graders in a near-

by elementary school twice a week. The course had two thrusts: the tutoring experience (and the weekly class meeting that supported it), and the reading and writing that the student athletes did on their own time. We assumed that, if you want to help someone else learn to read and write, you have to be a reader and writer yourself. And so these student athletes were expected to read for pleasure for approximately four hours a week any book of their own choosing and write a weekly entry in their response journals, which I would collect and respond to before our next class meeting when I would return the journals to begin the cycle again.

You may wonder what Kenny and his three classmates are doing in a collection focusing on children's responses to literature. When I think of readers deeply involved with text, the adult-child distinction is not that important. In any case, four student athletes—

Daniel, Kim, Kenny, and Rod—are the focus of this piece. In the "book talk" in their reading response journals, they did what effective readers do: they brought their "ownselves" into the texts they constructed as they read and wrote. The "speaking personality" that Bakhtin (1981) calls "voice" was loud and clear in each of these student athletes' responses to literature. Each one made meaning in text through what was most meaningful in his or her own life.

Daniel

What was most important to Daniel was the experience he was having as Octavio's tutor. Like all the student athletes, Daniel described his reading and writing self in his first entry, the only structured entry of the semester. I asked the students to begin their journals by responding to eight prompts:

- Describe a positive reading experience you have had (in or out of school).
- Describe a negative reading experience you have had.
- Describe a positive writing experience you have had.
- Describe a negative writing experience you have had.
- Describe the best teacher you ever had.
- Describe the worst teacher you ever had.
- Describe yourself as a reader.
- Describe yourself as a writer.

Here is Daniel's description of himself as a reader and writer:

> Myself as a reader is not real well but I just take my time and eventually understand or finish my reading. As a writer I am a slow starter but as I get into it I do just fine!

Throughout his public school experience, Daniel had worn the label "dyslexic." Like all the student athletes, he kept a record (on the inside front cover of his journal) of how many pages and how many hours he read each week. Daniel read his one book, *To Kill a Mockingbird* by Harper Lee, at the rate of five pages an hour. Yet no one has ever read this book with greater attention than Daniel. His first (unstructured) entry indicated what was to be his

Cover illustration from Harper Lee's To Kill a Mockingbird. *©1960 by Harper Lee. Reprinted by permission of Warner Books, Inc., and HarperCollins.*

major purpose in the journal: to relate the book to his tutoring experience, finding parallels between Octavio and the child characters in his book (Scout and Jem) and between the adult-child relationships in his book (Atticus with Scout and Jem) and his relationship with Octavio. This was what he cared about most deeply, and it came into his reading response journal from the beginning. In that first (unstructured) entry, written before his first tutoring session with Octavio, Daniel wrote:

> The Book *To Kill A Mockingbirds* is a really great Book. I think that it will help me alot in this class, because their are some things Scouts dad helps her with that would help me with the kids at the school. Scout like the children we are going to help are in the same grade. The Book is real interesting to me and I look forward to reading it Durning the week...

Daniel met with Octavio for the first week (two sessions) and then wrote:

> I really don't know if we write about this, becouse it is not really pertaining to my book. I just wanted to let you know how things are going with Octavio my tutee. Octavio is a great kid and is a little behind in reading but he is really trying hard. I can tell as this sommester comes to an end Octavio and I will have a close relationship and become good friends. When I can't see Octavio anymore I know I will miss him. This reminds me about when Scout misses Dill after he leaves to go back home.

Daniel seems a little uncertain here. Is it acceptable to write about Octavio in the journal, or must he confine himself to commenting on the book he is reading? He is not sure, so he scurries to safety in his final sentence. In my response, I encouraged him to write about Octavio, and throughout the semester he did.

However, Octavio was not the only child Daniel wrote about. He was fascinated with the character Scout. She and Octavio shared the spotlight in his journal entries as the semester progressed, and Daniel got more deeply involved both in his reading and his tutoring.

> I know that I talk about Scout a lot, but I find her very interesting. Scout is a little girl who acts like a boy and gives Atticus a very interesting life. Scout is a girl who will stood up to what she believes and sometimes foght over it. Like at a Christmas party she fought a boy for calling Atticus a negro lover. Since she is so interested in everything she has alot of questions for Atticus to answer. Scout wonders why townspeople do not think Atticus is normal because he doesn't participate in regular town activities. And Atticus has to explein why jest like he has to explain everything else. Also I am glad that you like Octavio he is a great kid and I enjoy going over there to see him, and how happy he is when he is with me.

> In my journal I would also like to keep you informed with Octavio as well as my reading. In these last few weeks I have seen major improvement in Octavio. I can tell that he is actually starting to like reading the same as me and I think we both owe it to this class, because before I never felt like reading and now it is an everyday event for me and as well as Octavio. But back to the book...

The semester was ending as Daniel finished his book:

> Well I finally finished the book *To Kill A Mockingbird*. I found this book to be a very interesting learning experience. I found ways to work with little children through Scout, Jem and Dill and the way Atticus worked with them. Like I said before Atticus has a way with children, and I think that that has helped him to be the great dad he was.... Also I thought I would tell you how Octavio is doing since I have kept you in touch with him. Octavio was the happiest little boy I have seen the other day. He read his first book to me this week, and me and him both thought that was great. He has really come around since September.

I am glad Daniel knew that there was a place for Octavio in his journal. If there had not been a place for Octavio, perhaps there would not have been a place for Daniel, either.

Kim

Kim's is a success story of sorts. She wrote in her first entry:

> I don't like to read, especially if the book is big and thick and boring. I like reading book with pictures used to illustrate what the book is about. Because of the type of English I used it is sometimes difficult for me to express myself in written words, therefore I prefer to express myself orally.

Her description suggested to me that it would be helpful for Kim to read books divided into manageable chunks that focused on personal relationships and family life, especially in black communities. As Kim responded in her journal to *The Color Purple* by Alice Walker, Lorraine Hansberry's *A Raisin in the Sun*, and Gloria Naylor's *Women of Brewster Place*, she showed herself to be an extraordinarily sensitive people watcher. She watched—and connected—characters in the books she read to people in her life. In the opening sentence of her first (unstructured) entry, she identified what was to be her central theme: "real life family situation." Her first three entries were responses to *The Color Purple*:

> Reading *the color purple* remends me of real life family situation in the world today. This book is very intresting it give you a inner drive that makes you want to read. Maybe its because I am use to the slang that are use write this book. I am almost throught with this book, I am not a fast reader but i just love this book. Some pointers that I've seen so far:
>
> 1. Problems with father and daughter
> 2. The problem of finding a good husband and for the husband to take good care you and family
> 3. Children disobying parent
> 4. Women brutality
>
> Againg this story is very intresting I love I wish I had read the book before watching the movie.

> ─────
>
> I am still trying my best to finish *The Color purple*...the more I read the more intresting the book gets. It telling me more and more about what people go through in life its like a every day thing. This book is real indept, I am happy am reading it.

> ─────
>
> I enjoyed reading *the color purple* its a very good story & really makes you wander and realize alot in life and what life can be about or is all about.... If you are willing to read slangs and understand slangs the book you will find it very intresting.

Kim's next two entries, responses to *A Raisin in the Sun*, brought vivid memories of her home (Jamaica) into her text:

> I feel very confortable reading this Story it remindes me of some family back home in Jamaica where I am from we have big yards in Jamaica and you can always pass by the road side and hear families talking just like what I've read so far. Always want their kids to be good and go to school and wife and husband argueing about something, I am enjoying this book so far.

> ─────
>
> When you read *a Raisin In The Sun* its just like real life, one can alway find a family that thing like that happen to. The play is also intresting because it deals with different dialets that we speak in every day life weather with family or friends. I am disapointed it such a short play mainly because it so very intresting to read...

The last two excerpts come from Kim's responses to *Women of Brewster Place*. Kim's way into the texts she read continued to be through people—living, breathing, feeling people.

> Thanks for suggesting this book already I am enjoying the quality and most of all the story itself. Again this story reminds me of people living in New York, because those appartment are so close together people can live like that looking through windows etc. It also bring me back when I was at home in Jamaica at the age of 14-16 my mother whom I was grown up with alway watch me if I was talking are walking with any guys on the street she would always tell me who I must "not" talk to. I love these story I know I am going to like the rest of the book.

> ─────────

> This story is overwhelming. I love it very much it teaches and remindes of so much things I have seen in life. Its also reminds me of some part in the story A *Raisin in the Sun* maybe this story is somewhat alike...

Kim's connection of *Women of Brewster Place* with *A Raisin in the Sun* is a good example of intertextuality—the connecting of one text with another. But for me, an even more important kind of intertextuality for Kim was her connection of the texts she read with those that she watched people live. It was this latter "intertextuality" that made Kim's success story possible, enabling her to go from "I don't like to read" to "I love it very much."

Kenny

I met Kenny (mentioned at the beginning of this chapter) through his description of himself in his first journal entry in which he responded to my prompts:

> Myself being a reader will enjoy it and read more of it if it has to do something with me or what I like. If it is above my vocabulary level, it will be frustrating and I will eventually put it down. As a writer, I don't mind writing if the writing are not that long. I could use some help on my grammar, but when I want to I can be good at grammar also.

Kenny was a thinker—reflection was his "thing." He especially focused on social issues in his journal responses to the books he read, the first of which was *Bloods: An Oral History of the Vietnam War by Black Veterans* by Wallace Terry.

> For this journal entry I would like to write about the context and words that were used in this book called "Bloods." Well the name itself describes how the book sounds and what was mentioned most of the time; blood. The book should be for adults only because of the nasty & violent issues discussed in some chapters. I do feel that this is no wrong doing; but that everyone should not be allowed to read it. Someone has to put it in text what really goes on but the young kids growing up would probably vomit on the incidents that goes on in the book. For an example, one man talks of when he shot another man in the head & it just exploded. I was shocked when I first read it but after a while I began to realize if someone don't write down the way times used to be; of course, they will never see them.

I tend to think of reflection as cool, logical, and existing at a safe remove from its object. But Kenny's reflection was not cool; it was warm and intense—a feeling, evaluative kind of reflection.

> *The Color Purple* was one of the best books I have ever read in my entire life. This is just an incredible book to read. It talks about black households after they had been out of slavery and the role of the black man. This is the part that I did like the most. The way this book shows how much power the man did have in the house. In the end the man was brought down & everything was taken away from him. That is basically what happens; but there are some good little spots in between. One incident that showed how much power the male did have in the household was when Shug Avery came to town, the male went after her and brought her

back home to be with him. This was done in front of his wife. I don't want to sound male-shovanist but this book gives a great example of the way things used to be.

Kenny's concern with social issues—rights and wrongs—was most impassioned when he focused on race relations:

> In the book, "Brothers: Black Soldiers in the Nam," it is different [from Bloods]. This book explains how the blacks were drafter to the war. They went to boot camp to train & the blacks hung out among the blacks, whites with whites, & so on. But when there was time for war, people had to survive. In order to do so, one had to put aside his or her ethnic views of a person and come together and fight. The coming together of units to survive is the whole issue that I receive from this book. It should not take a war to make people of different races unite. The world would be more powerful as one and also less problems in this world. So WHY CAN'T AMERICANS BE AS ONE?

In his final entry, Kenny showed himself to be something of a literary critic as well as a social one:

> "Although a tragic story of man's inhumanity to man, this is also an uplifting tale of courage, human dignity, and love.... An outstanding book." The name of the book is called *Sounder* by William H. Armstrong. I'm not yet finished with this book; but I am very close to the end. So far, this book has been nothing but trouble, sorry, and alot of shedding of tears. The purpose of my quote at the beginning was to write down what was written on the cover of the book. I truly honestly disagree with this quote except for the last statement. It is truly an outstanding book. But the whole book, things are happenning that is negative. The dogs gets the maines and he is away from the home for a while; the husband (man) gets put in to jail, and he is there for Christmas. This leaves the family back at home to suffer and shed their tears. Now let

me ask you. How can this book seem to be an uplifting tale of courage? This is how I felt.

Kenny did, indeed, bring his "ownself" into his reading—and into his writing, too. It was the self that enabled Kenny to play the parts of the characters within text as he read and wrote.

Rod

Rod's description of himself as a reader and writer was brief: "If I'm reading something boring then I fall asleep. As a writer I'm very lenient and can go in any direction." It was the first word of Rod's next entry that told me what the journal meant to him. That word was "Hi!," and it signalled the beginning of the friendship we would build through our writing. Of the 25 student athletes in the class, Rod wrote the most dialogically. In fact, his text—sentence by sentence—was so closely tied to mine that I cannot present the following selected excerpts from Rod's journal without also providing my own text that he was responding to. For Rod, the writing really was a conversation—a "convo," as he called it.

> Rod: Hi! I'm back again. This time I'm gonna tell you a little 'bout my book. Benjie, the main character in the story, is a young black boy who is thirteen years old. He is well on his way to being hooked on heroin. He thinks he isn't hooked, but family and friends say he's lost it. The drug pusher isn't worried. He thinks its better for kids to buy from a young pusher like himself cause the older pushers take a cut from the boy themselves. He says he doesn't feel sorry for a living. Benjie really has a problem though. It's a great book. Sometimes I just hate to put it down. I get wicha later! Peace,
>
> Sir Rod

Me: I'm really glad you're getting really drawn into *Benjie*, Rod. (Wait a minute. I think I'm mixed up. I was thinking "Benjie" was the name of your book. Is it the name of your book or just the name of the main character?)

It sounds like your book is dealing with important social issues—drugs, family relationships and so on. What is it that makes this a "great book" for you, Rod? Why do you sometimes "hate to put it down"?

Sometimes when I think about the kids you all are tutoring at [the elementary school], I wonder how many of them come from families where there's a drug problem. It's really something to think about. Will any of those kids be Benjies some day?

See you in class.

Rod: Once again I'm back to express myself on my book. Yep, you misunderstood. The title of my book is "A Hero Ain't Nothin' But a sandwich." Benji is really the main dude in the book. It's a great book for me because I've been around this type of thing basically all my life. I have *never* had a problem with it, but I have family and friends whom has seen plenty of action. I don't want to put the book down because I can't wait to see how Benji handles his problem. Some kids at [the elementary school] may start off like Benji, but hopefully they will detour away from it. Though, from my observation and from speaking to a few of the kids, I know that there is some of it going on in the family and neighborhood. That's really terrible, too. Don't worry though, cause as long as Sir Rod is behind the wheel, then everything will B-A-O-K.

Peace,
Sir Rod

Rod: Well, I guess I'm back before you could write, but I'ma go ahead and write anyway. I had written, but when I went to [the elementary school], I forgot to turn it in.

I'm very sorry though. But anyway, to update you on my book, I have read that Benji's grandmother is very old and saved with the Lord.... Next, I'll be reading about his (Benjie's) teacher. I'll tell ya about him in the next convo. This book is gettin' mo betta, mo betta, mo betta!

I'm gone.
Sir Rod

Me: I'm glad your book is getting "mo betta, mo betta, mo betta." I think our conversations in this journal are too.... I can see that you're able to relate to the issues raised in *A Hero Ain't Nothin' But a Sandwich.* (Why does the author give the book this title?) Do you think this book would be a good one for [the elementary school] kids to read later on, when they're in their teens? Authors who write realistic fiction for adolescents these days must really have to struggle with the problem of how realistic to be. Surely today's world is full of drugs, violence, poverty, abuse, etc. But just how should you present this in a book for young people? You want it to ring true for the reader, but you don't want it just to be shocking or hopeless. A difficult question, I think.

Rod: Hello, Howdy, & Hi!!! I'm in my room (very tired) resting up for another hard game. You "otta" come. Anyways, the book is going fine and dandy. I think the author gives this book that title (depending on how much I've read so far) because it really doesn't take much to be someone. You don't have to [be] a high-class, money making dope dealer to be a hero. I think (so far) that he is expressing that even the smallest, most simplest thing such as a sandwich can be a hero. This would be a great book for the [elementary school] kids to read in their later lives. Being in the area that it is in, I know that they would definitely benefit from it. I think the authors who write books like this don't just see it & write it. Nor do they visit an area for a while or read about familiar areas for their information. I actually think that they really have lived there in that type of neighborhood before. Maybe the author is the main character, but he just changed the names. Do you think older, "more adults," could benefit from reading this book. What about celebraties, or money making business boomers? Do you think they could read this book & understand the situation & offer to help in their surrounding areas to help prevent such drug trafficing? Well, once again "I'm gone."

P ositive   Peace,
E ducation   Sir Rod!!!
A lways
C orrects
E rrors

Through Rod's journal, we became friends. We came together as we created text about text—and about each other and the first graders we both cared about. It is what friends do: they have "convos" about the significant experiences they share.

Becoming Journal Writers

Before I met Daniel, Kim, Kenny, and Rod, I saw their grades, reading test scores, and college entrance examination results. The scores said these four students were disabled readers, but their reading response journals suggested otherwise. In their journals these students showed themselves to be deeply and personally engaged with text. Each responded to and created text from a caring center that Kenny called "ownself." Daniel's ownself was Octavio's tutor; Kim's ownself was people watcher; Kenny's ownself was social critic; and Rod's ownself was friend. Their reading response journals made possible a special kind of intertextuality by inviting these four students to connect the lives they lived with the texts they read and wrote.

Reflections

I used to teach second grade. That was long ago, and my students and I did not engage in written interactions about the books they were reading. I wish we had. But if tomorrow I were to walk away from my university teaching and become a second grade teacher again, I know that the children and I would write interactively about the books they were reading. We would do this for the same reasons that Daniel, Kim, Kenny, Rod, and I did. The writing would

- remove me from the lofty height of pedant—"delivering" instruction and dispensing "positive reinforcement"— and would position me instead in the role of teacher as I understand it, as a more experienced friend;

- enable me to listen and respond to each individual child revealed in the writing—and to do both reflectively;

- invite me again and again to affirm the child's act of making meaning through forging "ownself" connections with text.

The ongoing interaction would say to each child, "Yes. Keep bringing your ownself into the texts you read and those you write. It's what readers and writers do. Readers and writers like *you*."

Notes

All adult and child names have been changed except for Rod, who requested that I use his real name. In all excerpts from the students' journals, I have preserved the original text as closely as possible.

The course described was started in 1990 by Joanne Calhoun while she was a doctoral student taking a course taught by Connie Juel. Joanne initiated a cross-age tutoring project that brought together the student athletes she was mentoring for the Men's Athletic Department at the University of Texas (Austin) and the children in the elementary school in which she was supervising student teachers. When Joanne left the university to return to her teaching in Vermont, Connie and I team taught the course: Connie focused on the student athletes' tutoring of their first grade tutees, while I focused especially on the student athletes' own reading and writing. We shared the teaching of the weekly class meeting on campus. I thank my department chair, JoAnn Sweeney, for providing release time for Connie and me to teach this course and for providing teaching assistants.

Reference

Bakhtin, M.M. (1981). *The dialogic imagination*. Edited by M. Holquist. Austin, TX: The University of Texas Press.

Literature

Armstrong, W.H. (1969). *Sounder*. New York: Harper-Collins.

Childress, A. (1977). A *hero ain't nothin' but a sandwich*. New York: Avon.

Goff, S. (1986). B*rothers: Black soldiers in Nam*. New York: Berkeley.

Hansberry, L. (1987). A *raisin in the sun*. New York: New American Library.

Lee, H. (1961). *To kill a mockingbird*. New York: Harper-Collins.

Naylor, G.R. (1988). *Women of Brewster Place: A novel in seven stories*. New York: Penguin.

Terry, W. (1985). *Bloods: An oral history of the Vietnam war by black veterans*. New York: Ballantine.

Walker, A. (1982). *The color purple*. San Diego, CA: Harcourt Brace.

CHAPTER 21

"Leading from Behind": Dialogue Response Journals

Marcia F. Nash

I N CLASSROOMS CERTAIN situations sometimes take a direction not originally intended: the book introduced casually into the book corner catches your students' attention and stimulates unexpected responses; the response to literature activity takes on a life of its own and grows into a unit; or a chance question during a read-aloud session becomes a research project. That is how this dialogue response journal project evolved for Diane Smith, a fifth grade teacher, and for me, a teacher educator who was a frequent visitor in Diane's classroom.

At first, when I approached Diane about working with her and her class, I wanted her students to read books and write reviews about them. I write reviews of children's books for a professional journal, and I wanted to include some reviews by middle graders in an upcoming issue. Although the students did eventually publish reviews, the journal writing that we did in preparation for writing the reviews took on a life and importance of its own.

Getting Started

Initially, we wanted Diane's fifth graders to become comfortable with reading books and then with talking and writing about them. A dialogue response journal seemed a logical tool for that purpose. As discussed in earlier chapters, a dialogue journal is a written conversation between either the teacher and a student or two students (Atwell, 1984; Graves, 1983). A literature response journal is one in which students record their thoughts, feelings, and reactions to what they are reading (Golden & Handloff, 1993). For us, dialogue response journals combined both functions—allowing us to carry on written conversations with students as they wrote in response to what they were reading.

We began by reading aloud to the whole class at the beginning of a book sharing time. The first book was *Dolphin Adventure* by Wayne Grover—a true story about a diver's encounter with a dolphin family and some attacking

Illustration from Wayne Grover's Dolphin Adventure, illustrated by Jim Fowler. Illustrations ©1990 by Jim Fowler.
Reprinted by permission of Greenwillow Books, a division
of William Morrow & Company, Inc.

who takes care of dolphins, whales, mani-
tees...ect.)"

"ORP is a pretty good book I like reading the
lists he makes. Also Isis is a good Book for
peaple who like scientific things and old ships."

"I think that Dolphin Adventure was a very good
book. It had the direct feelings from the author,
and I like that. I think it would be fun to go div-
ing and see dolphins, because my favorite sea
animals are dolphins."

The first writer offered a personal evaluation of
the book and a piece of personal information
("I like nachur"); the second related a personal goal and a clarifying definition (of a marine
biologist). The third writer chose to recommend other books he had been reading instead of writing about Dolphin Adventure. The
fourth mentioned the author's style and made
a personal connection with the story.

After reading the first entries we knew we
were off to a good start. We were beginning to
understand that the journals would have a lot
to say about this class and their responses to
literature. We hoped that we could listen
closely enough to hear what they were saying.

sharks. After the reading and before we discussed the book, Diane and I wrote a "letter"
to the class on an overhead transparency asking them how they felt about the book. They responded in individual journals, and we, in turn,
responded individually to their responses.
That is how our weekly correspondence began.

We were struck by the range of responses in the journals. Some of those first entries
written about Dolphin Adventure follow:

"I thought it was a awsom Book. I like nachur
that's why I gave it a 10."

"If you really want to know, That story lifted my
future of being a Marine biologist. (A person

Fine Tuning

Every Friday morning for the next five
months Diane and I met with small groups of
seven or eight children to share books in a literature share circle. At the end of the share
time we collected their journals with their
writing for the week. We used the weekend to
respond and returned their journals each
Monday. As we worked to get the journals op-
erational, we talked about our questions and
concerns: How directive or instructive should
we be as respondents? How would the time
lag (the time between their entries and our responses) affect the students and their writing?

Toward addressing our first concern, we decided to be as genuine as possible: when we had questions—whether in response to something a student had written or something we had observed—we asked them. The rest of the entries were to be what Hickman (1992) calls free response—"what they are likely to do without prompting" (p. 186). Initially, we did not realize how often we would have opportunities to extend and deepen students' response to literature, so we did not put much thought into what we might extend, or how we might do it.

As the students began writing, our second concern seemed justified. We noticed differences in the amount of dialogue they actually invited and to which they would respond. Still, they all wrote. Some students consistently carried on written conversations; others did occasionally; a smaller number never did. Perhaps the time lapse between their writing and our response made it difficult for a few students to view this exchange as real conversation. Others seemed to simply have their own agendas for what they wanted to write.

Making Discoveries

Our original intent was to get the students accustomed to thinking and writing about the books they read, but as the journals evolved, we made discoveries about the students and ourselves. These discoveries subtly clarified, and then redefined, how we used the journals. Diane initially saw them as a vehicle for finding out more about individual student's reading behaviors. I was more interested in the nature of their free responses. We both became interested in class patterns of preference, choice, the students' perceptions of the author's role, and their awareness of literary elements.

Discoveries About Reading Behaviors

The journal entries revealed a great deal about individual student's reading behaviors. For example, one student consistently had trouble finishing books, while another frequently reread; still another always depended on a friend when deciding what book to read:

"It was surduve [sort of] Intreting because it has a suprise ending I like that In a book but sometimes I dont read the hole book and dont get to find out what its about."

"I reread books because I like the books and I enjoy reading them. The books just give me a good feeling when I read them again."

"Im waiting to read a book thats called *Football Photos* right now my friend has it he said it was a good book so Im going to try it out but for righ now Im reading *the seven treasure hunts* I like it I pick it becuse the cover look interesting and the title sounded pritty good...the other book is *El Chino* I picke *El Chino* becuse my freind told me aubout it."

Sometimes these discoveries were simply interesting details about the reader, as in the case of the student who enjoyed rereading books. As fellow readers, we shared our own experiences with books reread. At other times these discoveries led to teacher interventions, as in the case of the student who had adopted a book-selection strategy that was not working well (taking the advice of one friend who did not seem to share his literary taste). In this case the intervention was simple: in the sharing circle participants were encouraged to talk about their book-selection strategies, so the student was exposed to various strategies used successfully by his classmates.

Discoveries About Book Choices

As choice strategies began to emerge, we noticed patterns. Although a few students discussed their choices spontaneously, many did not. To find out more, we asked students directly about their choices: "I have noticed that you read a variety of different kinds of books. How do you decide on a book?" One student replied, "lots of people always tell me not to judge a book by it's cover. I do. That's how I usually do my choseing. And I usualy get pretty good books."

Although favorite authors, illustrations, and teacher recommendations were all mentioned as selection strategies, relying on the cover—both the picture and descriptive information—was mentioned most often as the way in which these students were choosing their books:

> "I have really got an iterst in this book because of the cover. It kind of looked like main [Maine]."

> "The reason that I picked it is beacause I like adventures and wierd stuff and the cover looked really wierd."

> "I'm starting a book called *Something Big Has Been Here* by Jack Prelutsky one of the reasons I was interested in It because It was by the same creators of the bestselling *The New Kid on the Block* SO FAR ive only read four Poems and I only Like 2." [The student believed the book was going to be about the singing group "New Kids on the Block."]

> "I pick it becuse the cover look interesting and the title sounded pritty good to me."

Although authors were less frequently mentioned, it was apparent that individuals often read many books by the same author. In this class, Ellen Conford, Matt Christopher, Gary Paulsen, Ann M. Martin, and Robert Peck were repeatedly chosen:

> "When I look for a book, I don't look for the cover. I look for the authors like Gary Paulsen and especially Paula Fox."

> "Jane Yolen Has a Very Good way of Writing. Her style's uniqui, but good."

> "I want to read more Books that Ellen Conford wrights. Because they are easy for me to Read. Can you please bring some more books in that she has writing."

> "I have read tons of books by Matt Christopher. I can't even remember how many I've read."

Picture books were also popular with these fifth graders. Illustrations were mentioned as a factor in choice for some students:

> "By reading back in my journal I think pretty much my favoriot book was *Manatee on location*. I guess I choice it bacuase I have a soft spot for endernerged animals. But also beuase of the photograhs too."

> "It has silly pictures and I like because I like books that, rhyme. I'ts easy to read, and I like to pretend that the charaters are people in my family."

In addition to the weekly literature share circle, Diane periodically did informal book talks. These talks convinced at least a few readers to try books that she introduced and highlighted: "I chose the book cause of the way Mrs. Smith Descriibed it."

The journals provided us with opportunity to explore book-choice strategies through both prodding and free response; they gave the students a forum for self-reflection.

Discoveries About Author's Craft and Literary Elements

The students were able to see beyond the action of the story to the author's role (Hickman, 1992). Their comments allowed opportunities for Diane and me to deepen their responses and to extend our own responses. The following journal exchange started with the student commenting on a book she had begun:

Student: I've started to read *The Flawed Glass* so far I think it's very interesting so far. But I though that the beginning was a little slow.

Teacher: I agree that *Flawed Glass* starts out a little slowly. The author spends a lot of time describing things and sort of getting everything ready to tell the story. Sometimes it's hard to stick with a book like that. Let me know if you continue to read it.

Student: I have continued reading *Flawed Glass*, and I don't regret it. I think the book gets alot better. I still think it's very weird the way the arthur rapidly switches back and forth from the eagle's to the humans. I also think the arthur gets pretty dramatic, like when Carl almost dies, I didn't like the way they described it. I would of liked to have had more of a choice to amagin my own feelings.

Teacher: I am so glad that you hung in there with *The Flawed Glass*. I wondered about the switch back and forth between the eagles and the people too. I couldn't see the point in spending so much time with the eagles. Then I started to think about how the eagle family was like the human family. The eagle family had a weak, sickly child just like the human family. If you have finished the book by the time you read this, think about what happens to the eagle and what happens to the humans. Are they both threatened by the same thing? Sometimes authors tell the same story twice.

Both these writers (teacher and student) explored their responses to a developing storyline. Both discovered that the other felt the parallel plots that the author had developed were initially disconcerting. By exploring and sharing, both were able to deepen and extend their responses.

Discoveries About Endings

Endings were the most important, or at least the most discussed, part of a plot for these fifth graders. They wanted complete closure, particularly in reference to the fate of the characters:

"I don't like books with bad endings beacause it leaves me wondering what happened and I feel like I read the book for nothing."

"One thing about this book is, I wish it had a scrule [sequel]. It is a good book but the end, I think is bad."

"I love the action and the suspence. But my freind said that the ending ruins the whole book, so I'll just enjoy it while it lasts."

This concern for endings may account, in part at least, for the popularity of series such as Baby-Sitters Club. In series books, there is no need to part with characters long term or worry that they may not live happily ever after because you will encounter them again in the next book. In fact, one of the fifth graders verified that speculation in response to Diane's inquiry about reading series books. Diane said, "I should have known that you would say you like series books best. I know you read a lot of Nancy Drew and Baby-Sitters Club. Can you tell me why? What makes series books so much fun to read?" The student replied in her journal,

Well seriries books are useful for entertaint and are usuly good for book reports. Like the Baby Sitters Club Ann M. Martian she writes in a good format. Series books are fun becuase they go on and on, the people will contium to have adventures.

After becoming aware of how important it was to these fifth graders that endings have what they perceived as being complete closure, Diane and I began to look at endings differently. As readers, we became more keenly aware of endings and our responses to them; and as teachers, we became interested in exposing the students to more "open" endings to extend and deepen their awareness of the range of endings beyond happily ever after.

One attempt to extend their responses to endings involved the book *The Black Falcon* by William Wise. Its main character is a poor knight who must order his pet falcon killed to feed a noble lady with whom he has fallen in love. After we had read the story to the class, the students expressed disappointment in the ending, even though the knight and the lady were married and lived more or less happily ever after. Several students thought the knight's servant should have come in at the story's end to announce that he had not really killed the falcon but had instead substituted a lowly—and presumably anonymous—chicken. The class agreed unanimously that saving the falcon would greatly improve the story.

By sharing the book and discussing the ending, we obviously did not instantly change the students' opinions about what makes a good ending, but it did challenge them to consider a different kind of ending. In so doing, we may have stretched their awareness of ironic endings. But just as important, we all participated on an equal footing in a lively discussion of authors' choices for endings.

Discoveries About Plot Development

These students frequently wrote about aspects of plot development beyond endings. The "stuff" that made a good plot for them was probably best described in a formula that one fifth grader shared in her journal. The formula emerged over a month of written conversations, which began with her response to *Dolphin Adventure.*

Student: *Dolphin Adventure* is a Good Book But it was missing some Good "stuff" I look for. I probably wouldent chose this Bok on my own.

Teacher: Can you tell me what good stuff you look for in a book that *Dolphin Adventure* didn't have?

Student: I can't relly desribe the "stuff" I look for. [and later] I also read *Mandie and the Cherocke ledgend.* I thought that was good but it neaded more of that "stuff" I like.

Teacher: If we could only figure out what that "stuff" is that makes a book good we would probably become famous. People have been trying to come up with a definition of what makes good literature for centuries. Still I think it is interesting to think and talk about. For instance, what was it about Joan Carris's style that you liked enough to make you want to read another book by her after you read *Just a Little Ham*?

Student: What a Great Book! [*Aunt Morbelia and the Screaming Skull,* the other Joan Carris book referred to in the previous entry] "stuff" poped out every where! I can define "stuff": comedy mixed in with adventure and drama=Good Book!

In her initial response, this student could not quite define what constituted the "stuff" of a good book. Although we prodded, hoping she could more clearly articulate what she meant, it was the student who continued to try to define what makes for a good book in her subsequent entries. The catalyst for her eventual definition seemed to be a suggestion from the teacher that she reflect on a favorite author's style across books she had just read. This student used what Lindfors, in the previous chapter, referred to as intertextuality— "the process of making meaning through connections across present and past texts and life experiences" (Short, 1993, p. 286). In this case, the student used intertextuality to deepen her own definition of the "stuff" of a good book.

Overall, these students favored plots that developed quickly and contained lots of action. Humor was often mentioned as an important component of a good story as was personal involvement:

> "A good book has a lot of action in it. When I say action it means the book is really exciteing and it kind of had a fast pace to it."

> "They like them ("Jenny Archer" books) becuase they always have a mystery or something for you to figer out. And kids Just like to keep readng till they find the answer to the problem, or mystery."

> "I am currently reading *Village By the Sea* wich is a very interesting book by a famous author named Paula Fox. I think it is good for 5th graders becuase it is adventureous and well detailed. I can't keep it down."

> "Mystrs just kep you going they are so exiting and some are very scary I rather have exitment then be scard out of my pants."

Discoveries About Characterizations

Characterization worked for these fifth graders if the characters seemed real to them. A good character was someone to whom they could relate directly, was very much like themselves, or at least like someone they could imagine existing in their worlds:

> "this book was "Excellent" this book was a defenate ten but I felt bad for the cousins Bonnie and Sylvia. This was good Because the author made you feel like one of the characters."

> "I just finished a book about a girl who never listens and just talks. I felt like I wanted to jump into the book and beat her untill she listens."

> "I find what I enjoy reading most is fiction about girls my age. I guess I never really reliezed that."

Other journal entries that showed that students understood characters contained comments that made connections between characters they were reading about and life experiences:

> "I liked *Stepbrother Sabotage*. It was realy good book. my Feelings about the story is like at home my oan stepbrither drives me crazy just like the one in the book."

> "I really like it cause it has reall fellings like a reall preson would feal. Like Lorna I would hate to eat all those healthe food."

Diane and I noticed a more subtle concern for the gender of the protagonists. Through observations and review of reading logs, which students kept in the back of their journals, we rediscovered the maxim that boys do not often choose to read books with girls as central characters. However, the girls did choose books with boys as central characters. We asked students to confirm or dispute this in our oral and written conversations with them. Although both boys and girls confirmed our observations in oral conversations, none chose to discuss the issue in writing. The following open-minded entry by a boy was as close as any of them came to discussing "gender of character" preference in their journals.

> Fifth graders like diffrent books about boys and some like magazines like boys they mostly like fishing, sports, mysryes books. I'm not saying girls dont like those book. But girls like romance book Im not a girl I can't tell and boys mite like those books too I don't but mabe somene else does.

Discoveries About Point of View

Discussions of point of view often related to comments about characterization. These fifth graders were concerned with which character the author let tell the story. They seemed to prefer stories told by characters close to their own age.

> "The name of the author of *Hang Tough Paul Mathers* is Alfred Slote. I forgot to tell you that in my last letter. He did a good job on that book, he told it in the kids point of view, so he relley didn't get very "sentimental.""

> "I like the way ANN M. Martin does each book from a diferent Girl's Pont of Veiew.""

> "I relley liked the book [*The Whipping Boy*] because I think it was descriptive. I also liked it becuase it was in the eyes of the wipping boy."

> *"Through students' journal entries, we learned about their reading behaviors, book-selection strategies, and responses to the crafting of literature."*

We found these fifth graders very willing and able to discuss the author's craft and literary elements. Their free responses informed us about what was important to them. Our conversations and inquiries helped us to deepen their responses and our own.

Reflections

Because of our schedules, Diane and I had very little time for reflecting together on the students' responses. Much of what we shared as we made discoveries about the students and ourselves was done in a casual, informal way: brief conversations as the class exited to recess or came in from the bus; hurried conversations as we exchanged books after school; and notes stuck on the front of journals or scribbled into our journal used for keeping anecdotal notes. While this was frustrating, it was also realistic. We had the advantage of being a team with shared concerns, but we had no more time to reflect on our discoveries than any classroom teacher.

Even with time constraints, we felt that the journals provided some valuable insights about the students and us as responders. Through their entries we learned about their reading behaviors, book-selection strategies, and responses to the crafting of literature. The journals also provided Diane and me opportunity to make discoveries about ourselves as readers and teachers. Often, these written conversations, particularly the more extended ones, allowed us to extend our own responses to books. We were constantly challenged to balance the skills of gentle prodding with thoughtful reception. By the end of the year, we hoped we had reached a point of "leading from behind"—letting the students set the direction with their responses yet occasionally influencing that direction with our questions and comments. And we are satisfied that we have allowed the journals, and our use of them, to grow and develop over time.

Notes

I would like to thank Diane Smith, fifth grade teacher at Cascade Brook School in Farmington, Maine, for sharing her classroom, her students, her insights, and her considerable expertise with me throughout this project.

References

Atwell, N. (1984). Writing and reading literature from the inside out. *Language Arts*, 61, 240–252.

Golden, J., & Handloff, E. (1993). Responding to literature through journal writing. In K.E. Holland, R.A. Hungerford, & S.B. Ernst (Eds.), *Journeying: Children responding to literature* (pp. 175–186). Portsmouth, NH: Heinemann.

Graves, D. (1983). *Writing: Teachers and children at work.* Portsmouth, NH: Heinemann.

Hickman, J. (1992). What comes naturally: Growth and change in children's free response to literature. In C. Temple & P. Collins (Eds.), *Stories and readers: New perspectives on literature in the elementary classroom* (pp. 185–193). Norwood, MA: Christopher-Gordon.

Short, K. (1993). Making connections across literature and life. In K.E Holland, R.A. Hungerford, & S.B. Ernst (Eds.), *Journeying: Children responding to literature* (pp. 284–301). Portsmouth, NH: Heinemann.

Children's Literature

Byars, B. (1991). *The seven treasure hunts.* New York: Harper-Collins.

Carris, J. (1989). *Just a little ham.* Boston, MA: Little, Brown.

Carris, J. (1990). *Aunt Morbelia and the screaming skull.* Boston, MA: Little, Brown.

Darling, K. (1991). *Manatee on location.* New York: Lothrop, Lee & Shepard.

Fleischman, S. (1986). *The whipping boy.* New York: Greenwillow.

Fox, P. (1988). *Village by the sea.* New York: Orchard.

Grover, W. (1990). *Dolphin adventure.* New York: Greenwillow.

Kline, S. (1989). *Orp.* New York: Putnam.

Leppard, L. (1983). *Mandie and the Cherokee legend.* New York: Bethany House.

Prelutsky, J. (1990). *Something big has been here.* New York: Greenwillow.

Say, A. (1990). *El Chino.* Boston, MA: Houghton Mifflin.

Slote, A. (1985). *Hang tough, Paul Mathers.* New York: HarperCollins.

Strachan, I. (1990). *Flawed glass.* Boston, MA: Little, Brown.

Wise, W. (1990). *The black falcon.* New York: Philomel.

Wittman, S. (1991). *Stepbrother sabotage.* New York: Harper-Collins.

Afterword

WHAT DO YOU want to do the moment you finish reading a good book? If you're like me, you want to talk about it. If I have enjoyed a book, I can't wait to tell somebody about it or see what another reader thinks of it. I don't want to leave the book's world; I just want to live in the spell of a good book a little longer. That's how I feel about Nancy and Miriam's book. First, I want to talk with them and ask them questions about the book: How did you plan for this excellent outline? How did you get such talented writers? How did you achieve such a nice balance among chapters? Then I want to tell other teachers about it; I want them to read the book so we can talk about it.

I learned many new ideas that I want teachers to try out. I want to tell teachers that Taffy Raphael's team found that students change their literacy behavior when they are in book clubs: they read more books, they talk about books inside and outside of school, they go to libraries. In general, they make books a part of their lives. I want to ask teacher readers, did you notice the part about language charts as a way to compare across books? Did you see that clever unit on books about foxes? Did you notice all the different ways you can use webbing? I liked the way Wells showed us the difference between grand conversations and gentle inquisitions. She showed us how a teacher can facilitate grand conversations through encouragement, synthesis, and inquiry. She called encouragement and synthesis "conversational maintenance" and said that inquiry is a way to model thought processes.

Roser and Martinez start the conversation in this book; now it is up to *Book Talk* readers to continue it. The authors give us a lot to think about and begin us on a long journey. They have shot literary arrows into our paths; the books they describe hit their mark and illuminate our lives as good literature can do.

Accept Nancy Roser and Miriam Martinez's invitation to talk about books—and beyond. It leads to grand conversations.

Bernice E. Cullinan
New York University

AUTHOR INDEX

Note: An "i" following a page number indicates that the reference may be found in an illustration.

Frasier, D., 131
Frost, R., 128, 130

G

Gaffney-Kessell, W., 130
Galda, L., 36, 41, 109, 114, 183, 184, 189, 190
Galdone, P., 64, 165, 166
Gallimore, R., 152, 156
Gamil, M., 49
Garland, S., 39
Garza, C.L., 162, 166
Gavelek, J.R., 67, 78
George, J.C., 40
Gilles, C., 67, 78
Gilliland, J.H., 40, 43, 49
Gimmestad, B., 188, 190
Ginsburg, M., 39, 64
Giovanni, N., 116, 130
Goatley, V.J., 67, 68, 78
Goble, P., 158, 159i, 166
Goff, S., 213, 216
Golden, J., 217, 224
Goldstein, Z., 166
Gombrich, E.H., 192, 199
Gorog, J., 40
Gowin, D.B., 90, 101
Graves, D., 217, 225
Greenfield, E., 43, 49, 189, 190
Grifalconi, A., 130
Grimm, J., 199, 200
Grimm, W., 199, 200
Groff, P., 192, 199
Grover, W., 217, 218i, 225

H

Hale, C., 131
Hamilton, V., 39
Handloff, E., 217, 224
Hansberry, L., 211, 216
Hansen-Krening, N., 44, 45, 49
Harris, J.C., 64
Harrison, P., 117, 119, 120, 123, 124, 126, 129
Harste, J., 54, 64, 142, 143, 149
Hartman, G., 5, 6i, 9
Hastings, S., 60, 64
Hauschildt, P., 68, 78
Haviland, V., 60, 64

Hays, M., 161i
Heard, G., 121, 129
Hearne, B., 199
Heath, S.B., 67, 78
Heide, F.P., 40, 43, 49
Heiden, D., 202, 207
Heimlich, J.E., 90, 101
Helbig, A., 130
Henkes, K., 38
Hepler, S., 54, 63, 81, 89, 197, 199
Hickman, J., 3, 9, 54, 63, 81, 88, 166, 197, 199,
    219, 220, 225
Hiebert, E.H., 67, 78
Hill, A., 130
Himler, R., 39
Hoffman, J.V., 81, 88, 157, 166, 169, 178
Hoffman, M., 37, 41, 158, 167
Hogrogian, N., 64, 172i
Holabird, K., 158, 167
Holland, K.E., 3, 9, 63, 149, 224, 225
Holquist, M., 216
Hooks, W., 64
Hopkins, L., 127, 130
Huck, C.S., 81, 88
Hughes, L., 119, 125, 129, 130
Hungerford, R.A., 3, 9, 63, 149, 224, 225
Hurston, Z.N., 43, 49
Hutchins, P., 110, 115
Hyman, T.S., 35i
Hymes, D., 156

I

Ingham, R., 118, 129
Iraqi, J., 166
Isami, I., 60, 61i, 64
Iser, W., 109, 115

J

Jarrell, R., 120, 130
Jeffers, S., 130
John, V., 156
Johnson, A., 43, 49
Johnson, D.D., 90, 101
Jones, M., 64
Jordan, C., 152, 156
Joyce, W., 36, 41
Juster, N., 40

SUBJECT INDEX

Note: An "f" following a page number indicates that the reference may be found in a figure; an "n," that it may be found in a note; a "t," that it may be found in a table.

CONFERENCES: teacher/student, 54
CONFORD, ELLEN: 220
CONTRERAS, CRIS: 158–164
CONVERSATION: 16; and dialogue contrasted, 136, 147; inner, ix; nature of, ix; response journal entries as, 213–214; student, 136; as student log entry, 69. *See also* Book talk
COONEY, BARBARA: 91
COSTUMES: class-play, 4
COVERS, BOOK: readers attracted to, 220
CROSSHATCHING: 193
CURRICULA: teacher/student-devised, 141

D

DANCE: as Focus Unit element, 57; story drama and, 185
"DANIEL" (Lindfors student): 209–211, 215
DAY NO PIGS WOULD DIE, A (Peck): 20–22
DEATH: classroom focus on, 21–22; Language Chart focus on, 176; literary focus on, 48
DEBATES: Language Chart–inspired, 85–86
DEPAOLA, TOMIE: 6, 161
DESIGN, BOOK: 38–39
DESKS: arrangement of student, 175
DEVIL'S ARITHMETIC (Yolen): 143
DIALOGUE (conversation). *See* Conversation
DIALOGUE (level of insight): 12, 13; and conversation contrasted, 136, 147; defined, 10; Focus Unit–generated, 54–58
DIALOGUE JOURNALS: 54, 56; defined, 217. *See also* Dialogue response journals
DIALOGUE RESPONSE JOURNALS: 208–215
DICEY'S SONG (Voigt): 174
DINOSAURS: 159
DIORAMAS: Focus Unit–generated, 57
DISCUSSION GROUPS, LITERARY: ix, 6, 9, 46–47, 67–68; hallmark of, 136; teacher, 42; teacher role in student, 136–149. *See also* Book clubs; Book talk; Community share; Interpretive (reading) communities; Literature circles
DISPLAYS: poetry-related classroom, 120
DOCTOR DESOTO (Steig): 58–59
"DOG" (Worth): 128
DOLPHIN ADVENTURE (Grover): 217–218, 222
DOMINIC (Steig): 12–18, 22

DRAMA, CLASSROOM: x, 3, 4, 74, 107, 115, 183–190; evaluation of, 189; Focus Unit–generated, 57; ideal conditions for, 186–187; Language Chart–inspired, 86; teacher involvement in, 187. *See also* Characters, story—student imitation of; Improvisation; Pantomime; Readers Theatre; Stories, reenactment of
DRAWINGS: as Focus Unit journal element, 56; in student logs, 69. *See also* Illustrations; Sketches
"DREW, NANCY": 221
DRUGS: as story topic, 213–215; as webbing consideration, 100f, 101
"DRUM, THE" (Giovanni): 116–117
DYSLEXIA: 209

E

ECOLOGY: 143
EGG CARTONS: as art resource, 5
EHLERT, LOIS: 39
EMPATHY, READER: 11, 17
ENDINGS, STORY: 221–222
ENDPAPERS: 192
EVALUATION SHEETS: book club, 77

F

FABLES: 59–62, 85. *See also* Myths; Tall tales
FABRIC: as art resource, 4
FAMILY PICTURES (Garza): 162
FANTASY: realism vs., 62
FICTION: as classroom drama subject, 185; historical, 85; nonfiction vs., 63. *See also* Fables; Folktales; Ghost stories; Mysteries; Myths; Novels; Short stories; Tall tales
FIELDTRIPS: literature comprehension-enhancing, 158
FIGURES OF SPEECH: poet use of, 125, 126–127. *See also* Imagery; Metaphors; Similes
FILIPINOS: 46, 48
FIRST DOG, THE (Brett): 159–160, 163
FLAME OF PEACE, THE (Lattimore): 174
FLASHBACKS: as storytelling device, 15
"FLASHLIGHT" (Thurman): 127
FLAWED GLASS (Strachan): 221
FLUENCY: as Book Club Project goal, 74; writing, 207

INSTRUCTION: as Book Club Project element, 74–76. *See also* Teachers
INTERPRETIVE (reading) COMMUNITIES: 108–109
INTERTEXTUALITY: 212, 222–223
IRA SLEEPS OVER (Waber): 162
I-R-E (initiation-reply-evaluation): 135
IT'S A DOG'S LIFE (Hopkins): 127

J

JARGON: 30
JINGLES, ADVERTISING: 118
JOHN BROWN: ONE MAN AGAINST SLAVERY (Everett): 142, 143, 147
JOURNALS: book club–related, 45f, 46; Focus Unit, 56–58; response (*see* Response journals); teachers', 171, 174–175, 177 (*see also* Notes, teacher); teacher/student (*see* Dialogue journals). *See also* Dialogue journals; Learning logs; Literature response journal logs; Reading logs; Response journals.
JUEL, CONNIE: 208, 215n

K

KAUFFMAN, GLORIA: 141, 144–148
KEATS, EZRA JACK: 80
KELLER, HELEN: 183
"KENNY" (Lindfors student): 208, 209, 212–213, 215
KIBILDIS, CAROL: 46–48
KIDS' CAT BOOK, THE (dePaola): 172, 173f
"KIM" (Lindfors student): 209, 211–212, 215
KINDERGARTEN(S): bilingual, 157–167; libraries of, 4; reading in, 169; response journals in, 171; story drama in, 187
KING, KAREN: 105, 111

L

LANGUAGE: classroom drama enhancement of oral, 184; of poetry, 119; second (*see* Bilingualism); thinking and, 67; visual image and, 192. *See also* Speaking; Words
LANGUAGE ARTS: 170. *See also* Reading; Writing
LANGUAGE CHARTS: 80–89, 169–171, 175–177; format of, 81, 83f, 86. *See also* Charts, Focus Unit

LANGUAGE TO LITERACY (LtL) Project: 80–83, 169–178. *See also* Language Charts
LEARNERS, TEACHERS AS: 31
LEARNING, INTEGRATED: 7
LEARNING DISABLED STUDENTS: journals as aid to, 201
LEARNING LOGS: 188
LEGEND OF THE BLUEBONNET, THE (dePaola): 84
LEGEND OF THE INDIAN PAINTBRUSH, THE (dePaola): 84
"LEO" ("Slower Than the Rest"): 25–29
LEO THE LATE BLOOMER (Kraus): 174
LETTERS (missives): as class effort, 6; Language Charts and, 86
LET THE CIRCLE BE UNBROKEN (Taylor): 95, 96f
LIBRARIES: book club–enhanced school, 45–46; classroom, 4, 5, 75, 158, 169, 171, 177; home, 55; public, 4, 7, 54, 55, 75, 158; school, 4, 45–46, 54, 69, 75 (*see also* Libraries, classroom)
LIBRARY CENTERS. *See* Libraries, classroom
LIMERICKS: 118
LINDFORS, JUDITH WELLS: 213–214, 222
LINDSEY (Handloff student): 201, 203–207
LIONNI, LEO: 38
LISTENING: story drama and, 185
LITERACY: nature of, 67
LITERATURE: multicultural, 42–49; personal experience as link to, x, 10, 17, 18, 24, 26–29, 36, 38f, 45f, 47, 53, 54, 57, 73, 107–108, 122, 126, 127, 145, 156, 161, 174, 189, 204t, 207, 211, 223, (*see also* Focus Units); selection of, x, 67, 75, 109–110, 144, 158, 166, 169, 202, 219–220, 222, 224; techniques of, 10–23. *See also* Books; Genre, literary; Fiction; Nonfiction; Poetry; Response(s), of children to literature
LITERATURE (SHARE) CIRCLES: ix, 218–220; reading strategies for, 143; teacher role in, 141–149
LITERATURE RESPONSE JOURNALS/LOGS: 148, 217
LITERATURE STUDY CIRCLES/GROUPS. *See* Discussion groups, literary
LITERATURE UNITS, THEMATIC: 81, 82f, 170–172
LITTLE RED HEN, THE (Galdone): 165

"LONE DOG" (McLeod): 127
LOPEZ (kindergarten teacher): 34, 37, 38
LUNCHROOMS: conversation in school, 136

M

"MAGIC IN A GLASS JAR" (Bacmeister): 150–155
MAIN (story) IDEAS: 25, 107
MANATEE ON LOCATION (Darling): 220
MANIAC MAGEE (Spinelli): 36, 174
MAPPING: in reading logs, 76
MAPS: 6; as student log element, 69. *See also* Character maps; Charts
MARSHALL, JAMES: 55
MARTIN, ANN M.: 224
MATHEMATICS: reading and, 169
MEANING, STORY: 14; art and, 193; illustrator spin on, 193; literature circle approach to, 144; reading for, 59, 107; webbing approach to, 91. *See also* Comprehension, reading
MEANING-SPACE: 109
MELE, MICHELE: 94
MEMORIZATION: of figures of speech, 125; of poetry, 118; as Readers Theatre element, 186
MESSAGE, STORY: 34, 36, 39f
METAPHORS: 34, 125; art-related, 192; character delineation through, 14; extended, 17–18, 21, 98; literature-inspired, 18; poetic, 128
MEXICAN AMERICANS: 46, 48, 157–166, 208
MISS RUMPHIUS (Cooney): 91–93
MOBILES: as Focus Unit resource, 57
MODELING, TEACHER: 34, 73, 76, 149, 160; LtL-related, 174; poetry-related, 121; of response journal-keeping, 171; of webbing, 91, 93
MONEY: as classroom topic, 134
MOOD (story element): 16–17, 21
MORPHEMES: 192
MORRISON, TONI: 48
MOTHER GOOSE RHYMES: 118
MOVIES: as literature circle referent, 144; as talk story element, 155
MR. POPPER'S PENGUINS (Atwater/Atwater): 183
MTV: ix
MUFARU'S BEAUTIFUL DAUGHTERS (Steptoe): 193–195

MULTICULTURALISM: 42–49
MURALS, CLASSROOM: 6; Focus Unit–generated, 57
MUSIC: as reading resource, 5; story drama and, 185
MYERS, BRENDA: 91–93
MYSTERIES: 206, 223
MYTHS: 85. *See also* Fables; Ghost stories; Tall tales

N

NATIVE AMERICANS: art of, 199; as classroom drama subject, 185
NAYLOR, PHYLLIS REYNOLDS: 6, 39
NAZISM: Book Club Project focus on, 73
NONFICTION: as classroom drama subject, 185; fiction vs., 63; as Language Chart element, 85; as story drama resource, 188–189. *See also* Biography
NOTEBOOKS, TEACHER: 77
NOTES, TEACHER: 148, 224; on classroom dramatizations, 189
NOVELS: x, 4, 169, 201; book club focus on, 45f, 77
NUMBER THE STARS (Lowry): 73
NURSERY TALES: 4. *See also* Mother Goose rhymes

O

OBJECT, STORY AS: 39, 40f
OCTAVIO ("Daniel" tutee): 209–211, 215
ORIGAMI: as Focus Unit resource, 57
ORP (Kline): 218
OUTSIDE OVER THERE (Sendak): 195–198
OVERHEAD PROJECTORS: 93, 112, 218

P

PAIN AND THE GREAT ONE, THE (Blume): 105, 106, 110, 111, 114
PANTOMIME: by students, 185
PAPERBACKS: 170
PAPER BAG PRINCESS, THE (Munsch): 133
PARDO, LAURA: 75–77
PARENTS: as reading teachers/critics, 106, 170
PARK'S QUEST (Paterson): 70, 71f, 72f
PAULSEN, GARY: 220

TRANSLATION: English/Spanish, 165
TUBMAN, HARRIET: 189
TUCK EVERLASTING (Babbitt): 37, 136–137,
    138–139
TUTORS: student athletes as first grade,
    208–211, 214–216n
"TV LIVE": ix
TWO BAD ANTS (Van Allsburg): 36, 98, 99f

U
UP AND DOWN ON THE MERRY-GO-ROUND
    (Martin/Archambault): 37–38

V
VALUE (art element): 193
VERY BUSY SPIDER, THE (Carle): 38–39
VIDEOTAPES: as Book Club Project resource, 76;
    as literature circle resource, 148; as talk
    story resource, 152, 155
VIET NAM WAR: 212
VIEWPOINT: authorial, 16, 34, 54, 85, 184,
    223–224; illustrator, 193, 194
VILLAGE BY THE SEA (Fox): 223
VOCABULARY: Book Club Project focus on, 69,
    74; reading-enhanced, 25; worksheet con-
    centration on, 169
VOICE (Bakhtin concept): 209
VYGOTSKY, L.: 183–184

W
WALLPAPER: as art resource, 4–5
WAR: as Book Club Project subject, 70f, 73–74,
    77. See also Civil War, U.S.; Viet Nam war
WASHES, COLOR: 193
WEBBING: x, 90–101, 114; defined, 90; as litera-
    ture circle element, 143, 148; prereading,
    93–94, 94f, 95f

WEBS: character, 92, 93, 94f; event, 96; personal,
    93
WEDNESDAY SURPRISE, THE (Bunting): 37
WHERE THE WILD THINGS ARE (Sendak):
    107–108
WHIPPING BOY, THE (Fleischman): 224
"WHY" STORIES. See Pourquoi tales
"Wilbur" (Charlotte's Web): 187
WOMEN OF BREWSTER PLACE (Naylor):
    211–212
WOMEN'S RIGHTS: literature circle focus on,
    143
WOODMAN, DEBORAH A.: 69, 73–77
WORDS: unfamiliar poetry, 126
WORKSHEETS: figures of speech "taught" via,
    127; literary comprehension assessed
    through, 124, 169
WOROBEY, BARBARA: 98, 101
WRETCHED STONE, THE (Van Allsburg): 98,
    100f
WRITER(S): professional (see Authors); reader re-
    lationship to, ix
WRITING, STUDENT: x, 3, 57, 63, 74, 77; audience
    as factor of, 202; as Book Club Project ele-
    ment, 68, 69, 74, 77; collaborative, 53, 63;
    emergent, 87; and literary response, 67,
    201–207; postreading, 33; reading and, 170;
    story drama and, 184, 185. See also Fluency,
    writing; Free writes; Poetry, student; Read-
    ers Theatre
"WRITTEN CONVERSATION": 143

Y
YOLEN, JANE: 220